SPIRIT
of TRUTH

"But when He comes, the Spirit of Truth,
He will guide you to all truth."

JOHN 16:13

STUDENT WORKBOOK
Sacred Scripture

SOPHIA
INSTITUTE
FOR TEACHERS

About Sophia Institute for Teachers

Sophia Institute for Teachers was launched in 2013 by Sophia Institute to renew and rebuild Catholic culture through service to Catholic education. With the goal of nurturing the spiritual, moral, and cultural life of souls, and an abiding respect for the role and work of teachers, we strive to provide materials and programs that are at once enlightening to the mind and ennobling to the heart; faithful and complete, as well as useful and practical. Sophia Institute is a 501(c)(3) nonprofit organization founded in 1983.

Printed in the United States of America
Design by Perceptions Design Studio
Cover image: Saint Matthew the Evangelist (San Matteo Evangelista), by Guido Reni.
Image courtesy Ellyn Juritz / Alamy Stock Photo.

Spirit of Truth: Sacred Scripture Student Workbook
ISBN: 978-1-622824-366
Fifth Printing

Inside this Book

UNIT 1

What is Sacred Scripture?

In this unit, you will learn about...

> The written record of God's revelation of Himself.
> The purposes of Scripture.
> How Scripture is used at Holy Mass.
> How to pray with Scripture using *Lectio Divina*.
> How to use the Bible.

Introduction

God reveals Himself to us in His Word. We encounter His Word in Sacred Scripture and Sacred Tradition as taught to us by the Magisterium of the Catholic Church who guards and protects the truths of our faith. Sacred Scripture is the written record of God's revelation of Himself throughout Salvation History. From the very beginning, God chose to make Himself known to us through words and deeds, gradually and in stages. This revelation culminated in the Incarnation, when God became man in the Person of Jesus Christ. Jesus is the Word of God. In Him, God has fully revealed Himself and has said all that needs to be said. He has spoken His one, perfect, unsurpassable Word. In Scripture, we meet our Lord Jesus Christ. St. Jerome famously said, "Ignorance of Scripture is ignorance of Christ." Therefore, the Church has always asked the faithful to know the Scripture in order to know Christ.

Scripture is very powerful in our lives. As St. Paul wrote, it is useful for "teaching, for refutation, for correction, and for training in righteousness" (2 Timothy 3:16) and it is able to speak to the deepest "reflections and thoughts of the heart" (Hebrews 4:12). The Scriptures are our guidebook for living the Christian life, for teaching others about the faith, and for defending the faith. It speaks directly to our souls and reveals to us our truest self. In order to achieve all of this, we must read Scripture frequently and reflect on its meaning for our lives. Just as we spend time with friends in order to know them better, we must spend time with the Lord in order to hear His voice in His Word.

What questions do you have right now about the topics you will be learning about in this unit?

_____

_____

_____

_____

Alleluia: Praise the Lord! A song or acclamation of praise before the Gospels are read at Mass.

Biblia: Latin for "a collection of books." The word Bible is derived from this word and refers to the fact that Scripture is not a single book to be read from cover to cover, but rather is a library of books and other writings.

Deposit of Faith: The whole content of the Christian faith formed by Sacred Scripture and Sacred Tradition together. The deposit of faith was revealed by God through Jesus Christ and has been faithfully guarded and interpreted by the Magisterium of the Catholic Church.

Duality: When one thing has two or more natures. Scripture is both the Word of God and the written words of humans.

Homily: A teaching drawn from the day's readings given by a priest (or deacon) at Mass.

Lectio Divina: Latin for "divine reading." It is an ancient form of praying with Scripture that is a slow and thoughtful encounter with the Word of God.

Liturgy of the Eucharist: The second part of the Mass in which we receive the Body and Blood of Jesus Christ in the Eucharist. In this part of the Mass, the priest prays the words of consecration and changes the bread and wine into the Body and Blood of Christ. We also come to the altar of the Lord and receive Holy Communion.

Liturgy of the Word: The first part of the Mass in which we receive the written Word of God. In this part of the Mass, the Scriptures are proclaimed and the priest teaches us in his homily. We also join together in prayer for others and profess our faith.

Magisterium: The teaching authority of the Church and those who exercise that authority, the pope and all of the world's bishops in union with the pope. The Magisterium of the Church authentically teaches and interprets the Word of God so that the faithful might be saved.

Profession of Faith: A public statement of belief made by the faithful during Sunday Masses and Holy Days of Obligation. It can either be the Nicene Creed, the Apostles' Creed, or a renewal of baptismal promises.

Revelation: An act of making known divine truth. From the beginning, God made Himself and His plan for us known gradually and in stages and in words and deeds.

Sacred Scripture/The Bible: The written record of God's revelation of Himself. It is the speech of God put down in writing under the breath of the Holy Spirit. The Word of God.

Sacred Tradition: The mode of transmission of the Word of God. The Word of God was given to the Apostles by Jesus and the Holy Spirit. The Apostles in turn handed it on to their successors, the bishops. With the help of the Holy Spirit, the Church has kept the Word of God whole and safe over the centuries so we can know and believe in the whole Faith today. Sacred Tradition and Sacred Scripture make up a single deposit - or one gift--of the Word of God. We accept and honor Sacred Tradition equally with Sacred Scripture.

Salvation: Being freed from the power and effects of sin. From the beginning, God promised us freedom from sin. He revealed His plan to save us from sin throughout Salvation History and Jesus Christ completed the plan of salvation by His sacrifice on the Cross and Resurrection from the dead. Sacred Scripture is our primary source for the truth we need to know for the sake of our salvation.

Theology: The study of God and the things of God. The study of God is different than the study of other things. Rather than learning a list of facts about God, theology is about learning to know, trust, and love God in order to grow in relationship with Him.

Universal Prayer or Prayer of the Faithful: The prayer of the assembly during every Mass that concludes the Liturgy of the Word. The faithful entrust the needs of the Church, the needs of the world, and their own needs to God.

Word of God: A title for Jesus Christ and a title for Sacred Scripture. Jesus is the Word of God become flesh in the Incarnation. In Him, God has revealed all that is necessary for the sake of our salvation. We meet Jesus in Sacred Scripture, the Word of God written down to preserve and communicate the Good News of salvation.

The Annunciation
BY LUIS JUAREZ (C. 1610)

National Museum of Art, Mexico City, Mexico.

The Annunciation

The Annunciation, by Luis Juarez (c. 1610)

Directions: Take some time to quietly view and reflect on the art. Let yourself be inspired in any way that happens naturally. Then think about the questions below, and discuss them with your classmates.

Conversation Questions

1. Identify the figures in the painting and describe what they are doing.

2. Artists use placement and light to draw our eye to important things. When you look at this painting, where did your eye naturally go? What or whom do you look at first? Next? What or whom are you drawn to focus on the longest? Why do you think the artist might have been drawing your attention in this way?

3. Why do you think the angel is holding a white lily? What might that represent?

4. Read Luke 1:26-38. How does this painting illustrate this Gospel story? Which specific moment from the story is depicted in the painting? What makes you think so?

5. What is on the desk in front of Mary? Why do you think the artist included that in this painting?

6. Read John 1:1 and John 1:14. How does this painting illustrate this passage from John's Gospel?

7. Which story from the Gospels you just read does this painting best illustrate? Why do you think so?

John 1:1

In the beginning was the Word, and the Word was with God, and the Word was God.

_____

_____

_____

_____

_____

_____

_____

_____

John 1:14

And the Word became flesh and made his dwelling among us, and we saw his glory, the glory as of the Father's only Son, full of grace and truth.

_____

_____

_____

_____

_____

_____

_____

_____

2 Timothy 3:16-17

All Scripture is inspired by God and is useful for teaching, for refutation, for correction, and for training in righteousness, so that one who belongs to God may be competent, equipped for every good work.

_____

_____

_____

_____

_____

_____

_____

_____

_____

Luke 11:28

He replied, "Rather, blessed are those who hear the word of God and observe it."

Psalm 46:11

"Be still and know that I am God!"

Hebrews 4:12

Indeed, the word of God is living and effective, sharper than any two-edged sword, penetrating even between soul and spirit, joints and marrow, and able to discern reflections and thoughts of the heart.

_____

_____

_____

_____

_____

_____

_____

_____

God Reveals Himself in His Word

Directions: Read the Scripture passages below and answer the focus questions. Then respond in writing to the given prompt.

John 1:1-5, 14

In the beginning was the Word, and the Word was with God, and the Word was God. He was in the beginning with God. All things came to be through him, and without him nothing came to be. What came to be through him was life, and this life was the light of the human race; the light shines in the darkness, and the darkness has not overcome it. And the Word became flesh and made his dwelling among us, and we saw his glory, the glory as of the Father's only Son, full of grace and truth.

1. Who was in the beginning with God and is God Himself?

   _____

   _____

2. What came to be through this person?

   _____

   _____

3. What did the Word become, and what did the Word reveal when He became that?

   _____

   _____

Luke 4:16-21

He came to Nazareth, where he had grown up, and went according to his custom into the synagogue on the Sabbath day. He stood up to read and was handed a scroll of the prophet Isaiah. He unrolled the scroll and found the passage where it was written: "The Spirit of the Lord is upon me, because he has anointed me to bring glad tidings to the poor. He has sent me to proclaim liberty to captives and recovery of sight to the blind, to let the oppressed go free, and to proclaim a year acceptable to the Lord." Rolling up the scroll, he handed it back to the attendant and sat down, and the eyes of all in the synagogue looked intently at him. He said to them, "Today this scripture passage is fulfilled in your hearing."

4. What did Jesus read from in the synagogue?

_____

_____

5. What did the Scripture that Jesus read from claim the Spirit of the Lord sent Him to do?

_____

_____

6. What did Jesus claim after reading the Scripture?

_____

_____

Reflection Question

In a well-written five- to seven-sentence paragraph, support the following statement using both of the above Scripture passages:

God reveals Himself in His Word.

_____

_____

_____

_____

_____

_____

_____

Divine Revelation Note-Taking Template

Directions: Read the selection and then fill in the blanks as you listen to your teacher.

In Sacred Scripture, the Church constantly finds her nourishment and her strength, for she welcomes it not as a human word, "but as what it really is, the word of God." "In the sacred books, the Father who is in heaven comes lovingly to meet his children, and talks with them" (CCC 104).

1.   God chose to reveal Himself and make known _____.

2.   A mystery is a truth that cannot be discovered by _____.

3.   God revealed Himself to invite us into _____ with Him.

4.   The _____ ensures that God's revelation of Himself will

     remain _____ and _____ for all

     time.

5.   The Tripod of Truth is made of _____,

     _____, and the _____.

6.   The core content of the Christian faith is found in _____,

     _____ and _____. Together,

     these are called _____.

7.   Tradition means to _____.

8.   Jesus told His Apostles to preach to all the _____, which they

     and their successors, the _____, have faithfully done for over

     2,000 years, under the guidance of the _____.

9.   The written record of God's revelation is called _____. It consists

     of the _____ and the _____ that make

     up the Bible.

10. Sacred Tradition came before _____.

11. The _____ refers to the authority of the Church to teach in
Jesus' name. It also refers to those who possess that authority, the
_____ alone, and all of the world's
_____ together in union with the pope.

12. Sacred Scripture and Sacred Tradition together form one Sacred
_____, or the whole content of the Christian faith.

These descriptions are not complete, but they help you see how God reveals Himself to us
through Sacred Tradition and Sacred Scripture. We will spend a lot more time studying the
written record of God's revelation, the Bible, this year.

Reflection Questions

1. Have you ever read a story from the Bible? Which one? What was it like?

_____

_____

2. How do you think we encounter the Word of God directly in the Bible?

_____

3. Which book of the Bible or biblical character or story are you most interested to
learn more about this year? Why?

_____

_____

_____

_____

The Body of Christ

THE LAST SUPPER, BY ANDREY MIRONOV (C. 2009)

MOND CRUCIFIXION, BY RAPHAEL (C. 1502-1503)

The Body of Christ

The Last Supper, by Andrey Mironov (c. 2009)

Mond Crucifixion, by Raphael (c. 1502-1503)

Directions: Take some time to quietly view and reflect on the art. Then think about the questions below, and discuss them with your classmates.

Conversation Questions

1. What do you first notice about each painting?

2. What is happening in each painting?

3. Who are the figures in each painting?

4. In the *Last Supper* painting, where is the source of light in the painting? What does that tell us about Jesus?

5. In the *Mond Crucifixion* painting, what are the angels doing? Why?

6. How do the two paintings together deepen our understanding of the Eucharist? What do they show us about whom we receive in the Bread of Life?

Scripture and the Body of Christ

Part I

Directions: In the left part of the Venn diagram, list at least three unique characteristics of Scripture. In the right part, list at least three unique characteristics of the Eucharist. Then, in the center portion of the diagram, list at least three ways Scripture and the Eucharist are similar.

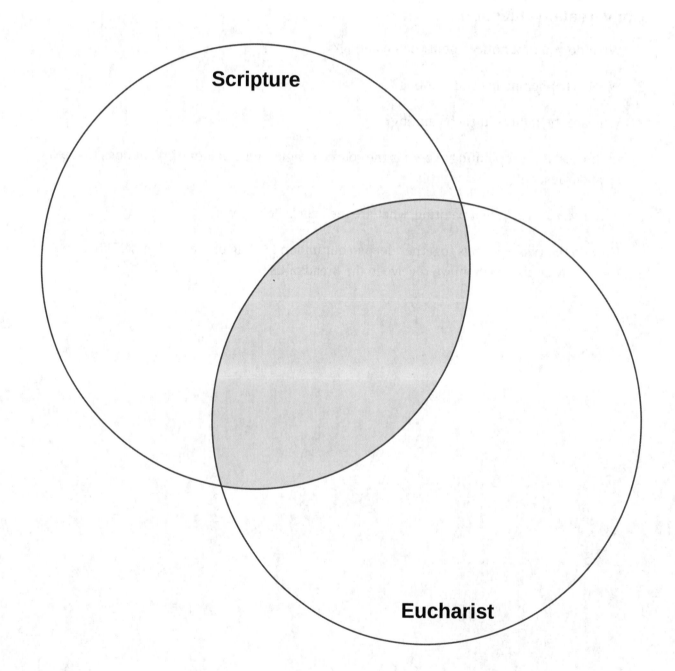

Scripture

Eucharist

Part II

Directions: In the boxes on the next page, draw a symbol for Scripture and one for the Eucharist to show how we encounter Jesus through each.

Scripture	The Eucharist

Uses of Scripture

Directions: List all the uses for Scripture St. Paul mentions to Timothy that you can find in this passage. Then, in your own words, write a single sentence that summarizes St. Paul's message to Timothy about the uses of Scripture.

But you, remain faithful to what you have learned and believed, because you know from whom you learned it, and that from infancy you have known [the] sacred scriptures, which are capable of giving you wisdom for salvation through faith in Christ Jesus. All scripture is inspired by God and is useful for teaching, for refutation, for correction, and for training in righteousness, so that one who belongs to God may be competent, equipped for every good work. (2 Timothy 3:14-17)

_____

_____

_____

_____

_____

_____

Summary Sentence:

_____

_____

_____

Choose one of the uses of Scripture St. Paul mentions to Timothy, and write two ways that you can you can put Scripture to this use in your own life.

Use of Scripture: _____

How can I do this in my own life?

1. _____

2. _____

Three-Sentence Autobiography

Directions: Read the three-sentence autobiography that you chose. Then answer the following questions.

1. What do you think the person most wanted you to know about him or her?

   _____

2. What more do you want to know about the person? How would you find out more about him or her?

   _____

   _____

3. What couldn't you know about or do with the person just from reading this autobiography?

   _____

   _____

4. Is this autobiography a complete picture of the person? Why or why not?

   _____

   _____

5. Read John 21:25:

   There are also many other things that Jesus did, but if these were to be described individually, I do not think the whole world would contain the books that would be written.

   What is John suggesting about Scripture in this passage?

   _____

   _____

6. Read the following quote from *Dei Verbum*, the Sacred Constitution on Divine Revelation from the Second Vatican Council:

   Scripture teaches "solidly, faithfully, and without error that truth which God wanted put into sacred writings for the sake of salvation."

What does Scripture teach without error?

_____

_____

_____

Reflection Question

Write a five- to seven-sentence paragraph that responds to the following: How do you think the experience of reading and reflecting on the three-sentence biographies is similar to studying Scripture? What do you think is the most important thing God wanted us to know through His revelation of Himself found in Scripture?

_____

_____

_____

_____

_____

_____

_____

_____

_____

Extra Question: Whose autobiography do you think you read?

_____

Salvation in Scripture

Directions: Read each Scripture passage and determine what truth it tells us about salvation.

1. Mark 1:15: _____

    _____

2. Luke 5:32: _____

    _____

3. John 3:18: _____

    _____

4. Acts 2:37-38: _____

    _____

5. Matthew 7:21: _____

    _____

6. John 15:10: _____

    _____

7. Matthew 22:37-40: _____

    _____

8. John 6:51: _____

    _____

9. Matthew 28:19: _____

    _____

Scriptural Roots of the Mass

Directions: Read through each of the prayers of the Mass, then look up each Scripture passage and determine which prayer of the Mass is found in each passage. Write the letter for each prayer next to the correct Scripture reference.

Prayers of the Mass

A. Hosanna in the highest. Blessed is he who comes in the name of the Lord. Hosanna in the highest.

B. Through him, and with him, and in him, O God, almighty Father, in the unity of the Holy Spirit, all glory and honor is yours, for ever and ever.

C. Glory to God in the highest, and on earth peace to people of good will.

D. Behold the Lamb of God, behold him who takes away the sins of the world. Blessed are those called to the supper of the Lamb.

E. The Word of the Lord. Thanks be to God.

F. Pray, brethren, that my sacrifice and yours may be acceptable to God, the almighty Father.

G. Our Father, who art in heaven, hallowed be thy name...

H. And with your spirit.

I. Let us offer each other the sign of peace.

J. Holy, Holy, Holy Lord God of hosts. Heaven and earth are full of your glory.

K. Lord Jesus Christ, who said to your Apostles: Peace I leave you, my peace I give you...

L. In the name of the Father, and of the Son, and of the Holy Spirit. Amen.

M. He took bread and, giving thanks, broke it, and gave it to his disciples, saying: TAKE THIS, ALL OF YOU, AND EAT OF IT, FOR THIS IS MY BODY, WHICH WILL BE GIVEN UP FOR YOU.

N. The grace of our Lord Jesus Christ, and the love of God, and the communion of the Holy Spirit be with you all.

O. Go in peace. Thanks be to God.

P. In a similar way, when supper was ended, he took the chalice and, once more giving thanks, he gave it to his disciples, saying: TAKE THIS, ALL OF YOU, AND DRINK FROM IT, FOR THIS IS THE CHALICE OF MY BLOOD, THE BLOOD OF THE NEW AND ETERNAL COVENANT, WHICH WILL BE POURED OUT FOR YOU AND FOR MANY FOR THE FORGIVENESS OF SINS. DO THIS IN MEMORY OF ME.

Q. When we eat this Bread and drink this Cup, we proclaim your Death, O Lord, until you come again.

R. Lord, I am not worthy that you should enter under my roof, but only say the word and my soul shall be healed.

Scripture References

_____   1.   Matthew 28:19

_____   2.   Corinthians 13:13

_____   3.   Timothy 4:22

_____   4.   Luke 2:14

_____   5.   1 Peter 1:25 and Romans 7:25

_____   6.   Hebrews 12:28

_____   7.   Isaiah 6:3

_____   8.   Mark 11:9-10

_____   9.   Matthew 26:26 and Luke 22:19

_____   10.   Luke 22:19-20, Matthew 26:27-28, and Mark 14:24

_____   11.   1 Corinthians 11:26

_____   12.   Romans 11:36

_____   13.   Matthew 6:9-13

_____   14.   John 14:27

_____   15.   Romans 16:16

_____   16.   John 1:29 and Revelation 19:9

_____   17.   Luke 7:6-7

_____   18.   Luke 7:50 and 2 Corinthians 9:15

Liturgy of the Word Fill-in-the-Blank

Directions: Read the "Liturgy of the Word" article by the USCCB located at **USCCB.org/ prayer-and-worship/the-mass/order-of-mass/liturgy-of-the-word**. Then complete the fill-in-the-blank activity with the correct words and phrases from the article.

1.   The Liturgy of the Word is made up of mostly _____.

2.   There are three Scripture readings on _____ and

_____.

3.   The first reading is taken from _____, and the second

reading is taken from _____.

4.   The last reading is always from _____.

5.   A _____ is sung between readings to help us meditate on

God's Word.

6.   The Gospels are the _____ of the Liturgy of the Word

because they tell the story of _____ life, ministry, and

preaching.

7.   Outside of Lent, the faithful stand and use an acclamation of praise called the

_____, which means

_____, to introduce the Gospel reading.

8.   A _____ ordinarily reads the Gospel; however, if one is

present at Mass, a _____ will do so.

9.   The _____ is preached by the

_____ after all the Scripture readings.

10.   The preacher of the homily draws from the readings to teach a lesson that may help us to

live _____ and grow in _____.

11. On Sundays, the _____ follows the homily. This is either

    the _____ Creed or the _____ Creed.

    Sometimes _____ promises are renewed instead, taking the

    place of the Creed.

12. The _____ concludes the Liturgy of the Word, in which the

    assembly entrusts their needs to the faithful and loving _____.

Silence and Prayer

Directions: Read the essay, then answer the questions that follow.

Think for a moment of all the times you are truly in silence throughout your day. Maybe your first thought is when you are asleep or taking a shower. Perhaps on your trips to and from school each day. Can you think of other times when no sounds creep into the peaceful silence around you? You might have trouble thinking of anytime at all that you find yourself in silence.

Our modern world makes it difficult to find silence. The TV is on even during mealtimes, the radio plays while we are in the car, and we put on earbuds when we study, walk the hallways of our schools, and maybe even when we sleep. Perhaps as a result, many of us are uncomfortable with silence. We think of it as a void that needs to be filled.

But are we really listening to the TV, or the radio, or even the music in our earbuds? Or are they functioning more like background noise? What is the difference between hearing something and really listening to it? How does background noise affect what we are able to *listen* to?

One of the great battles of prayer involves a question that many of us have asked at one point or another: Why can't I hear God speak to me? Perhaps it is because we are not listening. In any conversation with a close friend, one must stop speaking and listen attentively to the other. It is difficult to hear anyone, let alone God, speak when we are surrounded by sound.

Psalm 46:11 tells us, in God's own voice nonetheless, "Be still and know that I am God!" The *Catechism of the Catholic Church*, in describing contemplative prayer, says that it is first "hearing the Word of God," and then it is "silence" in which "the Father speaks to us His incarnate Word" (2716-2718). Silence, that state of being in which we so rarely find ourselves, is essential to knowing God and to hearing His voice.

You don't need to go to great lengths to hear God speak to you. First, you need to be deliberate about when and where you pray. Set aside a specific time to pray. It doesn't have to be a long time. Even just five minutes will do, especially if you're not used to praying. Then find a place that is comfortable and relatively free of distractions.

Second, you need to be in a quiet place. Turn off the TV, take off the headphones, and turn off the music. Prepare yourself to listen.

Third, as the *Catechism* tells us, we have to hear the Word of God. How do we do that? Thankfully, God has been speaking to us from the very beginning. He has spoken to us throughout human history and has said all that He needed to say when He sent His only Son to earth to become one of us and to save us from sin. We can hear this Good News of mercy and love in the Scriptures, the Word of God in writing. God is present in His Word. To hear God speak, read the Scriptures. Not all at once. Not even cover to cover. Begin with the Gospels, where we meet God's Word become flesh in Jesus Christ. A single passage will do, something manageable and not overwhelming. The goal should be quality, not quantity. The perfect place to start would be to read the Gospel reading from the upcoming Sunday Mass.

Lastly, reflect in silence. Be filled with God's Word, spoken to you. As in any conversation with a close friend, be attentive to what God has said. What is He telling you? Only in the silence will you be able to discover the answer.

1. Why is it difficult to find silence in our modern world?

    _____

2. The author suggests that there is a difference between hearing and listening. How would you describe that difference? Give an example of hearing rather than listening.

    _____

    _____

3. What is one of the great battles of prayer? What does the author suggest is the reason for this battle?

    _____

    _____

4. What is the main idea of the paragraph that begins "Psalm 46:11 tells us..."?

    _____

    _____

5. What are the four steps the author suggests for hearing God speak to us? Briefly define each step.

    _____

    _____

    _____

    _____

    _____

6. Where is a good place to begin reading Scripture?

    _____

Reflection Question

Are you comfortable with silence? In what ways do you fill the silence throughout your day? How might your own prayer experience be different if you took time to be in silence?

_____

_____

_____

_____

_____

_____

_____

Lectio Divina Expert Groups Worksheet

Directions: In your group, answer the questions about the step of *Lectio Divina* assigned to you. Then work with a new group to learn and answer the questions about the other steps of *Lectio Divina*.

Lectio

1. What is the English translation of this word? _____

2. What does one do in this step?

   _____

   _____

3. What are some tips for practicing this step?

   _____

   _____

4. How is this step related to the other three steps? (Save this question to be answered in your new groups.)

   _____

   _____

Meditatio

1. What is the English translation of this word? _____

2. What does one do in this step?

   _____

   _____

3. What are some tips for practicing this step?

   _____

   _____

4. How is this step related to the other three steps? (Save this question to be answered in your new groups.)

   _____

   _____

Oratio

1. What is the English translation of this word? _____

2. What does one do in this step?

   _____

   _____

3. What are some tips for practicing this step?

   _____

   _____

4. How is this step related to the other three steps? (Save this question to be answered in your new groups.)

   _____

   _____

Contemplatio

1. What is the English translation of this word? _____

2. What does one do in this step?

   _____

   _____

3. What are some tips for practicing this step?

   _____

   _____

4. How is this step related to the other three steps? (Save this question to be answered in your new groups.)

   _____

   _____

Bible Scavenger Hunt

Part 1: Bible Basics

1. Label the book, chapter, and verses in the following reference:

    Matthew   28 : 16-20.

2. Which books of the Bible do the following abbreviations stand for?

    Nm. _____   1 Sm. _____

    Ez. _____   Mt. _____

    Ex. _____   Eph. _____

    Bar. _____   Phil. _____

    Jer. _____   Neh. _____

Part 2: Fill in the Blank

Directions: Look up the given book and chapter of the Bible and skim the chapter to find the given verse. Then fill in the blanks with the missing words.

1. **1 Corinthians 13:** _____ is patient, _____ is kind. It is not jealous, (_____) is not pompous, it is not inflated, it is not rude, it does not seek its own interests, it is not quick-tempered, it does not brood over injury, it does not rejoice over wrongdoing but rejoices with the truth. It bears all things, believes all things, hopes all things, endures all things.

2. **Romans 12:** For as in one body we have many parts, and all the parts do not have the same function, so we, though many, are _____ in Christ and individually _____. Since we have gifts that differ according to the grace given to us, let us exercise them: if prophecy, in proportion to the faith; if ministry, in ministering; if one is a teacher, in teaching.

3. **Ephesians 1:** In him we have redemption by his _____, the forgiveness of transgressions, in accord with the riches of his grace that he lavished upon us.

4. **Proverbs 3**: For whom the LORD _____ he reproves, as a father the son he favors.

5. **Revelation 13**: Then I saw a beast come out of the sea with ten _____ and seven _____; on its _____ were ten _____, and on its heads _____ names.

6. **Proverbs 1**: _____ is the beginning of _____; fools despise _____ and _____.

7. **Luke 9**: He said to them, "Give them some food yourselves." They replied, "_____ are all we have, unless we ourselves go and buy food for all these people."

8. **Matthew 5**: Blessed are they who _____ for righteousness, for they will be satisfied.

Part 3: Who Said This?

Directions: Look up the given verses in the Bible to determine who made the statements listed. You may need to look in the verses surrounding the given passage to figure it out.

Bible Verse	Who said it
"Saul, Saul, why are you persecuting me?" –ACTS 9:4	1. _____
"I saw the Lord seated on a high and lofty throne, with the train of his garment filling the temple." –ISAIAH 6:1	2. _____
"You will soon persuade me to play the Christian." –ACTS 26:28	3. _____
"Go and search diligently for the child. When you have found him, bring me word, that I too may go and do him homage." –MATTHEW 2:8	4. _____
"Now shout, for the LORD has given you the city." –JOSHUA 6:16	5. _____

Bible Verse	Who said it
"By hearsay I had heard of you, but now my eye has seen you." –JOB 42:5	6. _____
"Fear God and keep his commandments, for this concerns all humankind." –ECCLESIASTES 12:13	7. _____
"How, then, could I do this great wrong and sin against God?" –GENESIS 39:9	8. _____
"If you are the Son of God, throw yourself down from here, for it is written: 'He will command his angels concerning you, to guard you,' and: 'With their hands they will support you, lest you dash your foot against a stone.'" –LUKE 4:9-11	9. _____
"Behold, half of my possessions, Lord, I shall give to the poor, and if I have extorted anything from anyone I shall repay it four times over." –LUKE 19:8	10. _____

Part 4: Random and Humorous

Directions: Look up the given passages of the Bible to answer each question.

1. What does a dog return to? –PROVERBS 26:11 _____

2. What does Jacob use as a pillow? –GENESIS 28:11 _____

3. What happened to the young man who grew bored of St. Paul's preaching? –ACTS 20:9

_____

4. What did Esau eat? –GENESIS 25:30 _____

5. How many times does St. Joseph (Jesus' earthly father) speak in the Bible? _____
   (Hint: count the number of times you find him speaking in the four Gospels. He appears only before Jesus is born and during His early childhood.)

How to Use the Supplemental Material in the Bible

Directions: Read the essay below, then follow the activity instructions and answer the questions that follow.

In addition to the Bible text, there is other valuable information in your Bible that can help you interpret and understand Scripture. At the beginning of most books, or before a group of books, you will find an introduction. This usually brief section will provide you with details about the authorship of the book, major themes or structures in the book, and other helpful information.

In each book you will find footnotes and cross-references at the bottom of pages. The footnotes provide additional information and valuable insights into the meaning of certain words or phrases in their original languages or certain ancient customs (that may have a different meaning in English or to our modern world). The cross-references direct you to other verses in Scripture that are similar, refer to the same thing, quote the same verse, or are helpful in interpretation. This information is the result of solid exegetical (interpretive) work done by and generally agreed upon by many scholars.

Every time you see an obelisk (†) in the Bible text, you will find a corresponding footnote labeled with the same chapter and verse numbers at the bottom of the page. Every time you see an asterisk (*) in the Bible text, you will find a corresponding cross-reference labeled with the same chapter and verse numbers at the bottom of the page. The cross-references direct you to similar Scripture passages.

Other versions of the Bible may use an asterisk (*) instead of an obelisk to indicate a corresponding footnote and small letters (a, b, c,...) to indicate a corresponding cross-reference. Regardless of the marking, the meaning is the same.

Let's practice! First, using a physical Bible:

1. Read the introduction to the book of Genesis.

2. Who wrote the book of Genesis? _____

3. What are the major sections of Genesis, and where does each section begin and end?

    _____

    _____

4. What are the major themes of the book of Genesis?

   _____

   _____

5. Look up Genesis 1:1-2. Which verse(s) indicates there is a footnote?

   _____

6. Which verse(s) indicates there is a cross-reference? (List the first five.)

   _____

   _____

7. Summarize the information provided for the first footnote given for this passage.

   _____

   _____

8. Look up the very last cross-referenced passage for verses 1-2. Why do you think this particular passage was cross-referenced?

   _____

   _____

UNIT 2

How is the Bible Different from Other Books?

In this unit, you will learn about...

> How the Holy Spirit inspired the human authors of Scripture.

> The writing styles of Scripture.

> The criteria for biblical interpretation.

> The senses of Scripture.

> The Old and New Testaments.

> The story of Salvation History and the covenants.

Introduction

Sacred Scripture is the inspired Word of God. That means that God spoke through human writers who wrote using their own abilities. God is the primary author of Scripture, but the human writers are also true authors. The human authors were inspired by the Holy Spirit to write what God wanted written for the sake of our salvation.

God reveals to us His plan for our salvation through both the Old and New Testaments of Scripture. The Old Testament prepares for the New and the New Testament sheds light on the Old. The Old Testament tells of the covenants God entered into with mankind throughout Salvation History. A covenant is a sacred permanent bond of family relationship.

In other words, throughout Salvation History, God has invited us to be a part of His divine family and prepared us to receive the gift of salvation. The New Testament tells of the New Covenant in Christ, in which Jesus won for us salvation from sin. By His Cross and Resurrection, we are freed from sin and made members of God's family in an everlasting covenant.

The proper interpretation of Scripture is guided by certain criteria given to us by the Church. In order to best know the meaning of Scripture, we must consider both the intention of the human authors and what God desired to be committed to writing for the sake of our salvation.

Are there any questions you still have about the topics you learned last month? What steps can you take to find out the answers?

_____

_____

_____

_____

What questions do you have right now about the topics you will be learning about in this unit?

_____

_____

_____

_____

_____

Apocalyptic: A writing style of Scripture. Apocalyptic writings communicate truths about God and our salvation through visions, often including strange imagery and symbolism.

Canon: The official list of inspired books that appear in the Bible. The Catholic canon of Scripture includes 46 Old Testament books and 27 New Testament books.

Covenant: A sacred unbreakable bond of family relationship. God entered in a series of covenants with mankind throughout Salvation History to invite us to be part of His divine family and to prepare gradually and in stages and in words and deeds to receive the gift of salvation.

Epistle/Letter: A writing style of Scripture. The epistles are letters written by St. Paul and other Apostles to early Christian communities and individuals to encourage them in their faith. They offer advice and teaching to their recipients that often apply to our situations today.

Foreshadow: To show, warn of, or indicate a future event before it happens. There are many stories, people, events, and ideas in the Old Testament that foreshadow later stories, people, events, and ideas in the New Testament, especially Jesus Christ and the events of salvation.

Genealogy: A writing style of Scripture. Genealogies record family ancestries and reveal important family connections between individuals in the Bible.

Inspiration: The human authors of Scripture were guided by God through the Holy Spirit in their writing. God's Spirit was present with them when they chose the words to write and how to write them. The Holy Spirit moved within them to write the truth God wanted written for the sake of our salvation.

Law: A writing style of Scripture. The Law, mostly contained in the first five books of the Bible, called the Pentateuch, are writings that communicate how to best love God and each other. The Law is necessary to free us from sin and direct us toward the ultimate goodness who is God.

Mediator: The person God chose to represent all those entering into a covenant with Him. Adam, Noah, Abraham, Moses, David, and Jesus Christ are the mediators of the primary covenants throughout Salvation History.

Narrative: A writing style of Scripture. Narratives tell a story in a straightforward way, recounting some event or story of an important person in Israel's history.

New Testament: The 27 books of Scripture that appear after the Old Testament that tell the story of the New Covenant. In the New Testament we meet God's Word Incarnate Jesus Christ, and we learn of His life, teachings, Passion, Death, Resurrection, and Ascension, as well as the story of the beginning of His Church guided by the Holy Spirit. The four Gospels hold a place of special importance in the New Testament and all of Scripture.

Old Testament: The first 46 books of Scripture that tell the story of the Old Covenant. The Old Covenant contains all the ways that God revealed Himself to us in Salvation History in order to prepare us for salvation in Jesus Christ.

Parable: A writing style of Scripture. Parables are short stories that communicate layers of truth. Jesus often used parables to teach His disciples.

Poetry: A writing style of Scripture. The poetic writings of the Bible use metaphorical and artistic language to communicate basic truths about God and human nature. Although they typically do not rhyme, they follow a certain rhythm and meter and employ characteristic literary devices such as parallelism and repetition.

Progression: The increase in the number of people included in each covenant, and God's family, throughout Salvation History.

Promise: Every covenant included a blessing from God that He assured His people He would fulfill. For example, God promised Abraham that His descendants would be more numerous than the stars and that they would bless the world.

Prophecy: A writing style of Scripture. The prophetic writings of the Bible foretold the consequences of the current course of action of the people of Israel and called them to repentance and right worship of God. Prophetic writings also warn us today of similar actions and consequences in our own lives and call us to turn away from sin and pursue holiness. These writings would also tell of the fulfillment of God's promises to His people and of His loving care for them.

Ruah: The Hebrew word for "breath" and "spirit." Just as God breathed His "breath of life" into Adam when He created Him to give him life, God's Spirit is present in the Scriptures, making them the living Word of God.

Salvation History: The story of God's love and mercy revealed to us throughout human history, culminating in Christ's sacrifice on the Cross and Resurrection from the dead which won for us salvation from sin and death.

The Senses of Scripture: The meanings of Scripture and the events described in it. There are two senses of Scripture: literal and spiritual. The literal sense is the meaning of the words of Scripture discovered by study of the text. The spiritual sense allows us to understand that, thanks to the unity of God's plan, the realities and events the text describes are themselves signs of our Faith. For example, the parting of the red sea is a sign of Baptism. The fullness of God's plan of revelation is revealed in Christ. All interpretation of Scripture must be guided by the judgment of the Church, which has the responsibility of protecting and interpreting the Word of God. The unity of the literal and spiritual senses allow the Church to interpret the riches of Sacred Scripture.

Sign: An external representation of the interior reality occurring within a covenant. Every covenant included a sign taken from human experience to represent the depth of God's love and mercy present at the heart of the covenant. Marriage between a man and a woman, the Sabbath, the rainbow, circumcision, the Law, Passover, the Temple, and the Eucharist are examples of signs of the covenants.

Three Criteria for Interpreting Scripture:
Guidelines given to us by the Church to help ensure that our interpretation of Scripture does not stray from the truth. First, we must look closely at the content and unity of the whole Scripture. Second, we must read Scripture within the living Tradition of the Church. Third, we must be attentive to the analogy of the faith.

Typology: The study of how a person or thing in Salvation History foreshadows a person or thing in Salvation History, especially as it relates to Jesus Christ and salvation. The earlier person or thing is a "type" of the later person or thing. For example: Noah's ark is a type of the Church. Isacc is a type of Christ.

Wisdom/Proverbs: A writing style of Scripture. Wisdom literature comments on the human condition using learned, quotable sayings. These often offer advice for a wide range of topics and situations.

Jonah and the Whale
BY JUSTUS JONAS D. Ä. (C. 1517)

Universitätsmatrikel in Erfurt Justus, Germany.

Jonah and the Whale

Jonah and the Whale, by Justus Jonas D. Ä (c. 1517)

Directions: Take some time to quietly view and reflect on the art. Let yourself be inspired in any way that happens naturally. Then think about the questions below, and discuss them with your classmates.

Conversation Questions

1. Read Jonah 2:1-11. How does the painting illustrate this story?

2. How did the artist depict the fish?

3. In Jonah 2:3, to what does Jonah compare being in the belly of the fish? In verse 7, what does Jonah believe God will do for him?

4. Who is the figure radiating light in the top center of the painting? Why do you think he is included in this image?

5. Read Matthew 12:38-40. How does this help clarify why this figure is in the painting? (Note: The figure kneeling in front of him is likely a wealthy patron who commissioned this painting.)

6. What do you think the figure on the back of the fish represents, and what is he doing?

7. Is there anything you would change about this painting? Why?

Biblical Foreshadowing

Directions: Look up each Scripture passage in the Bible and write in your own words a brief summary of each passage. Then determine what the Old Testament passage is foreshadowing and record your answer in the third column.

Old Testament Passage	New Testament Passage	What is foreshadowed?
1 Genesis 3:1-7, 22-24	1 Corinthians 15:20-22	
2 Exodus 16:1-15	John 6:48-51	

Old Testament Passage	New Testament Passage	What is foreshadowed?
3 Numbers 21:4-9	Luke 23:33-35	
4 2 Samuel 7:12-16	Luke 1:30-33	

2 Peter 1:20-21

Know this first of all, that there is no prophecy of scripture that is a matter of personal interpretation, for no prophecy ever came through human will; but rather human beings moved by the Holy Spirit spoke under the influence of God.

_____

_____

_____

_____

_____

_____

_____

_____

_____

Genesis 2:7

[T]hen the LORD God formed the man out of the dust of the ground and blew into his nostrils the breath of life, and the man became a living being.

_____

_____

_____

_____

_____

_____

_____

_____

_____

Romans 12:6

Since we have gifts that differ according to the grace given to us, let us exercise them: if prophecy, in proportion to the faith.

_____

_____

_____

_____

_____

_____

_____

_____

Matthew 5:17-18

Do not think that I have come to abolish the law or the prophets. I have come not to abolish but to fulfill. Amen, I say to you, until heaven and earth pass away, not the smallest letter or the smallest part of a letter will pass away from the law, until all things have taken place.

1 Corinthians 13:4-7

Love is patient, love is kind. It is not jealous, [love] is not pompous, it is not inflated, it is not rude, it does not seek its own interests, it is not quick-tempered, it does not brood over injury, it does not rejoice over wrongdoing but rejoices with the truth. It bears all things, believes all things, hopes all things, endures all things.

The Inspiration of Scripture

Directions: Read the essay, then answer the questions that follow.

In the first lines of the book of Genesis, the sacred author used the Hebrew word *ruah* to describe God's presence in the beginning before creation. This is often translated as a "mighty wind" that swept over the nothingness (Genesis 1:2). But the original meaning is clear. *Ruah* is used to describe the Spirit of God, the very presence of God Himself.

Later in Genesis, we read when God created Adam out of the dust of the ground, He "blew into his nostrils the breath of life" (Genesis 2:7). The Hebrew word chosen by the Sacred Author to describe the "breath" of God is a very specific one: *Ruah*. Again, this more accurately translates into "spirit." Our word *spirit* comes from the Latin *spiritus*, which means *breath*. God breathed into Adam His own spirit and gift of life. Put another way, God "in-spirited" Adam, or inspired him. It was the very presence of God placed within Adam that animated him and gave him life.

As Christians, we believe all of Scripture is inspired by God. In other words, just as the Spirit of God was present within Adam, so too is it present in the Scriptures. Scripture itself claims this truth. St. Paul, in his second letter to Timothy, writes: "All scripture is inspired by God and is useful for teaching, for refutation, for correction, and for training in righteousness, so that one who belongs to God may be competent, equipped for every good work" (2 Timothy 3:16-17). And St. Peter writes: "Know this first of all, that there is no prophecy of scripture that is a matter of personal interpretation, for no prophecy ever came through human will; but rather human beings moved by the Holy Spirit spoke under the influence of God (2 Peter 1:20-21). Clearly, these sacred authors understood that the Spirit of God is present in the Scriptures in a special way, animating them and giving them life. Therefore, we can say God is the primary author of Scripture.

God did not, however, put pen to paper Himself. To speak to us in a human way, God worked through human beings to write the truth that He wanted put down into writing. Thus, the Holy Spirit inspired the human authors of the Sacred Books of the Bible. The official Church document on Divine Revelation, *Dei Verbum*, tells us: "To compose the sacred books, God chose certain men who...made full use of their own faculties and powers so that, though He acted in them and by them, it was as true authors that they consigned to writing whatever He wanted written and no more" (11). In other words, the human authors of Scripture used their own powers and abilities to write. They chose the language, words, and writing style to communicate God's truth in writing. God's inspiration of Scripture did not lessen the authorship of the human authors. In fact, the human authors truly cooperated with the movement of the Holy Spirit in their lives, as all of us are called to do.

Just as the *ruah* of God dwelled within Adam and gave him life, so too did the Spirit of God dwell within the Sacred Authors of Scripture to move them to write. The same Holy Spirit is present to us today in the inspired Word of God, the Sacred Scriptures.

1. What word does the sacred author of Genesis use to describe God's presence in the beginning before creation? What does the word mean? How is it translated in English?

    _____

    _____

2. What word does the sacred author of Genesis use to describe how God brought Adam to life? How is it translated in English? How is its meaning similar to the word used to describe God's presence before creation?

    _____

    _____

    _____

    _____

3. What do we as Christians believe about the inspiration of Scripture? How is this similar to the way that God "in-spirited" Adam?

    _____

    _____

4. Describe one example from Scripture itself of how the sacred authors understood the inspiration of Scripture.

    _____

    _____

    _____

5. Why can we say that God is the primary author of Scripture?

    _____

    _____

6. How did God speak to us in a human way?

_____

_____

7. Can the human authors of Scripture be considered true authors of Scripture? Why?

_____

_____

8. What is one way the Holy Spirit is present to us today?

_____

_____

Reflection Question

If God is the primary author of Scripture and inspired the human authors to write the truth, what then should be our attitude toward Scripture? Have you ever read or heard proclaimed a particular Scripture passage that "spoke" to you? If yes, how did that make you feel? If no, how could you encounter God in a new way in Scripture in the future?

_____

_____

_____

_____

_____

_____

_____

The Truth of Scripture Anticipation Guide, Part 1

Directions: Based on what you may have heard or read, which of the statements below do you think are true, and which are false? Circle your answer for each statement.

	True or false?	
1. The stories in the Bible were made up by the human authors.	True	False
2. Every last detail in the Bible is literally true.	True	False
3. The human authors of the Bible wrote using their own powers and abilities.	True	False
4. The Bible contains what we need to know for the sake of our salvation.	True	False
5. The Bible is our only source of truth.	True	False

The Truth of Scripture Anticipation Guide, Part 2

Directions: Based on what you may have heard or read, which of the statements below do you think are true, and which are false? Circle your answer for each statement.

	True or false?	
1. The stories in the Bible were made up by the human authors.	True	False
2. Every last detail in the Bible is literally true.	True	False
3. The human authors of the Bible wrote using their own powers and abilities.	True	False
4. The Bible contains what we need to know for the sake of our salvation.	True	False
5. The Bible is our only source of truth.	True	False

Writing Styles of the Bible Worksheet

Part 1

Directions: Look up the following passages together with your teacher and discuss why they are examples of the given writing style of the Bible.

1. **Narrative:** Genesis 12:1-4

2. **Law:** Exodus 20:1-17

3. **Prophecy:** Jonah 3:4-5

4. **Poetry:** Psalm 78:1-4

5. **Wisdom/proverbs:** Proverbs 19:1

6. **Parable:** Mark 4:3-9

7. **Genealogy:** Matthew 1:1-17

8. **Epistle/letter:** Philippians 1:1-2

9. **Apocalyptic:** Revelation 12: 1-18

Part 2

Directions: Look up the following passages on your own or with a partner and determine which writing style of the Bible they are examples of. Briefly explain why you think so in the space provided. There are two examples of each writing style.

1. **Matthew 5:1-12** _____

Why?

_____

_____

2. **Luke 15:11-32** _____

Why?

_____

_____

3. **Jeremiah 25:8-19** _____

Why?

_____

_____

4. **Sirach 9:10** _____

Why?

_____

_____

5. **1 Samuel 16:10-13** _____

Why?

_____

_____

6. **Luke 1:46-55** _____

Why?

_____

_____

7. **Daniel: 2:31-45** _____

Why?

_____

_____

8. **Genesis 11:10-32** _____

Why?

_____

_____

9. **1 Timothy 1:1-2** _____

Why?

_____

_____

10. **Isaiah 53:4-6** _____

Why?

_____

_____

11. **Mark 10:17-22** _____

Why?

_____

_____

12. **Revelation 19:11-16** _____

Why?

_____

_____

13. **Ruth 4:17-22** _____

Why?

_____

_____

14. **Romans 12:1-2** _____

Why?

_____

_____

15. **Luke 1:39-45** _____

Why?

_____

_____

16. **1 Peter 1:1-12** _____

Why?

_____

_____

17. **Matthew 20:1-16** _____

Why?

_____

_____

18. **Psalm 1:2-3** _____

Why?

_____

_____

The Interpretation of Scripture
Note-Taking Guide

Directions: While listening to the lecture on the interpretation of Scripture, complete the sentences below.

1. St. Peter understood that Scripture is the _____ and therefore is not open to personal _____.

2. The interpreter of Scripture must seek to understand _____ _____.

3. A _____ helps us visualize how to interpret Scripture best: first close up with _____ itself, then outward to _____, and finally outward again to consider the _____ of the whole Catholic Faith.

4. The first criterion for interpreting Scripture is to _____ _____.

5. The footnotes and _____ included in most Bibles help direct the reader to other places in Scripture where a topic is addressed.

6. The first criterion for interpreting Scripture helps to avoid _____, which means trying to make a passage of Scripture mean or say something that is not supported by anything else in the Bible.

7. The second criterion for interpreting Scripture is to _____ _____.

8. The living Tradition of the Church consists of _____,

   _____, and _____

   _____.

9. The third criterion for interpreting Scripture is to _____

   _____.

10. The analogy of faith refers to all of the _____ and

    _____ of the Church and the whole of God's plan for

    _____.

Reflection Question

How should a person react if he finds that he has interpreted a passage of Scripture incorrectly? Why? Has this situation ever happened to you? How did you react?

_____

_____

_____

_____

_____

_____

Senses of Scripture Graphic Organizer

Directions: Fill out the graphic organizer with the correct information during the PowerPoint presentation on the senses of Scripture.

Sense	Definition

Identifying the Senses of Scripture

Directions   Look up and read each of the given Scripture passages. Then read the brief commentary and determine which sense of Scripture is being addressed.

Senses of Scripture			
Literal	Allegorical/ Typological	Moral/Tropological	Anagogical

Which sense of Scripture is the commentary addressing?

_____   1. **Genesis 22:1-19**
God calls Abraham to sacrifice his only beloved son, Isaac, as a test of his faith. On the journey, Isaac carries the wood for his own sacrifice up one of the mountains that would become Jerusalem, on which Jesus would later be crucified. Along the way, Isaac asks Abraham where the sheep for the offering was, to which Abraham responded: "God will provide the sheep." Later, God's only Son, Jesus, the Lamb of God, offers Himself in sacrifice on the Cross.

_____   2. **Genesis 1:26-27**
God creates man and woman in His image and likeness and gives humanity dominion over all of creation.

_____   3. **Psalm 122:1**
David sings of the joy that awaits us when we enter into the house of the Lord.

Which sense of Scripture is the commentary addressing?

_____ 4. **Genesis 4:8-16**

Cain kills his brother Abel and is punished for his actions even while God still loves Him and seeks to protect him from further violence.

_____ 5. **Isaiah 53:1-12**

The prophet Isaiah tells of one who suffers for the sins of others, who is punished and wounded to take on the guilt of the sin of others. He was led "like a lamb to the slaughter" and accepted his fate. It is because of this that this person will be exalted above all others. Jesus fulfills this prophecy by being beaten, flogged, and crucified for the sins of all.

_____ 6. **Matthew 22:37-40**

Jesus teaches that the greatest commandment is to love God above all else and the second greatest is to love our neighbor as ourselves.

_____ 7. **Mark 9:2-8**

Jesus' divinity is revealed to Peter, James, and John as He ascends a mountain and is transfigured. Then Elijah and Moses appear, and Jesus converses with them.

_____ 8. **Revelation 21:22-27**

John's vision describes the heavenly Jerusalem that has no need for a Temple because God is its center. His glory shines across the heavenly city and all who dwell within it.

Senses of Scripture Relay

Complete the steps below as quickly as you can — the
first group to fill out the worksheet correctly wins!

Step 1: Rapid Summary!

Directions: With your partner(s), read each selection from Scripture and summarize it in the space provided.

1. 1 Samuel 17:40-51 _____
_____
_____
_____

2. 1 Corinthians 3:16-17 _____
_____
_____
_____

Step 2: Fast Match!

Directions: One person from your group should go up to the teacher, who will hand you a commentary card. Read the card and write down which Scripture passage it describes. Then write down which of the four senses of Scripture it refers to and why you think so. When your group is finished with one card, another person from your group should go back to the teacher and trade the finished card for a new card. Continue this way until you have completed the answers for all cards.

When you have completed your worksheet, have one person bring the paper up to the teacher to check the answers. First group to complete the worksheet correctly wins!

A

Scripture related to this card: _____

Sense of Scripture: _____ Why?

B

Scripture related to this card: _____

Sense of Scripture: _____ Why?

C

Scripture related to this card: _____

Sense of Scripture: _____ Why?

D

Scripture related to this card: _____

Sense of Scripture: _____ Why?

E

Scripture related to this card: _____

Sense of Scripture: _____ Why?

F

Scripture related to this card: _____

Sense of Scripture: _____ Why?

G

Scripture related to this card: _____

Sense of Scripture: _____ Why?

H

Scripture related to this card: _____

Sense of Scripture: _____ Why?

Prediction Guide on the Old and New Testaments

Directions: Before reading **The Old and New Testaments**, put a check mark next to the statements below that you predict the author will confirm in the reading. Then, after reading, put a check mark next to those statements that the author did indeed confirm in the reading.

Your prediction	Statement	Confirmed by author
	1. The Bible is made up of seventy-three books.	
	2. The Holy Spirit guided the Church to choose the various writings included in the Bible because they measure up to the truth of the Christian faith.	
	3. Only the writings of the New Testament are inspired by God.	
	4. Jesus was unaware of the ways in which the Old Testament pointed to and prepared for His coming.	
	5. There is nothing for us to learn from the Old Testament today.	
	6. The most important things contained in the Old Testament are the signs, symbols, and prophecies that foreshadow the coming of Jesus Christ.	
	7. The only way to know about Jesus Christ is through the Gospels.	
	8. We can better understand the New Testament by reading the Old Testament.	

The Old and New Testaments

Directions: Read the following essay and use it to complete **Prediction Guide on the Old and New Testaments** on the previous page.

The Bible is divided into two parts: the Old Testament and the New Testament. Each part is made up of many different books. The Old Testament contains 46 books, and the New Testament contains 27 books. That means the Bible is made up of 73 books.

In the first centuries of the Church, the Holy Spirit guided the Church to determine the official list of inspired books that appear in the Bible. This official list is called the canon of Scripture. The word *canon* means "measuring rod." The canon of Scripture is literally the books of the Bible that "measure up." In other words, the 73 books of the Bible consistently and faithfully present the revealed truths of the Christian faith in written form.

The Old Testament is not called the Old Testament because it is outdated or no good anymore. Rather, it is called the Old Testament because it tells the story of the Old Covenant. The Old Covenant contains all the ways that God revealed Himself to us in human history in order to prepare us gradually and in stages for salvation. God revealed Himself first to Adam and Eve, then to the Chosen People, fathered by Abraham. He was proclaimed by the prophets, who prepared the way for the coming of the Messiah. The New Testament tells the story of the New Covenant, that is, the story of salvation won for us by Jesus Christ. Therefore, both the Old and New Testaments

Abraham and Isaac, by Rembrandt

are essential parts of the Bible. The books of the Old Testament are no less inspired by God than the books of the New Testament.

In fact, the Old Covenant is just as important today as it was thousands of years ago. Jesus says in Matthew 5:17-18, "Do not think that I have come to abolish the law or the prophets. I have come not to abolish but to fulfill. Amen, I say to you, until heaven and earth pass away, not the smallest letter or the smallest part of a letter will pass away from the law, until all things have taken place." When Jesus says "the law or the prophets," He is referring to what we call the Old Testament today. He makes it clear that He did not do away with the Old Covenant, but rather fulfilled it. It is still an important part of our faith today.

Because God is the primary author of the Bible, the Old Testament was intentionally written using prophecy, signs, and symbols that foreshadow and prepare for the coming of Christ. Although the typological meaning of the Old Testament is perhaps of most importance, the Old Testament also has great value in its own right. *Dei Verbum*, the Church's document on Divine Revelation explains that the writings of the Old Testament "are a storehouse of sublime teaching on God and of sound wisdom on human life, as well as a wonderful treasury of prayers." In other words, the Old Testament collects the beautiful and inspiring knowledge of God, offers guidance for our lives, and teaches us how to pray. Therefore, Christians everywhere honor the Old Testament as the true Word of God.

The New Testament is the Word of God in a way that is unique from the Old Testament. In the New Testament, we meet God's Word Incarnate, Jesus Christ. The New Testament has at its center the life, teachings, Passion, death, and Resurrection of Jesus, as well as the story of the beginning of His Church guided by the Holy Spirit. Of special importance in the New Testament are the four Gospels, which contain the written record of the New Covenant and the life of Christ. Therefore, we venerate the Gospels above all other Scripture, not only at Mass, but in our own spiritual lives.

Together, the Old and New Testaments form an organic unity of Scripture. That means that we read the Old Testament in the light of the Crucified and Risen Christ, and we read the New Testament in the light of the Old. The *Catechism of the Catholic Church* no. 129 puts it this way: "the New Testament lies hidden in the Old, and the Old Testament is unveiled in the New." Thus, both Testaments of Scripture are essential to each other and to our Christian faith.

The Old and New Testaments Statement Support

Directions: For each confirmed statement from the prediction guide, rewrite the statement and then write two or three sentences in your own words that describe how the reading confirms the statement. For each unconfirmed statement, write two or three sentences in your own words that describe what the reading does say about each statement.

Confirmed Statements

1. Rewrite the statement:

   _____

   _____

   What supporting evidence confirms the statement?

   _____

   _____

   _____

2. Rewrite the statement:

   _____

   _____

   What supporting evidence confirms the statement?

   _____

   _____

   _____

3. Rewrite the statement:

_____

_____

What supporting evidence confirms the statement?

_____

_____

_____

4. Rewrite the statement:

_____

_____

What supporting evidence confirms the statement?

_____

_____

_____

Unconfirmed Statements

5. Rewrite the statement:

_____

_____

What does the reading say about the unconfirmed statement?

_____

_____

_____

6. Rewrite the statement:

_____

_____

What does the reading say about the unconfirmed statement?

_____

_____

_____

7. Rewrite the statement:

_____

_____

What does the reading say about the unconfirmed statement?

_____

_____

_____

8. Rewrite the statement:

_____

_____

What does the reading say about the unconfirmed statement?

_____

_____

_____

Old and New Testament Quick Write

Directions: Using the entire time allowed, write a response in your own words to the following prompt:

One important thing a person should know about
the Old and New Testaments is...

_____

_____

_____

_____

_____

_____

_____

_____

_____

_____

_____

_____

_____

Consequences and Relationships

Directions: Briefly describe what you think the consequence might be for each of the following scenarios.

1. You hire someone to put in new windows and siding on your house. He does a very poor job and causes damage to your home.

    _____

    _____

    _____

2. You accept a new job that will pay you a salary. You fail to show up for work regularly, and when you do show up, you are late and you fail to meet deadlines.

    _____

    _____

    _____

3. A student brings a gun to school and threatens other students.

    _____

    _____

    _____

4. Your parents give you a curfew. You get home two hours late.

    _____

    _____

    _____

5. A wife goes out to run errands for the day and asks her husband to do some things around the house. He agrees. She posts the list of things she needs done on the refrigerator. He spends all day watching sports and relaxing on the couch and doesn't do any of the things on his wife's list.

_____

_____

_____

After reflecting on the above scenarios answer the following questions:

6. What are the differences between the first three scenarios and the last two?

_____

_____

_____

7. How do the consequences between the first set and the second set of scenarios differ?

_____

_____

_____

8. What set of scenarios is our relationship with God more like? Explain.

_____

_____

_____

Contracts vs. Covenants

Directions: Complete the chart using the information below, information from your teacher, and your own knowledge.

The *Catechism* defines mercy as "the loving kindness, compassion, or forbearance shown to one who offends." Mercy can also be defined as love that keeps on loving even when it is rejected. God has revealed His mercy to us through covenants in salvation history. Covenant comes from the Latin word *convenire*, which means "to come together" or "to agree," and it is the central theme throughout Scripture. A covenant is a formal and solemn pact or agreement permanently binding two or more parties to responsibilities toward each other.

	Contracts	Covenants
1	Exchange of _____.	Exchange of _____.
2	Sets up obligations, but they are not _____ obligations.	There are personal responsibilities that flow from a covenant. These responsibilities are based on _____.
3	The basis of contractual obligations is _____.	Covenants are based on _____.
4	Can be dissolved / cannot be dissolved. (circle one)	Can be dissolved / cannot be dissolved. (circle one)

The Covenant with Noah

Directions: Read Genesis 9:8-17, the story of God's covenant with Noah, then answer the questions that follow.

God blessed Noah and his sons and said to them: "Be fertile and multiply and fill the earth. Fear and dread of you shall come upon all the animals of the earth and all the birds of the air, upon all the creatures that move about on the ground and all the fishes of the sea; into your power they are delivered. Any living creature that moves about shall be yours to eat; I give them all to you as I did the green plants. Only meat with its lifeblood still in it you shall not eat. Indeed for your own lifeblood I will demand an accounting: from every animal I will demand it, and from a human being, each one for the blood of another, I will demand an accounting for human life.

"Anyone who sheds the blood of a human being, by a human being shall that one's blood be shed; For in the image of God have human beings been made. Be fertile, then, and multiply; abound on earth and subdue it."

God said to Noah and to his sons with him: "See, I am now establishing my covenant with you and your descendants after you and with every living creature that was with you:

the birds, the tame animals, and all the wild animals that were with you—all that came out of the ark. I will establish my covenant with you, that never again shall all creatures be destroyed by the waters of a flood; there shall not be another flood to devastate the earth."

God said: "This is the sign of the covenant that I am making between me and you and every living creature with you for all ages to come: I set my bow in the clouds to serve as a sign of the covenant between me and the earth. When I bring clouds over the earth, and the bow appears in the clouds, I will remember my covenant between me and you and every living creature—every mortal being—so that the waters will never again become a flood to destroy every mortal being. When the bow appears in the clouds, I will see it and remember the everlasting covenant between God and every living creature—every mortal being that is on earth."

God told Noah: "This is the sign of the covenant I have established between me and every mortal being that is on earth".

1. Who is the mediator of this covenant? How do you know?

_____

_____

2. What obligations or responsibilities are given in this covenant?

_____

_____

3. What commands does God give in this covenant?

   _____

   _____

4. What does God promise in this covenant?

   _____

   _____

5. What is the sign of this covenant? _____

6. What other Bible story/covenant does this story remind you of? Why?

   _____

   _____

   _____

Salvation History: A Love Story

Directions: Read the story of Salvation History, then complete the questions that follow.

The story of the Christian faith is a love story. The main characters are God and His people. Throughout human history God has pursued us. He has revealed Himself to us and made His love known to us. *The Catechism of the Catholic Church* no. 218 illuminates this mystery: "In the course of its history, Israel was able to discover that God had only one reason to reveal Himself to them, a single motive for choosing them from among all peoples as His special possession: His sheer gratuitous love. And thanks to the prophets, Israel understood that it was again out of love that God never stopped saving them and pardoning their unfaithfulness and sins." The only reason God does anything is because of His love for us. Like any epic love story, the story of our faith has its ups and downs. But unlike any other human story of love, God is unfailingly faithful to His beloved, us, despite our persistent unfaithfulness.

We encounter this love story first and foremost in Scripture. The Bible is the written record of the story of our salvation. We call this salvation history. God made Himself known in specific ways, to prepare us, His people, for the gift of salvation. Salvation history is the story of God's saving actions in human history. God entered into a series of covenants with mankind. A covenant is a sacred bond of family relationship. When two parties enter into a covenant, the family relationship that is formed is permanent. It cannot be dissolved.

Through each covenant, God gradually and in stages, in words and deeds, revealed more of Himself and drew us deeper into relationship with Him. God chose certain mediators, or individuals, who represent all those entering into the covenant with God. God first revealed Himself to Adam and Eve, and then continued His self-revelation with Noah and his family. Then God promised great blessings to the world through Abraham's descendants. God freed His Chosen People from slavery through Moses and established them as a nation and then, under David, as a kingdom. Finally, God fully revealed Himself in Jesus Christ and saved His people from sin.

As God's relationship with His people progressed, each covenant brought more people into the covenant family. From the original couple, to a faithful family, to a holy tribe, to a chosen nation and later a royal kingdom, culminating in one, holy, catholic, and apostolic Church, God drew the entire human race to Him.

Each new covenant contained a sign, or an external representation of an internal reality. These signs were taken from human experience, to represent the depth of God's love present at the heart of each covenant. Marriage between a man and a woman, the Sabbath, the rainbow, circumcision, the Law, Passover, and the Temple all took on greater meaning in their communication of God's love and mercy.

At the appointed time, God Himself entered into human history by sending His only beloved Son as a man. Jesus, the Second Person of the Blessed Trinity, was like us in all things but sin. He fully revealed the Father and communicated His grace to us in and through His life and teaching. Jesus performed miracles as signs of God's love and mercy and to announce the coming of the Kingdom of God. And then He offered Himself as a sacrifice for our sins. By His Cross and Resurrection we are set free from sin, our salvation is won, and we are made holy.

Jesus tells us to love one another, saying, "This is my commandment: love one another as I love you." To love as Jesus loved is far from the warm, fuzzy feelings of the modern notion of love. How did Jesus love us? St. John the Evangelist explains: "In this is love: not that we have loved God, but that he loved us and sent his Son as expiation for our sins." Further, Jesus says, "No one has greater love than this, to lay down one's life for one's friends." The greatest expression of love is self-sacrifice, giving oneself as a gift to another.

On the night before He died, Jesus gathered with His Apostles for their last meal together. He took bread, said the blessing, broke the bread, and gave it to them, saying, "Take and eat; this is my body" (Matthew 26:26). Similarly, He took the cup of wine, gave thanks, and gave it to them, saying, "Drink from it, all of you, for this is my blood of the covenant, which will be shed on behalf of many for the forgiveness of sins" (Matthew 26:27-28). The next day, Jesus sacrificed Himself on the Cross, fulfilling His words by His actions. Christ loved us by giving Himself freely and completely to us in an act of mercy.

Rather than being an end to the love story, Christ's Passion, death, Resurrection, and glorification is a new beginning. Through this ultimate, undeserved act of love, each of us is invited to be a son or daughter of God, to receive salvation, and to enter into eternal life with a Father who loves us and has pursued us from the beginning of time.

1. What is the best way to describe the story of the Christian faith? Who is involved in this story?

   _____

   _____

2. For what reason did God reveal Himself, choose a people as His special possession, and save the entire human race by sending His only Son to die for us?

   _____

3. What is salvation history? How is it enacted?

   _____

   _____

4. What is a covenant? _____

5. What did God do through each covenant? _____

_____

6. What is a mediator? Give two examples.

_____

_____

7. What is a sign? Give two examples.

_____

_____

8. What did Jesus fully reveal to us, and how did He do this? What did He announce, and how did He do this? What did He accomplish on the Cross?

_____

_____

9. What is Jesus' commandment to us? How do we do this?

_____

_____

10. How is the Eucharist an example of Christ's love for us?

_____

_____

11. Why is Christ's Passion, death, and Resurrection not an end to the story of the Christian faith, but a beginning?

_____

_____

Reflection Question

On your own paper, describe a time that you felt loved by someone else. How did you know that you were loved? What signs were there of that love? What did you do in response? How is this time similar to or different from the way that God loves us? Why?

God's Covenants and Mercy

Directions: Every covenant has a promise, a mediator, and a sign. Each covenant also signifies a progression or growth in God's family. Fill in the following chart by placing the squares you receive in the appropriate space.

Covenant Mediator	Covenant Promise	Covenant Sign	Covenant Progression
Adam			
Noah			
Abraham			

Covenant Mediator	Covenant Promise	Covenant Sign	Covenant Progression
Moses			
David			
Jesus			

UNIT 3

The Early World of Genesis

In this unit, you will learn about...

- The story of creation and what it teaches us about God and man.
- The story of Adam and Eve.
- The Original Sin and fall of man.
- God's promise of a savior.
- The spread of sin and wickedness through the human family.
- The story of Cain and Abel.
- The Great Flood and God's covenant with Noah.

Introduction

The Book of Genesis begins with the words, "In the beginning, when God created the heavens and the earth…" This reveals to us that God is the Creator of all things; everything that is visible and material, and everything that is invisible and spiritual. From the story of creation, we learn that God is all-powerful and all-knowing, and that He goes beyond His creation and yet is intimately involved in it. God keeps the universe in existence by His Word, Jesus. As we recite at each Sunday Mass in the Nicene Creed, through Him all things were made. In fact this is one reason why we give the Holy Spirit the title, "The Giver of Life." We learn that God made many different creatures, and He gave each one unique and good qualities. We learn that creation has an order: all of God's creatures, from the tiniest bacterium to the most intricate flower petals to the most fearsome lion, are dependent on each other. All are made for the good of humanity. We learn that we are made in His image and likeness as male and female, which means that out of all of creation we are unique and capable of knowing ourselves and our Creator and of giving and receiving love.

From the very beginning God had desired that the human race come together in a loving relationship with each other and with Him. He wrote this truth into our very bodies as male and female. He ordered the universe in such a way as to be a place for the covenant between human beings and God to be lived, a Temple of creation. And He made human beings to be the priests, prophets, and kings of this Temple. In this paradise there was peace between human beings and all of creation, harmony between men and women, and no suffering or death.

Our original parents, Adam and Eve, lived in friendship with God. Out of that friendship came their perfectly happy existence. God is holy, and Adam and Eve were holy and were partakers in the divine life–this was called Original Holiness. They had nothing to fear from nature or from each other. Everything was in perfect order–this is called Original Justice. But Adam and Eve gave in to temptation from the devil, disobeyed God, and rejected His love. This disobedience was the Original Sin, which caused sin, suffering, and death to enter the world. Adam and Eve lost the Original Holiness that had been theirs, and lost it for all generations that would come after them. God, however, did not leave us in our sin and promised the human race a savior. Thus began the story of salvation, as sin and wickedness spread through the human family and God worked in word and deed to make His love and mercy known and to prepare us to receive salvation.

As you can see, the Blessed Trinity created the world and human beings out of love. This was a sign to all of creation that God is good, wise, and loving. God's plan of loving goodness reaches its fruition for each of us personally when we are made a new creation in Jesus Christ!

Are there any questions you still have about the topics you learned last month? What steps can you take to find out the answers?

_____

_____

_____

_____

What questions do you have right now about the topics you will be learning about in this unit?

_____

_____

_____

_____

Unit 3 Vocabulary

Concupiscence: A tendency, or inclination, to sin that is an effect of Original Sin. Even though Baptism erases the stain of Original Sin, the tendency to sin remains.

Creation: Everything that God made, the heavens and the earth, all things visible and invisible. God created all things out of nothing. Everything that God makes is good. Therefore, all of creation is fundamentally good.

Dominion: Authority or rule. Kings have authority and rule over their kingdoms and subjects. Adam was given dominion over all of creation.

Ex nihilo: Latin for "out of nothing." This is the doctrine of creation, that God created all things out of nothing with only His Word. This fact teaches us that God is all-powerful, all-knowing, and goes beyond His creation.

Immutable: Unchanging. God does not change and, therefore, He does not experience emotion in a human way.

Infinite: Without beginning or end. God is the creator of all things, including time and space. Therefore, He is timeless, without beginning or end, and not bound by space.

King: One of the original roles God gave to Adam in the Garden of Eden. A king has dominion, or rules over, his kingdom and its subjects. God gave Adam dominion over all of creation. Adam, then, was the first king.

Leisure: Time free from work. Rather than idleness or doing nothing, true leisure is to engage in activities, such as art, philosophy, music, and most importantly worship of God, that enrich us as human beings. Authentic leisure is when we love God and the things of God, and love our neighbor. Leisure is the purpose of our work: we work so that we can have leisure.

Nahash: Hebrew word most often translated as "serpent," but more accurately translates to "leviathan," a large, ferocious sea monster. The Book of Genesis uses the word *nahash* to describe the serpent who tempted Adam and Eve.

Navi: Hebrew word for prophet, which means "mouth." Prophets speak for God. Adam was the first prophet when he named all of the animals.

Omnipotent: All-powerful. We know that God is all-powerful because all things came from Him.

Omniscient: All-knowing. We know that God is all-knowing because if He created all things, there is nothing that He would not know.

Original Justice: The original state of human beings before sin. In the beginning there was no suffering or death, man was at peace with himself, there was harmony between men and women, and there was peace between Adam and Eve and all of creation. Original Justice was lost due to the Original Sin.

Original Sin: The first sin of Adam and Eve that brought pain, suffering, and death into the world. Because we are all descendants of Adam and Eve we are all born with Original Sin in our souls. We need to be baptized to remove the stain of Original Sin. The effects of Original Sin remain, however. For example, we tend to sin, we suffer, and we die.

Priest: One of the original roles God gave to Adam in the Garden of Eden. The task of a priest in the Old Testament was to guard and protect God's dwelling place, the tabernacle, and to serve Him. This involved making sacrifices, even of their own life, if necessary. Adam's job, then, was to guard and protect the Garden of Eden, God's dwelling place with His creation, and to serve God by offering all of creation back to Him as a sacrifice. Adam was the first priest.

Prophet: One of the original roles God gave to Adam in the Garden of Eden. The task of a prophet in the Old Testament was to speak on God' behalf and be His spokesperson. Adam was given the job of naming all of the animals, a right reserved for their creator. Adam, then, was God's spokesperson and acted as the first prophet.

Protoevangelium: Means "first Gospel." In Genesis 3:15 God promises to send a savior to crush the head of the serpent and defeat sin and death. This is the first announcement of the Gospel, the Good News of salvation won by Jesus Christ.

Shamar: Hebrew word for "to guard and protect" or "to serve." This word indicates Adam's role as a priest in the Garden of Eden.

Sin: A deliberate offense against God. It is something we say, think, do, or fail to do that is against the eternal law of God. It is a failure to love God and neighbor.

Son/Daughter of God: One of the original roles God gave to Adam and Eve in the Garden of Eden. Adam and Eve were made in God's image and likeness. Among other things, according to Scripture, to be made in one's image and likeness is to be his or her child, a son or daughter. Therefore, Adam and Eve were God's children, a son and daughter of God.

Spouse: One of the original roles God gave to Adam and Eve in the Garden of Eden. God gave Adam and Eve one initial command: "Be fertile and multiply." That is, to come together as one man and one woman in marriage and to cooperate with God's creative power and have children. The marriage of the first man and first woman is a sign of the giving and receiving of love God desires to share with all of humanity.

The Church: The community of disciples founded by Jesus that will exist until the end of time. The Church is at the same time human and divine. It is the gathering of God's people on earth and it is the mystical Body of Christ. The Church is the means by which salvation is communicated to us in this age.

The Great Flood: God caused it to rain for forty days and forty nights, which flooded the earth and washed away the sin and wickedness of humanity. Only Noah and his family and two of every animal were spared in order to renew creation and for God to enter into a new covenant with the human race.

Transcendent: Beyond full understanding and limitation. God goes beyond and is greater than His creation.

Dejection of Noah from Mountain Ararat
BY IVAN AVIAZOVSKY (C. 1870)

Dejection of Noah from Mountain Ararat

Dejection of Noah from Mountain Ararat, by Ivan Aviazovsky (c. 1870)

Directions: Take some time to quietly view and reflect on the art. Let yourself be inspired in any way that happens naturally. Then think about the questions below, and discuss them with your classmates.

Conversation Questions

1. Read Genesis 8:15-19. How does the painting illustrate this story?

2. Is the overall mood of the painting happy or sad? How do the colors of the painting enhance the feeling conveyed by the painting?

3. Notice that both the sun and the moon appear in the painting. What time of day does it appear to be? What does the time of day suggest about what is happening in this moment captured by the painting?

4. Why do you think the artist chose not to show the ark in this image?

5. Read 1 Peter 3:19-21. How does the painting help you to understand this passage?

6. Imagine that you were Noah. What do you think would be the most important things to do in the new world created out of the Flood?

Images of the Church

Directions: Decorate the image of Noah's ark with at least three signs or symbols that represent the Church and salvation. These can be actual symbols used by the Church or symbols that you create yourself.

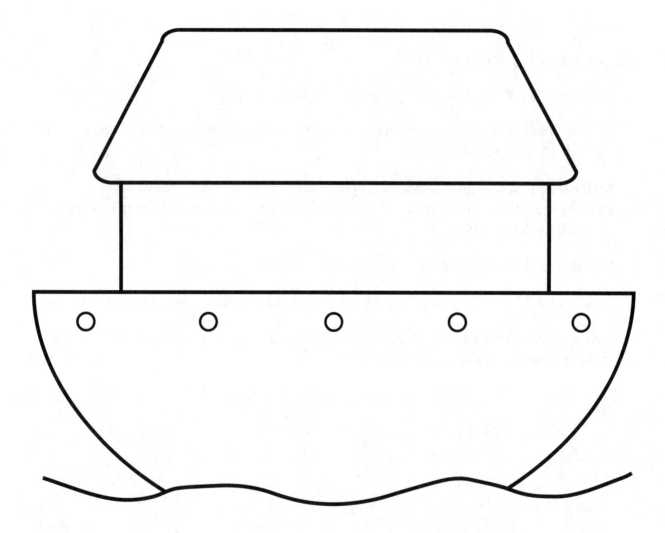

Genesis 1:31

God looked at everything He had made, and found it very good.

Psalm 8:4-6

When I see your heavens, the work of your fingers, the moon and stars that you set in place—What is man that you are mindful of him, and a son of man that you care for him? Yet you have made him little less than a god, crowned him with glory and honor.

_____

_____

_____

_____

_____

_____

_____

_____

_____

Romans 7:15

For I do not do what I want,
but I do what I hate.

Genesis 3:15

I will put enmity between you and the woman, and between your offspring and hers; They will strike at your head, while you strike at their heel.

Genesis 4:3-7

If you act rightly, you will be accepted; but if not, sin lies in wait at the door: its urge is for you, yet you can rule over it.

Acts 22:16

Now, why delay? Get up and have yourself baptized and your sins washed away, calling upon his name.

1 Peter 3:19-21

In it he also went to preach to the spirits in prison, who had once been disobedient while God patiently waited in the days of Noah during the building of the ark, in which a few persons, eight in all, were saved through water. This prefigured baptism, which saves you now.

_____

_____

_____

_____

_____

_____

_____

_____

_____

What Did God Make on Each Day of Creation?

Directions: Based on what you already know and without using a Bible or any other resource, create a list of what you think God created on each of the seven days of creation. Be specific and thorough. Where applicable, record how God made the things He made (for example, did He place the thing, form it out of something, or speak it into existence?).

	What Did God Create?	How Did God Create?
Day 1		
Day 2		
Day 3		
Day 4		
Day 5		
Day 6		
Day 7		

The Story of Creation Reading Guide

Directions: Read the story of creation in Genesis 1 and the commentaries below, then respond to the questions that follow.

Read Genesis 1:1-3, then read the following:

In Genesis 1:1, "the heavens" refers to all spiritual realities, and "the earth" refers to all physical/material realities. In other words, "the heavens and the earth" refers to all that exists. The first line of Genesis tells us that God created all that exists, spiritual and material.

The language used in Genesis 1:1-2 tells us that before the beginning there was God and the earth was "without form or shape, with darkness over the abyss." If something has no form or shape, it is nothing. Darkness is the absence of light, and an abyss is a vast emptiness. In other words, in the beginning there was nothing but God Himself.

Notice that the text mentions that, in the beginning, there were "waters" present over which a "mighty wind" swept. These waters were part of the ancient concept of the makeup of the universe and were not actual water as we think of it. These primordial waters were a way of describing the nothingness that existed before the beginning. Think of staring at the ocean on a pitch-black night and seeing literally a tangible nothing.

Since there was nothing that existed before the beginning, God created all that exists out of nothing. The Latin phrase *ex nihilo*, which means "out of nothing," describes this doctrine that God created out of nothing.

The fact that God created all that exists out of nothing tells us that He is omnipotent (all powerful) and omniscient (all knowing). It also tells us that He transcends (goes beyond) all things and is infinite (without beginning or end).

1. What does the first line of Genesis tell us that God created? What do the terms "heavens" and "earth" really refer to?

   _____

   _____

2. What does the text tell us existed before the beginning? How do we know?

   _____

   _____

3. What did God use to create? What is the Latin phrase for this doctrine of creation?

   _____

   _____

4. In knowing that God created all that exists, what else do we learn about Him?

_____

_____

Read Genesis 1:3-5, then read the following:

When God said, "Let there be light," He could not have been creating actual light as we think of it, considering the fact that the sun and the stars, the sources of light, were not created until the fourth day. The Tradition of the Church has long taught that when God said, "Let there be light," He created all the angels that would exist. The angels, pure spiritual beings, show forth the light of God in all they do. Tradition has also long taught that when the sacred author of Genesis tells us that God separated the light from the darkness, he is referring to the rebellion of Satan and the angels who followed him. The separation of light and dark is when Satan was cast out of Heaven with the angels who followed him, who became demons prowling the world, seeking the ruin of souls.

5. What is the Tradition of the Church regarding what God created when He said, "Let there be light"?

_____

6. What occurred when God separated the light from the darkness?

_____

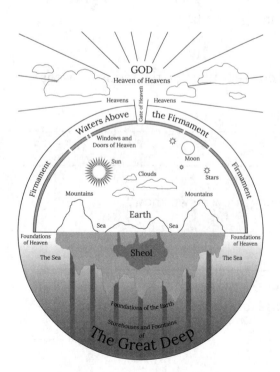

Read Genesis 1:6-13, then read the following:

Ancient people thought of the sky as a dome that covered the flat earth. While not an attempt at a scientific explanation, this description of the sky makes a kind of sense. If you stand in the middle of an open field and look all around you, you can see the sky touch the horizon at every point, like a dome. Ancient people then believed that the sun, the moon, and the stars were in fact stuck in this dome and revolved around it. Above the dome was heaven and below the earth was the underworld, *sheol*, or hell. The earth was supported by pillars that were rooted in foundations in the underworld.

7. How does the author of Genesis describe the sky? What does the sky separate?

_____

_____

8. Is the description of the sky and the formation of the land and sea a scientific explanation? Why or why not?

_____

_____

Read Genesis 1:14-19, read the following:

What do you notice about the passage of time so far in the story of creation? Four days have passed, but time ("the seasons, the days, and the years" marked by the sun and the moon, who are the "rulers" of day and night) was not created until the fourth day. So, how were there days if there was no time?

First, because of this fact, we can conclude that this account of creation is not science, nor is it meant to be. Clearly, the human author is not trying to give a scientific account of how the universe came to be. He is communicating other truths about God and His creation. We learn that God works not according to 24-hour days but gradually and in stages. He does not do things "all at once" but rather unfolds things gradually and systematically, using words and actions. This is always how God acts in human history, evidenced through the story of Scripture.

9. What is the "problem" with the Genesis accounting of the passage of time over the first four days?

_____

_____

10. What can we conclude about God by considering the passage of "time" over these first four days?

_____

_____

Read Genesis 1:20-31, then read the following:

Human beings are unique out of all the creatures God created. Only human beings were made in God's image and likeness, and they were given dominion over all the living things on earth, plants and animals.

To have dominion is to have authority or to rule over others. To have dominion is the role of a king, who has dominion over the subjects in his kingdom. A king can exercise his dominion as a good king or as a bad king. We call bad kings who abuse their authority "tyrants." God calls human beings to be good "kings" over creation and use our authority to care for and nurture all that God has made.

According to Genesis 1:27, to be made in God's image and likeness, at least in part, means to be made as male and female. The opposite and complementary nature of the sexes is a fundamental truth of human nature and part of how we directly image God.

After He finished with the work of creation on each day, God looked at what He had made and saw that it was good. This tells us that everything God makes is made fundamentally good. On the sixth day, however, God looked at what He had made and found it to be very good. This highlights the uniqueness of human life and the dignity (value) of the human person above all else in creation.

11. What is unique about human beings out of all the creatures that God created?

_____

12. What does it mean to have "dominion"?

_____

13. According to Genesis 1:27, at least in part, what does it mean to be made in God's image and likeness?

_____

_____

14. What did God say about each day after he finished with the work of creation on that day? What does that mean about what God makes?

_____

_____

15. What did God say about what He had made on the sixth day? What does that mean about humanity?

_____

_____

Read Genesis 2:1-3, then read the following:

It's easy to think that on the seventh day God did not create anything and simply lay back and relaxed. This is not the case, however. In fact, on the seventh day, God created what may be the most important thing: leisure. Leisure is not simply idleness or doing nothing; rather, leisure is the purpose of our work—that is, to engage in activity, such as philosophy, art, and, most importantly, worship of God, that enriches us as persons. Put another way, authentic leisure is when we love God and the things of God, and love our neighbor. In a certain sense, we work so we can have leisure.

Further, the Hebrew word for the number seven is the same Hebrew word for "covenant." In other words, on the seventh day of creation, God "sevens" Himself, or swears a covenant with all of creation through Adam. In this original covenant, God invites humanity to be a part of His family and to enter into covenant with Him. This invitation makes humanity greater than any of the other creatures God made. We are not pets, nor are we slaves. We are invited to be like God, in His image.

Notice that in the Genesis account, the seventh day of creation never actually ends. This is not a mistake or an oversight by the sacred author. We can understand this lack of an ending to mean that we are still in the seventh day, awaiting the eighth day, when God will make all things new. The seventh day, then, is the time set aside for us to be in relationship with God, to worship Him, and to fulfill the purpose for which we were made, which is to love God and to love one another.

16. What did God create on the seventh day? How is this the "purpose" of our work?

_____

_____

17. What is the alternate meaning of the Hebrew word for "seven"? How does this help us understand what happens on the seventh day of creation?

_____

_____

18. When does the seventh day end? What does this "ending" mean for us?

_____

_____

The Awesomeness of God

Directions: Read the Psalm, then answer the reflection questions that follow.

O LORD, our Lord,
how awesome is your name through all the earth!
I will sing of your majesty above the heavens

with the mouths of babes and infants.
You have established a bulwark against your foes,
to silence enemy and avenger.

When I see your heavens, the work of your fingers,
the moon and stars that you set in place–

What is man that you are mindful of him,
and a son of man that you care for him?

Yet you have made him little less than a god,
crowned him with glory and honor.

You have given him rule over the works of your hands,
put all things at his feet:

All sheep and oxen,
even the beasts of the field,

The birds of the air, the fish of the sea,
and whatever swims the paths of the seas.

O LORD, our Lord,
how awesome is your name through all the earth!

–PSALM 8

Reflection Questions

1. In what ways is the story of creation from Genesis 1 reflected in Psalm 8?

    _____

    _____

    _____

2. How does Psalm 8 expand on the description of the importance of human beings in creation?

    _____

    _____

    _____

3. In what ways does creation itself glorify God?

    _____

    _____

    _____

Two Stories of Creation?

Directions: Some scholars suggest that Genesis 1 and Genesis 2 are two different stories of creation. With a partner, read Genesis 2 and compare its version of the story of creation with the version found in Genesis 1. Then complete the following activities:

1. List at least three **similarities** between Genesis 1 and Genesis 2.	2. List at least three **differences** between Genesis 1 and Genesis 2.
‣ ‣ ‣	‣ ‣ ‣

Assuming that the theory that there are two different stories of creation in Genesis 1 and Genesis 2 is correct, with a partner, reflect on the following:

3. What is the main idea the author of Genesis 1 is communicating?	4. What does the author of Genesis 2 assume you already know?

5. Why is the author of Genesis 1 telling the story of creation in this way?	6. What does the author of Genesis 2 want you to understand?
7. What does the author of Genesis 1 apparently think is most important to know?	8. What does the author of Genesis 2 apparently think is most important to know?

Working on your own: Having read Genesis 1 and Genesis 2 and reflected on the content of each, do you agree with the scholars who suggest that Genesis 1 and Genesis 2 are different stories of Creation? If you agree that they represent different stories, explain why and support your answer with evidence from the text. If you disagree, and think they tell the same story from different perspectives, explain why and support your answer with evidence from the text. Write your answer on the lines below.

_____

_____

_____

_____

_____

_____

_____

_____

_____

_____

_____

_____

_____

_____

Adam Comes to Eden

BY LUIS JUAREZ (C. 1585-1639)

Mosaic in the Cathedral of Monreale, Italy.

The Roles of Adam Reading Guide

Directions: For each role, read the Scripture and the commentary, then answer the questions that follow.

Priest

Genesis 2:15: The LORD God then took the man and settled him in the Garden of Eden, to cultivate and care for it.

Numbers 3:5-8: Now the LORD said to Moses: Summon the tribe of Levi and station them before Aaron the priest to serve him. They shall discharge his obligations and those of the whole community before the tent of meeting by maintaining the tabernacle. They shall have responsibility for all the furnishings of the tent of meeting and discharge the obligations of the Israelites by maintaining the tabernacle.

God gave the man (Adam) a job: "to cultivate and care for" the Garden of Eden. The Hebrew word *shamar* describes Adam's job "to cultivate and care for" or "to guard and protect" the Garden and everything in it, including his wife, Eve.

To *shamar* is a priestly role. Numbers 3 describes the work of the Levitical priests pertaining to the tabernacle in the Israelite camp. At this time, the tabernacle was where God dwelled among His people as they wandered the desert for 40 years. Numbers 7 describes the priestly "obligations ... before the tent of meeting by *maintaining* the tabernacle," and the priestly "*responsibility* for all the furnishings of the tent of meeting ... by *maintaining* the tabernacle." The Hebrew word used in these passages, *shamar*, is the same word used to describe the work of Adam.

Therefore, we can conclude that Adam was the first priest, fulfilling the work of a priest in the garden. The Garden of Eden, then, can be understood to be the original tabernacle, God's dwelling place among His people.

1. What job did God give to Adam? Who will later have the same job? _____

2. What can we conclude about Adam after understanding the meaning of *shamar* and its use elsewhere in the Bible?

_____

Prophet

Genesis 2:18-20: The LORD God said: It is not good for the man to be alone. I will make a helper suited to him. So the LORD God formed out of the ground all the wild animals and all the birds of the air, and he brought them to the man to see what he would call them; whatever the man called each living creature was then its name. The man gave names to all the tame animals, all the birds of the air, and all the wild animals; but none proved to be a helper suited to the man.

From ancient times through today, the right to name something has belonged to its creator or discoverer. For example, parents name their children and scientists name the things they discover.

In Genesis 2, God brings all the animals to Adam to name. "He brought them to the man to see what he would call them; whatever the man called each living creature was then its name." In this instance, this means that God gave Adam the right to speak for Him.

The Hebrew word for "prophet," *navi*, means "mouth." In other words, a prophet speaks for God. He or she is God's spokesperson. Therefore, when Adam speaks for God in naming the animals, he is acting as a prophet.

3. Who usually has the right to name something? _____

4. What did God give to Adam when He brought all the animals to him?

   _____

   _____

5. What is the Hebrew word for "prophet," and what does it mean? What does this definition tell us about Adam?

   _____

   _____

   _____

King

Genesis 1:28: God blessed them and God said to them: Be fertile and multiply; fill the earth and subdue it. Have dominion over the fish of the sea, the birds of the air, and all the living things that crawl on the earth.

God gave Adam and Eve dominion over all creation. To have dominion is to have authority or to rule over, as in how a king rules over his kingdom and its subjects. Dominion is a kingly role. When God gave Adam and Eve dominion, He made them royalty: a king and a queen.

Kings can choose to exercise their dominion as either good kings or bad kings. Good kings rule their subjects by serving them and caring for them. This is seen in the kinds of laws they pass, the way those laws are enforced, and how justly the people are judged according to the law. Bad kings are tyrants. They do not serve their subjects and only take for themselves while abusing the rights of their subjects. God gave Adam and Eve dominion to be good rulers, royalty in the image and likeness of God.

6. What does it mean to have dominion? Who typically has dominion over others?

    _____

7. What is the difference between a good king and a bad king?

    _____

    _____

8. What kind of royalty did God call Adam and Eve to be? Why?

    _____

    _____

Sons and Daughters

Genesis 1:27: God created mankind in his image; in the image of God he created them; male and female he created them.

Genesis 5:3: Adam was one hundred and thirty years old when he begot a son in his likeness, after his image; and he named him Seth.

To discover the immediate meaning of being made in God's image and likeness, we must turn to the next time this language is used in Scripture, Genesis 5:3. There we learn that Adam "begot a son in his likeness, after his image." Thus, it becomes clearer that to be in one's "image and likeness" is to be his or her child, a son or daughter. Therefore, Adam and Eve, made in God's image and likeness, were His children, a son and daughter of God.

9. According to Genesis 5:3, what does it mean to be in another's image and likeness? What does this fact mean about Adam and Eve?

_____

_____

_____

Spouses

Genesis 1:28: God blessed them and God said to them: Be fertile and multiply.

Genesis 2:18-25: The LORD God said: "It is not good for the man to be alone. I will make a helper suited to him." So the LORD God formed out of the ground all the wild animals and all the birds of the air, and he brought them to the man to see what he would call them; whatever the man called each living creature was then its name. The man gave names to all the tame animals, all the birds of the air, and all the wild animals; but none proved to be a helper suited to the man. So the LORD God cast a deep sleep on the man, and while he was asleep, he took out one of his ribs and closed up its place with flesh. The LORD God then built the rib that he had taken from the man into a woman. When he brought her to the man, the man said: "This one, at last, is bone of my bone and flesh of my flesh; This one shall be called 'woman,' for out of man this one has been taken." That is why a man leaves his father and mother and clings to his wife, and the two of them become one body. The man and his wife were both naked, yet they felt no shame.

In Genesis 1, God gives Adam and Eve one initial command: "Be fertile and multiply." That is, to come together as man and woman in marital union as husband and wife, and to cooperate with God's creative power and have children, or procreate.

Later, this union between man and woman is explored more deeply in Genesis 2, where God tells Adam that it is not good for him to be alone. Then God brings all the animals to Adam in order to find a suitable mate. This is not to say that God thought Adam would find a companion in the animals. Rather, in bringing the animals to Adam, God helps Adam realize that he is unique among all of creation.

God creates woman as Adam's equal. This is evidenced by the fact that she was created from his side, from his middle, and more specifically, from a bone that is close to his heart, a rib.

When Adam first sees the woman, he instantly recognizes her as a being like him, made in God's image and likeness. He proclaims, "This one, at last, is bone of my bones and flesh of my flesh." In other words, "At last! One who is like me!" The two become one flesh, united as spouses in marriage, in order to give and receive love, and to fulfill God's first command: "Be fertile and multiply."

10. What was God's initial command to Adam and Eve?

_____

11. What does it mean to procreate?

_____

_____

12. Why does God bring the animals to Adam?

_____

13. How do we know that woman was created as man's equal?

_____

_____

14. What does Adam recognize about Eve when he first sees her?

_____

_____

15. Why are man and woman meant to become spouses in marriage?

_____

_____

_____

The Five Roles of Adam Diagram

Directions: In the space provided, write three important ideas about each role of Adam. Then using **The Five Roles of Adam Props** provided by your teacher, cut out the props and paste them in the appropriate place on the figure.

Priest

1. _____
2. _____
3. _____

Son/Daughter

1. _____
2. _____
3. _____

Prophet

1. _____
2. _____
3. _____

Spouse

1. _____
2. _____
3. _____

King

1. _____
2. _____
3. _____

The Fall of Man

Directions: Read the story of the Fall of Man in Genesis 3, and analyze the story to respond to the questions for each character.

Adam

1. What did Adam fail to do? (Recall the job that God gave to Adam.)

   _____

   _____

   _____

2. What did he do? _____

3. Whom did Adam blame? _____

4. What consequences did Adam receive for his choices and actions?

   _____

5. If you were Adam, what would you have done differently?

   _____

   _____

Eve

6. What did Eve fail to do? _____

7. What did she do? _____

8. Whom did Eve blame?_____

9. What consequences did Eve receive for her choices and actions?

   _____

10. If you were Eve, what would you have done differently?

   _____

   _____

God

11. Why do you think God didn't step in and help Adam and Eve when they were confronted by the serpent?

_____

12. What did God ask Adam and Eve after they ate the fruit? Why do you think He asked these questions?

_____

13. What consequences did God give Adam and Eve for their sin?

_____

14. What did God make for Adam and Eve?

_____

15. Why do you think God allowed the serpent to tempt Adam and Eve in the first place?

_____

_____

Serpent

16. How did the serpent lie? _____

17. Whom does the serpent threaten, and how? _____

_____

18. What consequences did the serpent receive for his choices and actions?

_____

19. What is prophesied to happen to the serpent's descendants in the end?

_____

_____

20. Why do you think the serpent tempted Adam and Eve in the first place?

_____

_____

Original Justice

Directions: Compare the characteristics of Original Justice to the list compiled by the class.

> **Original Justice ruled Adam and Eve's existence before Original Sin.
> The state of Original Justice was characterized by:**

No suffering or death

> ‣ Mankind was meant to live forever, free of suffering and death, with God in paradise.

Man was at peace with himself

Mankind had control over the spiritual powers of the soul: the intellect and the will.

> ‣ Intellect – The power to know and understand.

> ‣ Will – The power to choose freely based on what the intellect understands; specifically, the power to love.

Harmony between man and woman

> ‣ Men and women coexisted peacefully with each other, with no tensions between them.

> ‣ Man and woman saw each other for what they are, equal persons made in God's image and likeness.

> ‣ There was no temptation to mistreat the other.

Peace between Adam and Eve and all of creation

> ‣ Mankind cared for and protected creation, exercising dominion as good stewards of the earth.

1. What similarities did you find between the brainstormed list and Original Justice?

   _____

   _____

   _____

2. What was not included in the brainstormed list when compared to Original Justice? What should be removed from the list?

   _____

   _____

   _____

Original Sin

Directions: Read the following excerpts from the *Catechism of the Catholic Church* and then answer the questions that follow.

397   Man, tempted by the devil, let his trust in his Creator die in his heart and, abusing his freedom, disobeyed God's command. This is what man's first sin consisted of. All subsequent sin would be disobedience toward God and lack of trust in his goodness.

398   In that sin man preferred himself to God and by that very act scorned him. He chose himself over and against God, against the requirements of his creaturely status and therefore against his own good. Constituted in a state of holiness, man was destined to be fully "divinized" by God in glory. Seduced by the devil, he wanted to "be like God," but "without God, before God, and not in accordance with God."

399   Scripture portrays the tragic consequences of this first disobedience. Adam and Eve immediately lose the grace of original holiness. They become afraid of the God of whom they have conceived a distorted image – that of a God jealous of his prerogatives.

400   The harmony in which they had found themselves, thanks to original justice, is now destroyed: the control of the soul's spiritual faculties over the body is shattered; the union of man and woman becomes subject to tensions, their relations henceforth marked by lust and domination. Harmony with creation is broken: visible creation has become alien and hostile to man. Because of man, creation is now subject "to its bondage to decay." Finally, the consequence explicitly foretold for this disobedience will come true: man will "return to the ground," for out of it he was taken. Death makes its entrance into human history.

405   Although it is proper to each individual, original sin does not have the character of a personal fault in any of Adam's descendants. It is a deprivation of original holiness and justice, but human nature has not been totally corrupted: it is wounded in the natural powers proper to it, subject to ignorance, suffering and the dominion of death, and inclined to sin – an inclination to evil that is called "concupiscence." Baptism, by imparting the life of Christ's grace, erases original sin and turns a man back towards God, but the consequences for nature, weakened and inclined to evil, persist in man and summon him to spiritual battle.

1.   From where did temptation to sin first come? _____

2.   What died in Adam's and Eve's hearts because of the first sin? _____

3. How did Adam and Eve abuse their freedom? What does all other sin consist of?

   _____

4. What was the devils' "seduction"? _____

5. What was the immediate consequence of the first sin?

   _____

6. What was the distorted image Adam and Eve formed of God? (Hint: A prerogative is a privilege or a right.)

   _____

   _____

7. In what ways did the Original Sin reverse Original Justice?

   _____

   _____

8. Although Original Sin is not caused by our own fault, it is still transmitted to each of us. What are the effects of Original Sin on human nature?

   _____

   _____

9. How does Baptism affect Original Sin? _____

   _____

10. To what does Baptism summon us?_____

Cain and Abel Reading Guide

Directions: Complete the reading guide with a partner according to the given directions.

With a partner, take turns reading Genesis 4:1-16 aloud to get an initial perspective of the story of Cain and Abel. Alternate sections as indicated.

READER 1:   ¹The man had intercourse with his wife Eve, and she conceived and gave birth to Cain, saying, "I have produced a male child with the help of the LORD." ² Next she gave birth to his brother Abel. Abel became a herder of flocks, and Cain a tiller of the ground. ³In the course of time Cain brought an offering to the LORD from the fruit of the ground, ⁴while Abel, for his part, brought the fatty portion of the firstlings of his flock.

READER 2:   The LORD looked with favor on Abel and his offering, ⁵but on Cain and his offering he did not look with favor. So Cain was very angry and dejected. ⁶Then the LORD said to Cain: "Why are you angry? Why are you dejected? ⁷If you act rightly, you will be accepted; but if not, sin lies in wait at the door: its urge is for you, yet you can rule over it."

READER 1:   ⁸Cain said to his brother Abel, "Let us go out in the field." When they were in the field, Cain attacked his brother Abel and killed him. ⁹Then the LORD asked Cain, "Where is your brother Abel?" He answered, "I do not know. Am I my brother's keeper?" ¹⁰God then said: "What have you done? Your brother's blood cries out to me from the ground! ¹¹Now you are banned from the ground that opened its mouth to receive your brother's blood from your hand. ¹²If you till the ground, it shall no longer give you its produce. You shall become a constant wanderer on the earth."

READER 2:   ¹³Cain said to the LORD: "My punishment is too great to bear. ¹⁴Look, you have now banished me from the ground. I must avoid you and be a constant wanderer on the earth. Anyone may kill me at sight." ¹⁵"Not so!" the LORD said to him. "If anyone kills Cain, Cain shall be avenged seven times." So the LORD put a mark on Cain, so that no one would kill him at sight. ¹⁶Cain then left the LORD's presence and settled in the land of Nod, east of Eden.

Determine together and record your answers:

1. What was Cain's "job"? (What does the text say, and what does that mean in plain language?)

    _____

2. What was Abel's "job"? (What does the text say, and what does that mean in plain language?)

    _____

Reread verse 3-5 individually. Determine together and record your answers:

3. Whose offering does God accept?

    _____

4. What reason is given for God's accepting one offering and not accepting the other?

    _____

    _____

    _____

5. Do you think it's fair that God accepted one offering and not the other? Why or why not?

    _____

    _____

    _____

6. What key word shows there was a difference between the two offerings?

    _____

    _____

    _____

7. Why is the difference between the two offerings important? How did it affect God's acceptance of the offerings?

    _____

    _____

    _____

Reread verse 7 individually. Record your own answer:

8. What do you think God meant by saying what He said to Cain in verse 7?

_____

_____

_____

Reread verse 8 individually. Then read CCC 407:

> The doctrine of original sin, closely connected with that of redemption by Christ, provides lucid discernment of man's situation and activity in the world. By our first parents' sin, the devil has acquired a certain domination over man, even though man remains free. Original sin entails "captivity under the power of him who thenceforth had the power of death, that is, the devil." Ignorance of the fact that man has a wounded nature inclined to evil gives rise to serious errors in the areas of education, politics, social action and morals.

Together, consider and record an answer:

9. Recall the effects of Original Sin on human nature. How do Cain's actions toward his brother show these effects of Original Sin?

_____

_____

_____

On your own: Finish rereading the passage. Consider and record an answer on your own:

10. God punished Cain for his actions, but He also took steps to ensure that no one harmed Cain. What does God's reaction to Cain tell us about God?

_____

_____

_____

11. What do you think God's reaction to Cain means for us and our own sin?

_____

_____

_____

The Body of Abel Found by Adam and Eve
BY WILLIAM BLAKE (C. 1826)

Tate Gallery, London. Bequeathed by W. Graham Robertson 1949.

The Definition of Sin

Directions: Read the excerpts from the *Catechism of the Catholic Church*, then answer the focus and reflection questions.

1849   Sin is an offense against reason, truth, and right conscience; it is failure in genuine love for God and neighbor caused by a perverse attachment to certain goods. It wounds the nature of man and injures human solidarity. It has been defined as "an utterance, a deed, or a desire contrary to the eternal law."

1850   Sin is an offense against God: "Against you, you alone, have I sinned, and done that which is evil in your sight." Sin sets itself against God's love for us and turns our hearts away from it. Like the first sin, it is disobedience, a revolt against God through the will to become "like gods," knowing and determining good and evil. Sin is thus "love of oneself even to contempt of God." In this proud self-exaltation, sin is diametrically opposed to the obedience of Jesus, which achieves our salvation.

1.   What is sin an offense against? What is sin a failure in? What is it caused by?

\
\

2.   What does sin wound? _____

3.   Against whom is sin an offense? What does it turn our hearts away from?

\
\

4.   How is all sin like the first sin?

\
\

5.   What is sin a love of, even to contempt (despising or hatred) of God? How is this opposed to Jesus?

\
\

Reflection Question

How are all of the characteristics of sin present in the sin of Cain? In other words, in what ways does Cain's sin offend "reason, truth, and right conscience," fail to love God and neighbor, and wound the nature of man and human solidarity; and how is it an attempt to become "like god"?

_____

_____

_____

_____

_____

_____

_____

_____

All Things New

Directions: Christ makes all things new when we have been reconciled to Him. He forgives our sin and renews the work of our hands. With a partner, identify two ways that each of the elements of human civilization can be used to honor God and value the dignity of the human person.

So whoever is in Christ is a new creation: the old things have passed away; behold, new things have come. And all this is from God, who has reconciled us to himself through Christ and given us the ministry of reconciliation, namely, God was reconciling the world to himself in Christ, not counting their trespasses against them and entrusting to us the message of reconciliation.

−2 CORINTHIANS 5:17-19

Cities

1. _____

2. _____

Entertainment

1. _____

2. _____

Technology

1. _____

2. _____

The Great Flood Pre-Assessment

Directions: Write "T" if the statement is true and "F" if the statement is false.

True or False?

_____ 1. God sent the Flood because human beings were wicked and sinful.

_____ 2. Noah argued with God over His plans for the Flood.

_____ 3. Noah was the only one in his generation who remained faithful to God.

_____ 4. God commanded Noah to bring seven pairs of each animal onto the ark.

_____ 5. God entered into a new covenant with creation after the Flood.

The Great Flood Reading Guide

Directions: Read each section of the story of the Great Flood from Genesis 6:5-9:17 and complete the questions that follow.

Read Genesis 6:5-13.

1. The text describes God's heart as being "grieved" and that He "regrets" having made human beings. From the author's perspective, God is angry. What reasons does the author of Genesis give for God's anger?

   _____

   _____

2. Why does Noah (and his family) find favor with God?

   _____

3. What is God's plan for dealing with the reason for His anger with the human race?

   _____

   _____

Read Genesis 6:14-22.

4. What does God command Noah to build? Why?

   _____

   _____

5. What does God say He will establish with Noah and his family? _____

6. How many of each animal does God tell Noah to bring with him? _____

7. How does Noah respond to all of God's commands?

   _____

   _____

Read Genesis 7:1-5.

8. How is Noah unique in his generation of human beings?

   _____

9. How many of each animal does God tell Noah to bring with him? How is this different from God's command in Genesis 6:19-20?

   _____

   _____

10. In how many days does God tell Noah He will send rain? _____

11. Recall the dual meaning of the number seven in Hebrew, and God's words to Noah in Genesis 6:18. How does this understanding help to clarify what the author of Genesis intended to tell us by the answers to 9 and 10?

   _____

   _____

   _____

12. How does Noah respond to all of God's commands?

   _____

Read Genesis 7:6-24.

13. What happened after seven days were over?

   _____

14. Read Genesis 1:1-2. How are the words of Genesis 7:11 similar to Genesis 1:1-2? Why do you think the author of Genesis is making this comparison?

   _____

   _____

   _____

15. For how many days and nights did it rain? This is a significant number in our Christian faith. Read Matthew 4:1-2. How are these passages similar? What do you think the number in both passages represents?

_____

_____

_____

16. As the waters upon the earth swelled, what happened to the living things of the earth?

_____

Read Genesis 8:1-5.

17. What happened when God "remembered" Noah and the animals with him?

_____

18. In what month and day did the ark come to rest? Given the answer to question 11, why do you think this is significant?

_____

_____

Read Genesis 8:6-22.

19. What animals did Noah release from the ark to determine if there was dry land? How long did Noah wait between releasing these animals?

_____

_____

20. What is the first thing Noah did upon leaving the ark? What did God promise Noah after he did this?

_____

_____

Read Genesis 9:1-7.

21. What command did God give Noah and his sons after He blessed them?

    _____

    _____

22. Read Genesis 1:28. How is God's command to Noah and his family similar to His command to Adam and Eve? How is the command different?

    _____

    _____

    _____

23. What does God give Noah and his family to eat that He did not allow before? What does God demand in return?

    _____

    _____

24. Read Genesis 1:27. What essential truth about human beings does God reaffirm in Genesis 9:6?

    _____

    _____

Read Genesis 9:8-17.

25. What does God establish with Noah and his sons? In doing so, what does God promise?

    _____

    _____

    _____

26. What is the sign that God establishes?

    _____

The Great Flood Post-Assessment

Directions: Write "T" if the statement is true and "F" if the statement is false.

True or False?

_____ 1. God sent the Flood because human beings were wicked and sinful.

_____ 2. Noah argued with God over His plans for the Flood.

_____ 3. Noah was the only one in his generation who remained faithful to God.

_____ 4. God commanded Noah to bring seven pairs of each animal onto the ark.

_____ 5. God entered into a new covenant with creation after the Flood.

Noah and Adam Comparison Graphic Organizer

Directions: Read each of the given Scripture passages and summarize as instructed. Then read the related commentary cards and determine which commentary describes how Noah fulfills that particular role of Adam, marking the letter in the space provided on the chart.

Priest		Commentary
ADAM: Genesis 2:15 Summarize Adam's role:	**NOAH: Genesis 8:20** Summarize the passage:	
Prophet		**Commentary**
ADAM: Genesis 2:19–20 Summarize Adam's role:	**NOAH: Genesis 9:8–10** Summarize the passage:	

King		Commentary
ADAM: Genesis 1:28 Summarize Adam's role:	**NOAH: Genesis 9:7** Summarize the passage:	

Son/Daugher		Commentary
ADAM: Genesis 1:27 **and Genesis 5:3** Summarize Adam's role:	**NOAH: Genesis 9:6** Summarize the passage:	

Spouse		Commentary
ADAM: Genesis 1:27-28 Summarize Adam's role:	**NOAH: Genesis 8:15-16** **and Genesis 9:1** Summarize the passage:	

Commentary

A God gave Noah and his sons the command to "subdue" the earth. In other words, they were given dominion, or rule, over God's creation. This is the fulfillment of Adam's role of dominion over all of creation.

B The only remaining institution after the Flood was that shared between Noah and his wife and Noah's sons and their wives, and they were given the very same command as Adam and Eve, to be fertile and multiply and fill the earth. This recalls the making of human beings as male and female, united as one flesh.

C Noah was given the task of communicating to his descendants and all of creation the covenant God made with him and all of creation. This fulfills Adam's role of speaking for God in naming all the animals.

D God reaffirmed with Noah that he is made in God's image (as are all human beings). Adam, and his son after him, made in his image, were likewise made in God's image and likeness.

E Immediately upon leaving the ark, Noah built an altar and offered sacrifice to God. Offering sacrifice is the role of those who guard and protect the Temple and is an expectation of this role God gave to Adam.

Anointing at Baptism

Directions: Read the text taken from the Rite of Baptism, then respond to the prompt in a well-written five- to seven-sentence paragraph with supporting evidence.

The Baptismal Rite: Anointing with Chrism

At your Baptism, you were anointed with a holy oil called chrism and the priest said the following:

God the Father of our Lord Jesus Christ has freed you from sin, given you a new birth by water and the Holy Spirit, and welcomed you into his holy people. He now anoints you with the chrism of salvation. As Christ was anointed Priest, Prophet, and King, so may you live always as a member of his body, sharing everlasting life.

At our Baptism, we are made priest, prophet, king, sons/daughters, and spouses. When we pass through the waters of Baptism, we are restored to the roles of Adam given by God at creation and given to Noah after the Flood.

Considering that we are restored to the roles of Adam at our Baptism, how is the Great Flood similar to our own Baptism?

God's Anger

Directions: Read the excerpt below from St. Augustine's *City of God*, XV:15 on God's anger. Then respond to the focus and reflection questions.

The anger of God is not a disturbing emotion of His mind, but a judgment by which punishment is inflicted upon sin. His thought and reconsideration also are the unchangeable reason that changes things; for He does not, like man, repent of anything He has done, because in all matters His decision is as inflexible as His prescience is certain. But if Scripture were not to use such expressions as the above, it would not familiarly insinuate itself into the minds of all classes of men, whom it seeks access to for their good, that it may alarm the proud, arouse the careless, exercise the inquisitive, and satisfy the intelligent; and this it could not do, did it not first stoop, and in a manner descend, to them where they lie. But its denouncing death on all the animals of earth and air is a declaration of the vastness of the disaster that was approaching: not that it threatens destruction to the irrational animals as if they too had incurred it by sin.

1. What is God's anger not? What is it?

   _____

   _____

   _____

2. How is God's thought described?

   _____

   _____

   _____

3. Unlike man, what does God not do? Why? (Hint: the word *prescience* means to have foreknowledge of events.)

   _____

   _____

4. Why does St. Augustine suggest that Scripture must describe God as being "angry" when he has already suggested that God does not actually get angry? (Hint: the word *insinuate* means to hint at something.)

_____

_____

_____

_____

Reflection Question

What are some other human reactions and emotions that are attributed to God? If God is unchanging and does not experience emotion, how then might we explain these human reactions and emotions that are used to describe God?

_____

_____

_____

_____

_____

_____

_____

_____

UNIT 4

The Chosen People

In this unit, you will learn about...

> The covenants.

> The descendants of Cain and Seth.

> The Tower of Babel and the reuniting of God's people at Pentecost.

> God's Chosen People.

> God's calling of Abraham and His covenant with him.

> The renewal of God's covenant with the Patriarchs: Isaac, Jacob, and Joseph.

Introduction

God revealed Himself gradually and in stages and in words and deeds throughout Salvation History. He entered into covenants with the human race. He chose a people to begin His relationship with mankind and make Himself known. Through these Chosen People, God made His plan of salvation known to the entire world and invited all people to be a part of His divine family.

After His covenant with Adam and Eve and their disobedience, and after the renewal of all of creation through His covenant with Noah, God entered into a covenant with Abraham. God made great promise to Abraham and his descendants that they would become a great nation, that a line of kings would descend from Abraham, and that Abraham's descendants would be more numerous than the stars and that through them the world would be blessed. The people descended from Abraham became God's Chosen People to whom God continued to reveal Himself. Through them, God would prepare the whole world to receive salvation.

Abraham, Isaac, Jacob, and Joseph are the Patriarchs, the fathers of our Faith. Through them God continually renewed His covenant promises and showed the depth of His love and mercy. Through the Patriarchs, we receive a small foretaste of the fullness of God's plan of salvation.

Are there any questions you still have about the topics you learned last month? What steps can you take to find out the answers?

_____

_____

_____

What questions do you have right now about the topics you will be learning about in this unit?

_____

_____

_____

_____

Unit 4 Vocabulary

Abraham: "Father of a great many." He was the first Patriarch and the "father of faith" to whom God made great promises and entered into covenant. His descendants would become the Chosen People.

Blessing: God promised Abraham that his descendants would be more numerous than the stars and through them all the families of the earth would be blessed.

Chosen People: The people descended from Abraham to whom God chose to continue to reveal Himself and through whom He would prepare the whole world to receive salvation. The people of Israel.

Gratuitous love: Undeserved love. The Chosen People did nothing to deserve or earn God's love and mercy. Rather, like a father who loves his children unconditionally, solely because He loved them, God chose the people of Israel, continually forgave them, and tasked them with sharing His love and forgiveness with the rest of the world.

Heir: Someone who inherits another person's land, possessions, and titles after that person dies. In the ancient world, one's heir was typically his first-born son.

Hospitality: Generous and friendly treatment of guests, visitors, and even strangers. Abraham showed hospitality to an angel of the Lord who visited him with a message from God.

Isaac: "Laughter." He was the son born to Abraham and his wife, Sarah, in their old age and heir to Abraham and all of God's promises in the covenant.

Israel: "He who wrestles with God." God changed Jacob's name to Israel after he wrestled an angel of the Lord to a draw. God's Chosen People became known as the people of Israel.

Jacob: "Supplanter." He was the son of Isaac who tricked his older brother, Esau, into giving away his birthright as Isaac's heir.

Kingship: God promised Abraham that his descendants would have a great name, which means that they would be a dynasty of great kings.

Moral Evil: An objectively evil act that a person commits. The rejection and murder of God's only Son is the greatest moral evil ever committed.

Nation: God promised Abraham that his descendants would be a great nation. This includes possessing land.

Nephilim: Mysterious individuals from Genesis 6 who are described as the "heroes of old" and the "men of renown." Careful study of Scripture and the writings of Church Fathers reveals that they may actually be the children from the marriages between the sinful descendants of Cain and the faithful descendants of Seth. They were morally corrupt men who sought to honor themselves rather than God.

Pentecost: The day when Jesus sent the Holy Spirit upon Mary and the Apostles and the Church was born. 50 days after Jesus' Resurrection (10 days after His Ascension into Heaven), Mary and the Apostles had gathered in the upper room and were filled with the Holy Spirit, who came in a rush of wind and appeared as tongues of fire over their heads. The Apostles were strengthened by the Holy Spirit to proclaim the Gospel in many languages to the gathered crowd. 3,000 people were baptized and entered the Church that day. Pentecost is the birthday of the Church. The blessing of Pentecost reversed the curse of the Tower of Babel.

Shem/Shemite: Shem was one of Noah's three sons. The name Shem means "name." Shem's descendants were known as Shemites, "the people of the name." In other words, Shem and his descendants honored the name of God and sought to be faithful to Him. Abraham was a descendant of Shem and his descendants became the Hebrew or Jewish people, the Chosen People of God.

Tower of Babel: The human race attempted to build a tower to Heaven to make themselves like God. As punishment, God confused their language and scattered them all over the earth.

Type: Someone or something in Salvation History that foreshadows or points forward to a later person or thing in Salvation History. In the story of the sacrifice of Isaac, Isaac foreshadows Jesus Christ.

The Hospitality of Abraham Icon

BY UNKNOWN ARTIST (C. 1375 – 1400).

Benaki Museum, Athens, Greece.

The Hospitality of Abraham Icon

 The Hospitality of Abraham Icon, *by Unknown Artist (c. 1375-1400)*

Directions: Take some time to quietly view and reflect on the art. Let yourself be inspired in any way that happens naturally. Then think about the questions below, and discuss them with your classmates.

Conversation Questions

1. Read Genesis 18:1-14. How does this icon illustrate this story from Scripture?

2. Who are the people in this icon? Why do you think the iconographer might have chosen to depict the Lord, appearing as three men, with wings?

3. How would you describe Abraham's reaction to the three men in the icon? What does the icon show Abraham doing?

4. Hospitality means welcoming people and giving generously to guests. Why do you think this icon is called *The Hospitality of Abraham*?

5. Share about a time when it has been hard for you to believe something about God.

6. Share about a time when you have gladly welcomed God into your life.

7. Do you think God was pleased that Abraham welcomed Him to eat at his home? Why?

The Lord Appears to Abraham

Directions: Read the story of how the Lord appeared to Abraham and promised him a son in his old age from Genesis 18, then answer the questions that follow.

The LORD appeared to Abraham by the oak of Mamre, as he sat in the entrance of his tent, while the day was growing hot. Looking up, he saw three men standing near him. When he saw them, he ran from the entrance of the tent to greet them; and bowing to the ground, he said: "Sir, if it please you, do not go on past your servant. Let some water be brought, that you may bathe your feet, and then rest under the tree. Now that you have come to your servant, let me bring you a little food, that you may refresh yourselves; and afterward you may go on your way." "Very well," they replied, "do as you have said."

Abraham hurried into the tent to Sarah and said, "Quick, three measures of bran flour! Knead it and make bread." He ran to the herd, picked out a tender, choice calf, and gave it to a servant, who quickly prepared it. Then he got some curds and milk, as well as the calf that had been prepared, and set these before them, waiting on them under the tree while they ate. "Where is your wife Sarah?" they asked him. "There in the tent," he replied. One of them said, "I will return to you about this time next year, and Sarah will then have a son." Sarah was listening at the entrance of the tent, just behind him. Now Abraham and Sarah were old, advanced in years. ... But the LORD said to Abraham: "Why did Sarah laugh and say, 'Will I really bear a child, old as I am?' Is anything too marvelous for the LORD to do? At the appointed time, about this time next year, I will return to you, and Sarah will have a son." Sarah lied, saying, "I did not laugh," because she was afraid. But he said, "Yes, you did."

1. How did God appear to Abraham? _____

2. What do you think these three men represent? _____

3. What did Abraham do for the Lord when the Lord appeared to him?

   _____

   _____

4. How can welcoming someone into your life open up the possibility to have a friendship with him or her?

   _____

   _____

5. What did the Lord promise Sarah?

    _____

    _____

6. How did Sarah respond to the promise of a child?

    _____

    _____

7. How did God respond to Sarah?

    _____

    _____

Trusting God

Directions: On the lines below each pair of Scripture passages, write the key similarities and/or differences.

1. GENESIS 18:9-10

   "Where is your wife Sarah?" they asked him. "There in the tent," he replied. One of them said, "I will return to you about this time next year, and Sarah will then have a son."

   LUKE 1:30A, 31

   Then the angel said to her…"Behold, you will conceive in your womb and bear a son, and you shall name Him Jesus."

   _____

   _____

2. GENESIS 18:10B-11A, 12

   Sarah was listening at the entrance of the tent, just behind him. Now Abraham and Sarah were old, advanced in years. …So Sarah laughed to herself and said, "Now that I am worn out and my husband is old…?"

   LUKE 1:34

   Mary said to the angel, "How can this be…?"

   _____

   _____

3. GENESIS 18:13-14

   But the LORD said to Abraham: "Why did Sarah laugh and say, 'Will I really bear a child, old as I am?' Is anything too marvelous for the LORD to do? At the appointed time, about this time next year, I will return to you, and Sarah will have a son."

   LUKE 1:35, 37

   And the angel said to her in reply, "The Holy Spirit will come upon you, and the power of the Most High will overshadow you. Therefore the child to be born will be called holy, the Son of God. …For nothing will be impossible for God."

   _____

   _____

4. GENESIS 18:15

Sarah lied, saying, "I did not laugh," because she was afraid. But He said, "Yes, you did."

LUKE 1:38

Mary said, "Behold, I am the handmaid of the Lord. May it be done to me according to your word."

_____

_____

Sarah did eventually trust and believe in God's promise to her. Still, it is best to believe God right away, as Mary did.

Now write a prayer asking God to help you trust Him. If needed, use more sheets of paper.

_____

_____

_____

_____

_____

_____

_____

Luke 1:37-38

"For nothing will be impossible for God." Mary said, "Behold, I am the handmaid of the Lord. May it be done to me according to your word."

Exodus 4:22-23

So you will say to Pharaoh, "Thus says the LORD: Israel is my son, my firstborn. I said to you: Let my son go, that he may serve me."

Acts 2:4

And they were all filled with the Holy Spirit and began to speak in different tongues, as the Spirit enabled them to proclaim.

_____

_____

_____

_____

_____

_____

_____

_____

Genesis 12:1-3

The LORD said to Abram: "Go forth from your land, your relatives, and from your father's house to a land that I will show you. I will make of you a great nation, and I will bless you; I will make your name great, so that you will be a blessing. I will bless those who bless you and curse those who curse you. All the families of the earth will find blessing in you."

John 3:16

For God so loved the world that he gave his only Son, that whoever believes in him should not perish but have eternal life.

Genesis 22:8

"My son," Abraham answered, "God will provide the sheep for the burnt offering."

Genesis 30:22

God remembered Rachel. God listened to her and made her fruitful.

Genesis 45:7

God, therefore, sent me on ahead of you to ensure for you a remnant on earth and to save your lives in an extraordinary deliverance.

_____

_____

_____

_____

_____

_____

_____

_____

_____

Matthew 5:10

Blessed are they who are persecuted for the sake of righteousness, for theirs is the kingdom of heaven.

The Nephilim

Directions: Read about the Nephilim, then answer the questions that follow in complete sentences.

In Genesis 6, we read a peculiar story about a group of people called the Nephilim. In times past, people came up with some unique theories as to who or what the Nephilim were. Some suggested that they were actual giants, mythical creatures who roamed the earth. Others suggested they were angels who came down from Heaven. Given our understanding of the lines of Cain and Seth, an alternate, perhaps better, understanding of the Nephilim can be had. Read about the Nephilim in Genesis 6:1-4:

> When human beings began to grow numerous on the earth and daughters were born to them, the sons of God saw how beautiful the daughters of human beings were, and so they took for their wives whomever they pleased. Then the LORD said: "My spirit shall not remain in human beings forever, because they are only flesh. Their days shall comprise one hundred and twenty years."

> The Nephilim appeared on earth in those days, as well as later, after the sons of God had intercourse with the daughters of human beings, who bore them sons. They were the heroes of old, the men of renown.

Notice that at the beginning of the story, the human race had grown in number. There are two distinct groups of people mentioned: the sons of God and the daughters of human beings, or men. Church Fathers, including St. John Chrysostom, St. Cyril of Alexandria, and St. Augustine suggested that the sons of God refer to the descendants of Seth. The daughters of human beings (men) refer to the descendants of Cain. In other words, this story is telling us that the wicked and sinful descendants of Cain married the descendants of Seth, who were faithful to God. The two lines of Cain and Seth had mixed! The children that resulted from these marriages were the Nephilim, the "men of renown." Rather than being literal giants or mythical beings, these offspring of Cain and Seth were morally corrupt men who sought to "make a name" for themselves. They selfishly honored themselves and wanted others to honor them as well.

The very next line, Genesis 6:5, confirms this interpretation: "When the LORD saw how great the wickedness of human beings was on earth, and how every desire that their heart conceived was always nothing but evil, the LORD regretted making human beings on the earth, and his heart was grieved." This sets the stage very well for the next chapter of Genesis, in which we read about the Great Flood, Noah, and his family. It also prepares us for the Tower of Babel later, where the human race will fall into the same sinfulness of pride once again.

1. What did people in times past understand the Nephilim to be?

    _____

    _____

2. How can we describe the line of Cain and the line of Seth?

    _____

    _____

3. What do we learn about the human race at the beginning of this story?

    _____

    _____

4. How were the lines of Cain and Seth mentioned in this story? What happened between the two lines?

    _____

    _____

5. Who were the "men of renown," and where did they come from?

    _____

    _____

6. What did the Nephilim do?

    _____

    _____

7. How does Genesis 6:5 confirm this interpretation?

    _____

    _____

My Family Tree

Directions: Fill in this simple family tree with information about yourself, your siblings, your parents, and your grandparents. Include details such as birthdates and places each person was born, if you know them.

Grandmother

Grandfather

Grandmother

Grandfather

Mother

Father

Me

Siblings

Siblings

The Tower of Babel

Directions: Read about the Tower of Babel, then answer the questions that follow in complete sentences.

The book of Genesis tells us that the human race sought to make a name for themselves rather than honor God. Recall the lie the serpent told Adam and Eve. He deceived them into thinking that if they ate the fruit of the Tree of Knowledge of Good and Evil, they would become gods themselves. This pleased them, so they ate the fruit, seeking to honor themselves rather than God. Here, the human race attempted to do the same thing, to make themselves gods - except, instead of fruit, they built a tower to Heaven to try to replace God. This event has at the same time profound cosmic, social, and religious meaning. We read about the story in Genesis 11:1-9:

> The whole world had the same language and the same words. When they were migrating from the east, they came to a valley in the land of Shinar and settled there. They said to one another, "Come, let us mold bricks and harden them with fire." They used bricks for stone, and bitumen for mortar. Then they said, "Come, let us build ourselves a city and a tower with its top in the sky, and so make a name for ourselves; otherwise we shall be scattered all over the earth."

> The LORD came down to see the city and the tower that the people had built. Then the LORD said: "If now, while they are one people and all have the same language, they have started to do this, nothing they presume to do will be out of their reach. Come, let us go down and there confuse their language, so that no one will understand the speech of another." So the LORD scattered them from there over all the earth, and they stopped building the city. That is why it was called Babel, because there the LORD confused the speech of all the world. From there the LORD scattered them over all the earth.

The tragedy of the story is that the human race had, until this point, been united as one people, united by one language. After God confused their language, the human race was no longer one people. In fact, they scattered all over the earth. In a way, at this moment in human history, this was necessary. Sin continually crept into human action. A drastic step like this was needed to begin to save mankind from itself.

God, of course, had a plan. This was not the end of the story. When human beings sought to make a name for themselves, to honor themselves instead of God, nothing good ever came of it. But when human beings honor God, God blesses them abundantly. Although God punished the human race after the Tower of Babel by confusing their language and scattering them across the world, He would later bring us back together, as one people, united in His name by the power of the Holy Spirit. This happened at Pentecost, which we read about in Acts 2:1-13:

When the time for Pentecost was fulfilled, they were all in one place together. And suddenly there came from the sky a noise like a strong driving wind, and it filled the entire house in which they were. Then there appeared to them tongues as of fire, which parted and came to rest on each one of them. And they were all filled with the Holy Spirit and began to speak in different tongues, as the Spirit enabled them to proclaim.

Now there were devout Jews from every nation under Heaven staying in Jerusalem. At this sound, they gathered in a large crowd, but they were confused because each one heard them speaking in his own language. They were astounded, and in amazement they asked, "Are not all these people who are speaking Galileans? Then how does each of us hear them in his own native language. ...[W]e hear them speaking in our own tongues of the mighty acts of God."

At Pentecost, when the Holy Spirit descended upon the Apostles, all of the people gathered from all over the world heard the Apostles proclaim the gospel in their own language. It was as if the human race were once again speaking the same language and gathered together in one place. This was no mistake or coincidence. In the Church, the curse of the Tower of Babel is reversed! In the Church, the human race is united again by the Holy Spirit. In the Church, the human race honors God and is faithful to Him, instead of selfishly trying to make a name for itself. We become part of the people of God through faith and Baptism.

1. Where did the descendants of Ham migrate to? What did they do there?

   _____

   _____

2. Whose sin were the actions of the descendants of Ham similar to? How?

   _____

   _____

3. According to Genesis 11, what reason did the people give for wanting to build a tower to Heaven?

   _____

4. According to Genesis 11, what reason did God give for punishing the people for building the tower?

   _____

5. How did God punish the people?

_____

6. What was the tragedy of the story of the Tower of Babel?

_____

_____

7. Why was this punishment necessary?

_____

8. What happens when human beings seek to make a name for themselves? What happens when they honor God?

_____

_____

9. At what event in salvation history did God bring the human race back together as one people?

_____

10. What happened at this event?

_____

_____

11. How did this event reverse the curse of the Tower of Babel?

_____

_____

_____

God Chooses Abraham Reading Guide

Directions: Read the reading guide below and answer the questions as you go.

"Father of all who believe"

Abraham is one of the most important people in the Bible. The *Catechism of the Catholic Church* calls him "the father of all who believe" (146) because of his obedience to God. The three great monotheistic religions of the world are Judaism, Christianity, and Islam, which are all descended from Abraham. Monotheism means belief in one God.

1. Why is Abraham one of the most important people in the Bible?

    _____

    _____

2. What does monotheism mean? _____

3. What are the three great monotheistic religions of the world, and how are they related to each other?

    _____

    _____

    _____

"Father of many"

When we first meet Abraham in the Bible, he is called Abram, which means "father of many." God will later change his name to Abraham, which means "father of a great many" as a sign of the covenant God makes with him. Unfortunately, at this point in his life, which was likely in his middle age, Abram had no children – his wife, Sarai, was barren. That means she could not have any children.

Abram and his family were from a city called Ur, which is in modern-day Iraq. Ur was a wealthy trading city. At the beginning of Abram's story, he and his family leave their homeland to travel to the land of Canaan, which is in modern-day Israel. This land will be very important in the rest of salvation history. It is the land God promises to give to His people – the Promised Land. Abram and his family, however, settle in a place called Haran, in modern-day Turkey, about halfway to Canaan. There, Abram's father dies, as well as one of his brothers. Abram becomes the head of his family and also very wealthy.

4. Where was Abram's family originally from? _____

5. Who was Abram's wife? What do we know about her at the beginning of the story?

   _____

   _____

6. Where did Abram and his family intend to go after they left their homeland?

   _____

7. Where did Abram and his family end up settling? _____

"Father of a multitude of nations"

The *Catechism of the Catholic Church* no. 59 tells us that "in order to gather together scattered humanity God calls Abram from his country, his kindred and his father's house, and makes him Abraham, that is, 'the father of a multitude of nations.' 'In you all the nations of the earth shall be blessed.'"

8. Based on the above *Catechism* passage, what was God's purpose in calling Abram?

   _____

   _____

9. Where did God call Abram from? _____

10. What did God make Abram? _____

11. Through Abram, what would happen to all the nations?

   _____

   _____

God's promises to Abram

In his old age, God called Abram. He gave him a mission and made him three promises. Read about God's call to Abram in Genesis 12:1-5, 7:

> The LORD said to Abram: "Go forth from your land, your relatives, and from your father's house to a land that I will show you. I will make of you a great nation, and I will bless you; I will make your name great, so that you will be a blessing. I will bless those who bless you and curse those who curse you. All the families of the earth will find blessing in you." Abram went as the LORD directed him, and Lot went with him. Abram was seventy-five years old when he left Haran. Abram took his wife Sarai, his brother's son Lot, all the possessions that they had accumulated, and the persons they had acquired in Haran, and they set out for the

land of Canaan. When they came to the land of Canaan…[t]he LORD appeared to Abram and said: "To your descendants I will give this land." So Abram built an altar there to the LORD who had appeared to him.

12. What did God call Abram to do?

   _____

13. What three rewards did God promise to Abram?

   1. _____

   2. _____

   3. _____

14. How did Abram respond to God's call?

   _____

   _____

15. At the end of this passage, God makes a final promise to Abram. Describe this final promise and what Abram does in response.

   _____

   _____

   _____

God's Threefold Promise to Abram

Directions: Using the Genesis readings as a reference, answer the questions that follow, then use the answers to fill in the diagram below.

1. What are the three promises God makes to Abram in Genesis 12:1-3?

   _____

   _____

   _____

2. What promise is God affirming and raising to the level of a covenant in Genesis 15:18?

   _____

3. What covenant later in salvation history fulfills this promise?

   _____

4. What promise is God affirming and raising to the level of a covenant in Genesis 17:6?

   _____

5. What covenant later in salvation history fulfills the promise from Genesis 17?

   _____

6. What promise is God reinforcing and elevating to the level of a covenant in Genesis 22:17-18?

   _____

7. What covenant later in salvation history fulfills the promise from Genesis 22?

   _____

8. Why does it make sense to say that the promises made to Abraham begin God's plan of salvation?

   _____

   _____

God's Threefold Blessing to Abram
(Genesis 12:1-3)

Promises

Covenants
(What chapter?)

Fulfilled

1

2

3

Abraham's Son

Directions: Read the story of God's promise to Abraham that he would have a son to be his heir from Genesis 17, then complete the questions that follow.

When Abram was ninety-nine years old, the LORD appeared to Abram and said: "I am God the Almighty. Walk in my presence and be blameless. Between you and me I will establish my covenant, and I will multiply you exceedingly." Abram fell face down and God said to him: "For my part, here is my covenant with you: you are to become the father of a multitude of nations. No longer will you be called Abram; your name will be Abraham, for I am making you the father of a multitude of nations. I will make you exceedingly fertile; I will make nations of you; kings will stem from you. I will maintain my covenant between me and you and your descendants after you throughout the ages as an everlasting covenant, to be your God and the God of your descendants after you. I will give to you and to your descendants after you the land in which you are now residing as aliens, the whole land of Canaan, as a permanent possession; and I will be their God." God said to Abraham: "For your part, you and your descendants after you must keep my covenant throughout the ages."

God further said to Abraham: "As for Sarai your wife, do not call her Sarai; her name will be Sarah. I will bless her, and I will give you a son by her. Her also will I bless; she will give rise to nations, and rulers of peoples will issue from her." Abraham fell face down and laughed as he said to himself, "Can a child be born to a man who is a hundred years old? Can Sarah give birth at ninety?" So Abraham said to God, "If only Ishmael could live in your favor!" God replied: "Even so, your wife Sarah is to bear you a son, and you shall call him Isaac. It is with him that I will maintain my covenant as an everlasting covenant and with his descendants after him. Now as for Ishmael, I will heed you: I hereby bless him. I will make him fertile and will multiply him exceedingly. He will become the father of twelve chieftains, and I will make of him a great nation. But my covenant I will maintain with Isaac, whom Sarah shall bear to you by this time next year." When he had finished speaking with Abraham, God departed from him.

The LORD took note of Sarah as he had said he would; the LORD did for her as he had promised. Sarah became pregnant and bore Abraham a son in his old age, at the set time that God had stated. Abraham gave the name Isaac to this son of his whom Sarah bore him.

1. How old was Abram when God appeared to him in this story? _____

2. God told Abraham that He would establish a covenant with him. What did He promise Abram in this covenant? (List all that apply.)

_____

_____

3. What does the name Abram mean? What does God change his name to? What does his new name mean?

_____

_____

4. Abram's wife's name is Sarai. What does God change her name to? _____

5. What does God promise He will do for Sarai? _____

6. How does Abram respond to all that God has just promised him and his wife?

_____

7. What does Abram ask of God instead? What do you think this means?

_____

_____

_____

8. What does God tell Abram his son's name will be? What does He promise Abram's son?

_____

_____

9. What does God promise to Ishmael?

_____

10. When will Abram's son be born? _____

11. How did God come through with His promises to Abram?

_____

_____

_____

Reflection Questions

1. The name of Abraham's son means "laughter" or "he who laughs." Why is this name appropriate considering what happened in the story?

   _____

   _____

   _____

2. Describe a time that you had faith in God and He came through with His promises to you. Was it easy or difficult to put your complete faith in God? Why or why not?

   _____

   _____

   _____

   _____

   _____

   _____

   _____

   _____

   _____

Sacrifice of Isaac

BY CARAVAGGIO (17TH CENTURY)

(Later painting)
Piasecka-Johnson Collection, Princeton, New Jersey.

(Earlier painting)
Uffizi Gallery, Florence, Italy.

The Sacrifice of Isaac Reading Guide

Directions: Read the story of the sacrifice of Isaac from Genesis 22:1-18, then answer the questions.

1. What did God ask Abraham to do? Why?

    _____

    _____

2. What do you think it means that God "put Abraham to the test"? What was God "testing"?

    _____

    _____

3. What did Abraham do in response to God's calling?

    _____

4. What happened on the third day of their journey?

    _____

5. What did Abraham place on his son Isaac's back? _____

6. What did Isaac ask his father? _____

7. How did Abraham answer his son's question?

    _____

8. An alternate translation of Abraham's answer to Isaac's questions is "God will provide Himself, the sheep for the offering." What do you think Abraham might have meant by "God will provide Himself"? As Christians, what event can we interpret Abraham's answer as foreshadowing?

    _____

    _____

9. Although he doesn't speak, what can we say about how Isaac responds to his father?

    _____

    _____

10. What did Abraham do when they arrived at the place God had told him?

_____

_____

11. At the last moment before Abraham was about to slaughter his son, what happened?

_____

_____

12. What did Abraham demonstrate by his obedience to God's calling?

_____

_____

13. What did Abraham offer as a sacrifice instead of his son? _____

14. What did God promise to Abraham because of his faith?

_____

_____

God Keeps His Promises: Isaac and Christ

Directions: In Scripture, a "type" is a person or thing in the Old Testament that foreshadows a person or thing in the New Testament. Isaac is a type of Jesus Christ. Complete the chart below by matching the strips showing how Christ fulfills the sacrifice of Isaac. Note any additional connections you see in the space provided, then answer the questions that follow.

Sacrifice of Isaac	Sacrifice of Christ

Sacrifice of Isaac	Sacrifice of Christ
Additional ways Isaac foreshadows Jesus:	Additional ways Jesus fulfills the sacrifice of Isaac:

1. How does reflecting on the connection between these two sacrifices help you answer the question: "Why would God ask Abraham to sacrifice his son?"

   _____

   _____

2. How does knowing the connection between these two sacrifices bring us to a deeper understanding of God's plan for humanity?

   _____

   _____

3. How does that understanding lead us to a deeper appreciation of God's mercy?

   _____

   _____

The Story of Isaac and Rebekah

Directions: Read the story of how Isaac found his wife, Rebekah, from Genesis 24:1-32, 49-67, and complete the plot-summary chart that follows by summarizing the important events that happened in each set of passages.

Abraham was old, having seen many days, and the LORD had blessed him in every way. [2] Abraham said to the senior servant of his household, who had charge of all his possessions: "Put your hand under my thigh, [3] and I will make you swear by the LORD, the God of heaven and the God of earth, that you will not take a wife for my son from the daughters of the Canaanites among whom I live, [4] but that you will go to my own land and to my relatives to get a wife for my son Isaac." [5] The servant asked him: "What if the woman is unwilling to follow me to this land? Should I then take your son back to the land from which you came?" [6] Abraham told him, "Never take my son back there for any reason! [7] The LORD, the God of heaven, who took me from my father's house and the land of my relatives, and who confirmed by oath the promise he made to me, 'I will give this land to your descendants'—he will send his angel before you, and you will get a wife for my son there. [8] If the woman is unwilling to follow you, you will be released from this oath to me. But never take my son back there!" [9] So the servant put his hand under the thigh of his master Abraham and swore to him concerning this matter. [10] The servant then took ten of his master's camels, and bearing all kinds of gifts from his master, he made his way to the city of Nahor in Aram Naharaim. [11] Near evening, at the time when women go out to draw water, he made the camels kneel by the well outside the city. [12] Then he said: "LORD, God of my master Abraham, let it turn out favorably for me today and thus deal graciously with my master Abraham. [13] While I stand here at the spring and the daughters of the townspeople are coming out to draw water, [14] if I say to a young woman, 'Please lower your jug, that I may drink,' and she answers, 'Drink, and I will water your camels, too,' then she is the one whom you have decided upon for your servant Isaac. In this way I will know that you have dealt graciously with my master." [15] He had scarcely finished speaking when Rebekah—who was born to Bethuel, son of Milcah, the wife of Abraham's brother Nahor—came out with a jug on her shoulder. [16] The young woman was very beautiful, a virgin, untouched by man. She went down to the spring and filled her jug. As she came up, [17] the servant ran toward her and said, "Please give me a sip of water from your jug." [18] "Drink, sir," she replied, and quickly lowering the jug into her hand, she gave him a drink. [19] When she had finished giving him a drink, she said, "I will draw water for your camels, too, until they have finished drinking." [20] With that, she quickly emptied her jug into the drinking trough and ran back to the well to draw more water, until she had drawn enough for all the camels. [21] The man watched her the whole time, silently waiting to learn whether or not the LORD had made his journey successful. [22] When the camels had finished drinking, the man took out a gold nose-ring weighing half a shekel, and two gold bracelets weighing ten shekels for her wrists. ²³ Then he asked her: "Whose daughter are you? Tell me, please. And is there a place in your father's house for us to spend the night?" ²⁴ She answered: "I am the daughter of Bethuel the son of Milcah, whom she bore to Nahor. ²⁵ We have plenty of straw and fodder," she added, "and also a place to spend the night." ²⁶ The man then knelt and bowed down to the LORD, ²⁷ saying: "Blessed be the LORD, the God of my master Abraham, who has not let his kindness and fidelity toward my master fail. As for me, the LORD has led me straight to the house of my master's brother." ²⁸ Then the young woman ran off and told her mother's household what had happened. ²⁹ Now Rebekah had a brother named Laban. Laban rushed outside to the man at the spring. ³⁰ When he saw the nose-ring and the bracelets on his sister's arms and when he heard Rebekah repeating what the man had said to her, he went to him while he was standing by the camels at the spring. ³¹ He said: "Come, blessed of the LORD! Why are you standing outside when I have made the house ready, as well as a place for the camels?" ³² The man then went inside; and while the camels were being unloaded and provided with straw and fodder, water was brought to bathe his feet and the feet of the men who were with him. (Abraham's servant said…) ⁴⁹ "Now, if you will act with kindness and fidelity toward my master, let me know; but if not, let me know that too. I can then proceed accordingly." ⁵⁰ Laban and Bethuel said in reply: "This thing comes from the LORD; we can say nothing to you either for or against it. ⁵¹ Here is Rebekah, right in front of you; take her and go, that she may become the wife of your master's son, as the LORD has said." ⁵² When Abraham's servant heard their answer, he bowed to the ground before the LORD. ⁵³ Then he brought out objects of silver and gold and clothing and presented them to Rebekah; he also gave costly presents to her brother and mother. ⁵⁴ After he and the men with him had eaten and drunk, they spent the night there. When they got up the next morning, he said, "Allow me to return to my master." ⁵⁵ Her brother and mother replied, "Let the young woman stay with us a short while, say ten days; after that she may go." ⁵⁶ But he said to them, "Do not detain me, now that the LORD has made my journey successful; let me go back to my master." ⁵⁷ They answered, "Let us call the young woman and see what she herself has to say about it." ⁵⁸ So they called Rebekah and asked her, "Will you go with this man?" She answered, "I will." ⁵⁹ At this they sent off their sister Rebekah and her nurse with Abraham's servant and his men. ⁶⁰ They blessed Rebekah and said: "Sister, may you grow into thousands of myriads; And may your descendants gain possession of the gates of their enemies!" ⁶¹ Then Rebekah and her attendants started out; they mounted the camels and followed the man. So the servant took Rebekah and went on his way. ⁶² Meanwhile Isaac had gone from Beer-lahai-roi and was living in the region of the Negeb. ⁶³ One day toward evening he went out to walk in the field, and caught sight of camels approaching. ⁶⁴ Rebekah, too, caught sight of Isaac, and got down from her camel. ⁶⁵ She asked the servant, "Who is the man over there, walking through the fields toward us?" "That is my master," replied the servant. Then she took her veil and covered herself. ⁶⁶ The servant recounted to Isaac all the things he had done. ⁶⁷ Then Isaac brought Rebekah into the tent of his mother Sarah. He took Rebekah as his wife. Isaac loved her and found solace after the death of his mother.

Plot Summary Chart

Verses	Events
1-5	
6-9	
10	
11-14	
15-19	
20-21	
22-27	
28-32	

Verses	Events
49-51	
52-54	
55-58	
59-61	
62-66	
67	

Isaac Assessment

Directions: Answer the following questions using you have learned from this and the previous two lessons.

1. With what huge sacrifice did God test Abraham?

   _____

2. What makes this sacrifice so very difficult for Abraham?

   _____

   _____

3. The author of Hebrews 11:17-19 offers an explanation for why Abraham is willing to sacrifice his son, Isaac, when God tests him. Put the reason in your own words:

   > By faith Abraham, when put to the test, offered up Isaac, and he who had received the promises was ready to offer his only son, of whom it was said, "Through Isaac descendants shall bear your name." He reasoned that God was able to raise even from the dead, and he received Isaac back as a symbol.

   _____

   _____

   _____

4. Name three of the ways Isaac is like Jesus Christ.

   ➤ _____

   ➤ _____

   ➤ _____

5. From Genesis 24, why did Abraham not want Isaac to marry a woman from Canaan?

   _____

6. What role did prayer play in finding Isaac's wife Rebekah?

   _____

   _____

Jacob and Esau

Directions: Read the story of Jacob and Esau, then answer the questions that follow.

Before they were born, the twins Jacob and Esau fought in their mother's womb. They continued to struggle with each other after they were born. Genesis 25:24-28 gives details about the birth of Jacob and Esau.

> When the time of her delivery came, there were twins in her womb. The first to emerge was reddish, and his whole body was like a hairy mantle; so they named him Esau. Next his brother came out, gripping Esau's heel; so he was named Jacob. Isaac was sixty years old when they were born. When the boys grew up, Esau became a skillful hunter, a man of the open country; whereas Jacob was a simple man, who stayed among the tents. Isaac preferred Esau, because he was fond of game; but Rebekah preferred Jacob.

The name Esau means "hairy," and the name Jacob means "supplanter" or "holder of the heel." To supplant means to replace, and that's just what Jacob would do to Esau. Notice that Isaac favored his firstborn son, Esau, while Rebekah favored Jacob, the younger son. Recall the prophecy that stated "the older will serve the younger." This prophecy about the brothers' relationship will ultimately come true: Jacob will take Esau's place – supplant him – as his father's heir! The first story we learn about Esau and Jacob illustrates their different characters. We can see that Esau is more concerned with the here and now, while Jacob thinks of the future. Esau sells his birthright to Jacob for a bowl of stew! We read about this in Genesis 25:29-34:

> Once, when Jacob was cooking a stew, Esau came in from the open country, famished. He said to Jacob, "Let me gulp down some of that red stuff; I am famished." That is why he was called Edom [Edom means "red" and is a variation of the name Esau]. But Jacob replied, "First sell me your right as firstborn." "Look," said Esau, "I am on the point of dying. What good is the right as firstborn to me?" But Jacob said, "Swear to me first!" So he sold Jacob his right as firstborn under oath. Jacob then gave him some bread and the lentil stew; and Esau ate, drank, got up, and went his way. So Esau treated his right as firstborn with disdain.

Even though Esau sold his birthright to Jacob, it was unlikely that Isaac would go along with it. So Rebekah and Jacob plotted to trick Isaac into giving his blessing to Jacob instead of to Esau. We read this story in Genesis 27:5-10, 15-17:

> Rebekah had been listening while Isaac was speaking to his son Esau. So when Esau went out into the open country to hunt some game for his father, Rebekah said to her son Jacob, "Listen! I heard your father tell your brother Esau, 'Bring me some game and prepare a dish for me to eat, that I may bless you with the LORD's approval before I die.' Now, my son, obey me in what I am about to order you. Go to the flock and get me two choice young goats so that with these I might prepare a dish for your father in the way he likes.

Then bring it to your father to eat, that he may bless you before he dies."

Rebekah then took the best clothes of her older son Esau that she had in the house, and gave them to her younger son Jacob to wear; and with the goatskins she covered up his hands and the hairless part of his neck. Then she gave her son Jacob the dish and the bread she had prepared.

Jacob brought his old, blind father the food and pretended to be his brother Esau. Then, he tricked Isaac into giving him his blessing and making him his heir. The plan worked, and Isaac gave his blessing to Jacob. The blessing Isaac gave to Jacob (disguised as Esau) took the following form from Genesis 27:27-29:

See, the smell of my son is as the smell of a field which the LORD has blessed! May God give you of the dew of heaven, and of the fatness of the earth, and plenty of grain and wine. Let peoples serve you, and nations bow down to you. Be lord over your brothers, and may your mother's sons bow down to you. Cursed be everyone who curses you, and blessed be everyone who blesses you!

After Esau discovered his brother's trickery, he became very upset. From this moment forward, Esau desired to kill his brother, Jacob. And so, Jacob fled his home and Esau's wrath and went to live with his uncle Laban.

1. What was Jacob and Esau's relationship like even before they were born?

   _____

2. How does the book of Genesis describe the differences between Jacob and Esau?

   _____

   _____

3. What do the names Jacob and Esau mean? How were they appropriate names for the brothers?

   _____

   _____

   _____

4. Which brother did Isaac favor? _____

5. Which brother did Rebekah favor? _____

6. How do we know that Esau was more concerned with the here and now rather than the big picture or the future?

   _____

   _____

7. How did Jacob and his mother plan to trick Isaac into giving Jacob his blessing?

_____

_____

8. After Jacob tricked his father into giving him his blessing, what did Isaac pray God would give to his heir (Jacob, disguised as Esau)?

_____

_____

9. How did Esau feel after he discovered he was tricked? What did Jacob do in response?

_____

_____

Reflection Questions

1. The sacred author of Genesis makes it clear that Esau was not fit to be head of his family after his father, Isaac, died. Even so, he was tricked out of his birthright as the oldest son. Do you think it was fair how Jacob became his family's heir? Why or why not? Do you think Esau's response to being tricked was fair? Why or why not?

   _____

   _____

   _____

   _____

2. Describe a time when you were not chosen to be on a team or to do something that you felt you should have been chosen to do. What happened? How did you feel? How did you react? How did things turn out? If you could go back to that moment, what would you do differently?

   _____

   _____

   _____

   _____

Jacob and Laban

Directions: Read the story of Jacob and Laban, then answer the questions that follow.

In Genesis 29:9-14 we learn about what happened when Jacob went to the land of his mother's brother to seek a wife. The moment he first saw Laban's younger daughter, Rachel, he fell instantly in love with her. Jacob knew he wanted to marry Rachel. He struck a bargain with his uncle Laban to work for him for seven years if he would give him Rachel to be his wife. For Jacob, the years seemed like days because of the love he had for Rachel. At the end of seven years, Jacob asked for Rachel's hand in marriage. Laban threw a big wedding feast, but that night he substituted Leah for Rachel. Jacob married Leah unknowingly – at least until the next morning. We read about Jacob's discovery of being tricked in Genesis 29:25-27:

> In the morning, there was Leah! So Jacob said to Laban: "How could you do this to me! Was it not for Rachel that I served you? Why did you deceive me?" Laban replied, "It is not the custom in our country to give the younger daughter before the firstborn. Finish the bridal week for this one, and then the other will also be given to you in return for another seven years of service with me."

So Jacob agreed to serve Laban for another seven years so that he could marry Rachel also. After a week of marriage to Leah, Jacob also married Rachel and had to stay on and serve Laban for another seven years. Just as Jacob had tricked his family into receiving Esau's birthright, Jacob was tricked into marrying both of Laban's daughters!

Over the years, Jacob grew in righteousness with God. And God blessed him with great success and wealth. Jacob, knew, however, that Laban could not be trusted. He created a plan to trick his uncle and make him pay justly for his now 14 years of service. We read about Jacob's plan in Genesis 30:29-32:

> Jacob replied: "You know what work I did for you and how well your livestock fared under my care; the little you had before I came has grown into an abundance, since the LORD has blessed you in my company. Now, when can I do something for my own household as well?" Laban asked, "What should I give you?" Jacob answered: "You do not have to give me anything. If you do this thing for me, I will again pasture and tend your sheep. Let me go through your whole flock today and remove from it every dark animal among the lambs and every spotted or speckled one among the goats. These will be my wages."

In essence, Jacob asked Laban for any future offspring of the flock of sheep that were spotted or dark colored. Laban believed that only spotted or dark-colored animals gave birth to spotted or dark-colored offspring and only solid-colored animals gave birth to solid-colored ones. So, that very day, Laban had separated the dark and spotted sheep and goats from the solid-colored ones, leaving behind only the solid colored animals. Laban believed he had made a great deal! Solid-colored animals would not give birth to spotted ones. Therefore, Jacob would earn only a small number of animals from the flock.

Jacob, however, knew Laban would try to trick him again. So he had planned for this moment. With some creative breeding practices and God's blessing, Jacob had engineered the flock of sheep and goats so that the solid-colored animals would in fact give birth to spotted and dark-colored ones and not solid-colored ones. Genesis 30:43 describes the result:

So the man [Jacob] grew exceedingly prosperous, and he owned large flocks, male and female servants, camels, and donkeys.

At the end of Jacob's years of service, Laban was not too happy about being tricked. And so Jacob gathered his wives, children, and servants, and he assembled his now large flock and possessions and fled from Laban's land. They set out to return to the land of his father, Isaac, to take possession of his inheritance.

1. Where did Jacob go to find a wife? The land of his mothers brothers

2. What was the deal Jacob made with Laban so that he could marry his daughter Rachel? To work for seven years

3. How was Jacob first tricked by Laban? What reason does Laban give for his trickery? He married Leah because he thought that Rachel was Leah. He did that because the oldest has to get married first.

4. What did Jacob agree to do so that he could still marry Rachel? Work for 7 more years

5. What did Jacob ask Laban for as payment for his 14 years of service? He did not ask for anything

6. Why did Laban believe he had tricked Jacob again?

_____

7. How did Jacob end up tricking Laban?

_____

_____

8. Where did Jacob flee to after tricking Laban? To the land of his father

Reflection Questions

1. Describe a time when you had to work hard to achieve something you wanted. What was it like to work for what you wanted? Did the time go by quickly or slowly? Why? How did you feel after you had achieved your goal?

_____

_____

_____

_____

_____

_____

2. When we first met Jacob, he used his skills of trickery and manipulation for his personal gain. By the end of his time with Laban, however, Jacob had grown in maturity and righteousness in the eyes of God. God blessed Jacob and allowed him to use his skills so that justice was done. What special skills and talents do you have? Describe a time you used skills and talents selfishly. How did that situation turn out? Describe a time you used your skills and talents justly for God. How did that situation turn out?

_____

_____

_____

_____

_____

_____

_____

_____

_____

_____

God Remembers Rachel

Directions: Read about Rachel and the battle of prayer, then questions that follow.

Jacob's beloved wife Rachel was barren; she could not have any children. Her sister, Leah, who was also married to Jacob, had many children. She gave birth to six sons. Rachel was very upset because she was unable to have children of her own. She became jealous of her sister. Eventually, Scripture tells us that "God remembered Rachel. God listened to her and made her fruitful" (Genesis 30:22). Rachel, despite her frustration and jealousy of her sister, cried out to God and He heard her. Rachel eventually gave birth to two sons, one of whom, Joseph, would grow up to be the savior of his people and all of Egypt.

Sometimes, when things aren't going our way and we seem to be down on our luck, it can feel as if God has forgotten us. But this is not true. God cannot forget us. He is God, our Creator and our Father. Psalm 49:15 tells us, "Can a mother forget her infant, be without tenderness for the child of her womb? Even should she forget, I will never forget you." In a poetic way, the psalmist tells us that even in the unlikely event that our own mothers would forget us, God will not. He cannot!

So how do we make sense of God's "remembering" Rachel if He does not forget us? In those moments in life when things aren't going our way and we become angry at God and feel as if He has forgotten us, the truth is, we have forgotten Him. Often in those moments, we turn away from God, fall into sin, rely only on our own abilities, and fail to trust others or seek help. We abandon our faith in God's promises to us. We forget that

He has a plan of hope for our lives. That's not to say that everything will always be easy. But, in the end, God will fulfill all of His promises to us. When the sacred author of Genesis explains that God "remembered" Rachel and "listened" to her, that first required Rachel to come back to God and cry out to Him.

Our prayer lives can sometimes be similar to Rachel's experience. The *Catechism of the Catholic Church* no. 2725 describes prayer as a battle:

> Prayer is both a gift of grace and a determined response on our part. It always presupposes effort. The great figures of prayer of the Old Covenant before Christ, as well as the Mother of God, the saints, and he himself, all teach us this: prayer is a battle. Against whom? Against ourselves and against the wiles of the tempter who does all he can to turn man away from prayer, away from union with God. We pray as we live, because we live as we pray. If we do not want to act habitually according to the Spirit of Christ, neither can we pray habitually in his name. The "spiritual battle" of the Christian's new life is inseparable from the battle of prayer.

The opportunity to pray to God is first and foremost a gift, but it also requires us to do something: to respond to Him. The battle of prayer, then, is against our own weaknesses, temptations, failures, distractions, and laziness. It is also a battle against the work of the devil himself, who wants nothing more than to pull us away from God. To be successful in the battle of prayer, we must humbly recognize that we cannot do it alone. We must trust in God to hear our prayer, and persevere against all obstacles that stand in our way. In this way, we will "remember" God throughout our lives.

1. Why was Rachel jealous of her sister, Leah?

_____

2. How does Scripture describe what happened between God and Rachel?

_____

_____

3. Why will God not forget us?

_____

_____

4. What does Psalm 49 say about God's "forgetting" us?

_____

_____

5. If God does not forget us, how do we make sense of God's "remembering" Rachel?

_____

_____

6. What had to happen first before God "remembered" Rachel?

_____

7. The *Catechism* describes prayer as a battle. Whom are we fighting in this battle of prayer?

_____

_____

8. What three things must we do in order to win the battle of prayer?

_____

_____

_____

Jacob Wrestles with an Angel

Directions: Read the story of Jacob wrestling with an angel, then answer the questions.

After Jacob earns his pay in spotted sheep and goats from Laban's flock, God speaks to Jacob and tells him to return to the land of his ancestors, where he was born, in order to reclaim his inheritance from his brother, Esau. Jacob gathered his wives, children, flock, and possessions and set out for the land of Canaan. Along the journey, Jacob grew frightened of what would happen when he met his brother again. The last time they had seen each other, Esau had wanted to kill Jacob! So, the night before they were to meet, Jacob found himself alone and struggling with his feelings. Then, a strange event occurs. An angel appeared before Jacob, and the two wrestled until dawn. We read this peculiar story in Genesis 32:25-39:

> Jacob was left there alone. Then a man wrestled with him until the break of dawn. When the man saw that he could not prevail over him, he struck Jacob's hip at its socket, so that Jacob's socket was dislocated as he wrestled with him. The man then said, "Let me go, for it is daybreak." But Jacob said, "I will not let you go until you bless me." "What is your name?" the man asked. He answered, "Jacob." Then the man said, "You shall no longer be named Jacob, but Israel, because you have contended with divine and human beings and have prevailed."

In his distress, Jacob wrestles an angel of God to a draw, although he is wounded in the process. Because of this, the angel changes Jacob's name to Israel, which means "he who wrestles with God." Israel, of course, would become the name of the people that would grow from Jacob's 12 sons.

What happened that night? Did Jacob really wrestle with an angel? Perhaps. The greater truth of this story, however, is what it tells us about our experience of prayer. One way of understanding this story is that Jacob, in his fear, "wrestled" with God in prayer. Our prayer lives can sometimes be similar to Jacob's experience. The *Catechism of the Catholic Church* no. 2725 describes prayer as a battle:

> Prayer is both a gift of grace and a determined response on our part. It always presupposes effort. The great figures of prayer of the Old Covenant before Christ, as well as the Mother of God, the saints, and he himself, all teach us this: prayer is a battle. Against whom? Against ourselves and against the wiles of the tempter who does all he can to turn man away from prayer, away from union with God. We pray as we live, because we live as we pray. If we do not want to act habitually according to the Spirit of Christ, neither can we pray habitually in his name. The "spiritual battle" of the Christian's new life is inseparable from the battle of prayer.

The opportunity to pray to God is first and foremost a gift, but it also requires us to do something, to respond to Him. The battle of prayer, then, is against our own weaknesses, temptations, failures, distractions, and laziness. It is also a battle against the work of the devil himself, who wants nothing more than to pull us away from God. And God wants us to bring this battle directly to Him. To be successful in the battle of prayer, we must humbly recognize that we cannot do it alone. We must trust in God to hear our prayer and must persevere against all obstacles.

1. What did God call Jacob to do after he had earned his pay?

   _____

2. Why was Jacob afraid of meeting his brother again?

   _____

   _____

3. What happened the night before Jacob was to meet his brother?

   _____

   _____

4. What did the angel change Jacob's name to? What does his new name mean?

   _____

   _____

5. While Jacob may or may not have actually wrestled with an angel, what is one way of understanding this story that reveals a greater truth about our own experience of prayer?

   _____

   _____

6. The *Catechism* describes prayer as a battle. Whom are we fighting in this battle of prayer?

   _____

7. What three things must we do in order to win the battle of prayer?

   _____

   _____

8. What does God want us to do in our battle of prayer?

   _____

   _____

Joseph Dreams of Greatness

Directions: Read about Joseph and his dreams of greatness, then answer the questions.

In Genesis 37 we learn more about Jacob's family. Jacob and his wives ended up settling in the land of his father, the land of Canaan. Jacob had 12 sons, but his eleventh son, Joseph, was his favorite. Joseph's mother was Rachel, and Joseph was born miraculously to Jacob and Rachel in their old age. Jacob's other sons knew that he favored Joseph, and they hated Joseph for it and treated him poorly. Their hatred of Joseph grew even more when he received a beautiful coat from his father. (This coat is often described as a coat of many colors. The Bible, however, describes it only as an "ornamented tunic.") Joseph would bring his father bad reports of his brothers while they worked in the fields. Then one day, Joseph had a dream that he shared with his family. We read about this dream in Genesis 37:5-11:

> Once Joseph had a dream, and when he told his brothers, they hated him even more. He said to them, "Listen to this dream I had. There we were, binding sheaves in the field, when suddenly my sheaf rose to an upright position, and your sheaves formed a ring around my sheaf and bowed down to it." His brothers said to him, "Are you really going to make yourself king over us? Will you rule over us?" So they hated him all the more because of his dreams and his reports.
>
> Then he had another dream, and told it to his brothers. "Look, I had another dream," he said; "this time, the sun and the moon and eleven stars were bowing down to me." When he told it to his father and his brothers, his father reproved him and asked, "What is the meaning of this dream of yours? Can it be that I and your mother and your brothers are to come and bow to the ground before you?" So his brothers were furious at him but his father kept the matter in mind.

Joseph first dreamed that he and his brothers were binding sheaves of wheat, when suddenly his sheaf rose up and brothers' sheaves bowed down to his. Then, he dreamed that the sun, the moon, and eleven stars bowed down to him. His brothers and even his father and mother believed Joseph was saying that they would someday bow down to him and he would be lord over them. Jacob punished Joseph for his dreams of greatness, and his brothers hated him even more.

When they heard about these dreams, Joseph's brothers had had enough. One day soon after, they plotted to kill Joseph to be rid of him. Joseph's oldest brother, Reuben, however, stopped them from killing Joseph, saying, "We must not take his life," and then suggested a different plan. The brothers stripped Joseph of the coat his father had given him and threw him into an empty well, where they planned to leave him. Later that day, a caravan of traders came riding by on camels. Joseph's brothers hatched another plan, which we read about in Genesis 37:28-36:

> Midianite traders passed by, and they pulled Joseph up out of the cistern. They sold Joseph for twenty pieces of silver to

the Ishmaelites, who took him to Egypt. When Reuben went back to the cistern and saw that Joseph was not in it, he tore his garments, and returning to his brothers, he exclaimed: "The boy is gone! And I – where can I turn?" They took Joseph's tunic, and after slaughtering a goat, dipped the tunic in its blood. Then they sent someone to bring the long ornamented tunic to their father, with the message: "We found this. See whether it is your son's tunic or not." He recognized it and exclaimed: "My son's tunic! A wild beast has devoured him! Joseph has been torn to pieces!" Then Jacob tore his garments, put sackcloth on his loins, and mourned his son many days. Though his sons and daughters tried to console him, he refused all consolation, saying, "No, I will go down mourning to my son in Sheol." Thus did his father weep for him. The Midianites, meanwhile, sold Joseph in Egypt to Potiphar, an official of Pharaoh and his chief steward.

Joseph's brothers sold him into slavery! And, to make matters even worse, they tore his coat, dipped it in goat's blood, and told their father that Joseph had been killed by a wild animal. Jacob was very sad because he believed, as his sons had told him, that his favorite son, Joseph, was dead. But Joseph was not dead. The traveling traders had sold Joseph to an Egyptian official named Potiphar, for whom Joseph now worked as a servant.

1. Who was Joseph? _He is the 11th son's son_

2. What special item did Jacob give Joseph? _Tunic_

3. How did Joseph's brothers feel about him? Why? _They were jealous of them, he was a tattle tale._

4. What did Joseph dream about himself and his family? _His brothers are bowing down to him_

5. What did Joseph's brothers first plot against him? What did they end up doing instead? _They were going to kill him, but Rueben said "we should not take away his life" They sell them to traders_

6. Where did Joseph end up at the end of this part of his story? _Egypt house_

Reflection Question

Think about a time that you fought or disagreed with a family member or a close friend. How did you feel when you were fighting or disagreeing with that person? How was the situation resolved? How did you feel afterward? Looking back at the situation, how could you have avoided the fight or disagreement in the first place? What would you have done differently to make a bad situation better?

I got into an argament with my sister about our bathroom. I felt like we should not be fighting about who gets first shower. To avoid this argument, we relized one of us could shower in another bathroom. One of us should have just went in another bathroom.

God Blesses Joseph

Directions: Read about how Joseph was blessed by God and answer the questions that follow. Then, complete the chart detailing Joseph's dream interpretations.

Even though Joseph endured rejection and suffering and had been sold into slavery by his brothers, God blessed him because of his faithfulness. He was bought by an Egyptian official named Potiphar, who made Joseph his personal attendant and put him in charge of his entire household. And God blessed Joseph and his work, which in turn blessed Potiphar and his household with great success. Neither Joseph nor his master had cause to worry.

Joseph was a handsome man, and he caught the eye of Potiphar's wife. She continually tried to seduce Joseph, but he refused her, proclaiming what a great wickedness it would be against Potiphar and against God. One day, Potiphar's wife forced herself upon Joseph. She grabbed his cloak, but he ran outside, leaving his cloak behind in her hands. Potiphar's wife called out to the men of the house and accused Joseph of attacking her. When Potiphar learned of his wife's accusations against Joseph, he became angry and had Joseph thrown into prison. Even though Joseph had been falsely accused of wrongdoing and was imprisoned, God was with him. The chief jailer put Joseph in charge of all of the other prisoners!

While Joseph was in prison, two other prisoners, the former cupbearer and the former baker to the Pharaoh of Egypt, told Joseph of dreams they had had. Once again, Joseph was able to use his God-given gift to interpret their dreams. We read of these dreams in Genesis 40:

Then the chief cupbearer told Joseph his dream. "In my dream," he said, "I saw a vine in front of me, and on the vine were three branches. It had barely budded when its blossoms came out, and its clusters ripened into grapes. Pharaoh's cup was in my hand; so I took the grapes, pressed them out into his cup, and put it in Pharaoh's hand." Joseph said to him: "This is its interpretation. The three branches are three days; within three days Pharaoh will single you out and restore you to your post. You will be handing Pharaoh his cup as you formerly did when you were his cupbearer. Only think of me when all is well with you, and please do me the great favor of mentioning me to Pharaoh, to get me out of this place. The truth is that I was kidnapped from the land of the Hebrews, and I have not done anything here that they should have put me into a dungeon." When the chief baker saw that Joseph had given a favorable interpretation, he said to him: "I too had a dream. In it I had three bread baskets on my head; in the top one were all kinds of bakery products for Pharaoh, but the birds were eating them out of the basket on my head." Joseph said to him in reply: "This is its interpretation. The three baskets are three days; within three days Pharaoh will single you out and will impale you on a stake, and the birds will be eating your flesh."

Everything came to pass as Joseph had predicted from their dreams. The chief cupbearer was restored to his former position, and the baker was killed. Unfortunately for Joseph, the cupbearer did not think of Joseph once he was restored, and Joseph remained in prison for two more years.

Then Pharaoh had a series of dreams that troubled him. He called for his magicians to interpret the dreams, but none could do it. Pharaoh's cupbearer then remembered Joseph, and he told Pharaoh about how Joseph had correctly interpreted his and the baker's dreams. So Pharaoh had Joseph brought to him, and he told Joseph of his dreams. We read about this in Genesis 41:17-32:

> Then Pharaoh said to Joseph: "In my dream, I was standing on the bank of the Nile, when up from the Nile came seven cows, fat and well-formed; they grazed in the reed grass. Behind them came seven other cows, scrawny, most ill-formed and gaunt. Never have I seen such bad specimens as these in all the land of Egypt! The gaunt, bad cows devoured the first seven fat cows. But when they had consumed them, no one could tell that they had done so, because they looked as bad as before. Then I woke up. In another dream I saw seven ears of grain, full and healthy, growing on a single stalk. Behind them sprouted seven ears of grain, shriveled and thin and scorched by the east wind; and the seven thin ears swallowed up the seven healthy ears. I

have spoken to the magicians, but there is no one to explain it to me." Joseph said to Pharaoh: "Pharaoh's dreams have the same meaning. God has made known to Pharaoh what he is about to do. The seven healthy cows are seven years, and the seven healthy ears are seven years—the same in each dream. The seven thin, bad cows that came up after them are seven years, as are the seven thin ears scorched by the east wind; they are seven years of famine. Things are just as I told Pharaoh: God has revealed to Pharaoh what he is about to do. Seven years of great abundance are now coming throughout the land of Egypt; but seven years of famine will rise up after them, when all the abundance will be forgotten in the land of Egypt. When the famine has exhausted the land, no trace of the abundance will be found in the land because of the famine that follows it, for it will be very severe. That Pharaoh had the same dream twice means that the matter has been confirmed by God and that God will soon bring it about."

Joseph interpreted Pharaoh's dream to be a prediction of seven years of abundant crops followed by seven years of famine. And, rather than take credit for himself, Joseph gave credit for the interpretation to God. Because of his faithfulness even in the face of rejection, persecution, false imprisonment, and suffering, Joseph was blessed by God. Pharaoh made Joseph his second in command of all of Egypt. He was put in charge of storing grain to prepare for the seven years of famine. And when all that Joseph had predicted came true, Egypt was saved because of Joseph and his faith in God.

Joseph's interpretations chart

Directions: Fill in the chart, first with an outline of the butler's, the baker's, and Pharaoh's dreams, Joseph's interpretation of each, and the final resolution of each.

1. What did God do for Joseph despite his rejection, suffering, and being sold into slavery by his brothers?

   Blessed him because of his +faithfullness

2. What happened to Joseph after he was sold into slavery?

   He was a personal attendant of Potiphar

3. Why did neither Joseph nor his master have reason to worry?

   God blessed Joseph and his work, wich in turn blessed Potiphar and his household with great sucess

4. How did Joseph end up being thrown in prison?

   She grabbed his cloak, but he ran outside leaving his cloak behind in her hands

	Description of dream	Joseph's interpretation	Final resolution
Pharaoh's cupbearer	He saw a vine with 3 branches, that eventually grew into grapes, he squezzed the grapes into a cup for the Pharof	In three days he will be let go from prison and be a cupbearer	The cupbearer was let go from prison and returned to his job.
Pharaoh's baker	three bread baskets in my hand, the birds were eating the bread	He will be killed in three days and the birds will eat your flesh	He got killed, the birds ate his flesh
Pharaoh	standing on the bank of Nile, there were 7 healthy and 7 unhealthy cows the unheathy cows ate the heathy ones	There will be 7 years of abundance and 7 years of famine	They had great supply of food for 7 years, then there was famine.

Joseph and His Brothers

Directions: Read about Joseph and his brothers, then answer the questions that follow.

All that Joseph predicted came true. There were seven years of abundant crops followed by seven years of harsh famine throughout the land. Because of Joseph and his position of authority in Egypt, enough grain was stored during the seven years of abundance so that all of Egypt could survive and live well. Even those in the surrounding lands came to Egypt to buy grain during this difficult time. That included people from the land of Canaan—Joseph's brothers, whom he had not seen in many years. Joseph's brothers, along with their father, Israel, and the rest of the family, had been suffering in Canaan and finally ran out of food. So they came to Egypt with what little they had to buy food from Joseph, although they did not know it was he because they thought he had died long ago. Joseph, however, recognized them. He decided to test them, to see if they had learned anything over the years.

And so, on the brothers' second journey to Egypt for food, Joseph hid a silver cup in one of their bags. Then he accused them of stealing his cup. The brothers had no knowledge of the cup and proclaimed "If any of your servants is found to have the goblet, he shall die, and as for the rest of us, we shall become my lord's slaves." Joseph ordered his guards to search their bags, and, of course, they found the silver cup. Joseph had placed the cup in the bag of the youngest brother, Benjamin. Benjamin's mother was also Joseph's mother, Rachel, and he was favored by Israel. Joseph had Benjamin seized. The other brothers threw themselves at Joseph's feet and begged for mercy. Judah spoke up and asked if he could take his younger brother's place and bear his punishment instead. At this, Joseph knew his brothers had changed and were no longer the same men who had sold him into slavery many years before.

The time had come for Joseph to reveal himself to his brothers. Weeping, Joseph sent away all of his servants so that only he and his brothers remained in the room. We read about Joseph's revelation in Genesis 45:3-5:

> "I am Joseph," he said to his brothers. "Is my father still alive?" But his brothers could give him no answer, so dumbfounded were they at him. "Come closer to me," Joseph told his brothers. When they had done so, he said: "I am your brother Joseph, whom you sold into Egypt. But now do not be distressed, and do not be angry with yourselves for having sold me here. It was really for the sake of saving lives that God sent me here ahead of you. The famine has been in the land for two years now, and for five more years cultivation will yield no harvest. God, therefore, sent me on ahead of you to ensure for you a remnant on earth and to save your lives in an extraordinary deliverance. So it was not really you but God who had me come here; and he has made me a father to Pharaoh, lord of all his household, and ruler over the whole land of Egypt."

Joseph revealed himself to his brothers through his tears. But, despite the suffering he had endured because of them, Joseph felt no hard feelings toward them. He had forgiven them for what they had done. And he saw the events of his life, good and bad, from God's perspective. Joseph understood that God had sent him to Egypt and allowed him to endure the rejection, persecution, and suffering he faced so that he could save the lives of many—all of Egypt and even his own family.

Joseph had his entire family brought to Egypt, and Pharaoh gifted them with the best land in Egypt to settle in. There, Joseph's family, the people of Israel, would live throughout the rest of the famine and for centuries to come.

1. What came true that Joseph had predicted?

   There were 7 years of abundant crops and 7 years of harsh femine.

2. What did Joseph do because of his position of authority in Egypt?

   He stored enough grain to survive 7 years of femine

3. How did Joseph meet his brothers again after many years?

   They came to Egypt for grain because In Canaan they were suffering.

4. How did Joseph test his brothers?

   He hid a silver cup in one of their grain bags. Then he accused him of stealing the cup.

5. After Joseph revealed himself to his brothers, how do we know that he had forgiven them for what they had done to him many years earlier?

   Because if they did not send them here, none of this would have happened

6. How did Joseph understand the events of his life from God's perspective?

   He sent him to Egypt and allowed him to endure the rejection, persecution, and suffering.

7. What happened to Joseph's family at the end of the story?

   They came down to Egypt and lived in the palace.

UNIT 5

Exodus

In this unit, you will learn about...

> The Exodus.

> God's call to Moses.

> The revelation of God's name to Moses.

> The Passover.

> The Passover of the New Covenant.

> The parting of the Red Sea and the delivery of the Ten Commandments.

Introduction

The Exodus is the central saving event of the Old Testament. In the Exodus, God called Moses to be His prophet and to lead His people out of slavery in Egypt into the Promised Land to become a great nation. God revealed His name to Moses which was an invitation to His people to know Him and call upon Him. After fleeing Egypt and crossing the Red Sea, the Israelites sinned in the desert. As punishment for their disobedience, God made them wander the desert for 40 years before they were able to enter the Promised Land.

At the heart of the Exodus is the Passover. Through Moses, God sent ten plagues upon Egypt as a sign to the Egyptians and the Israelites that He is the God of the universe and has power over all things. The final plague God sent upon Egypt was the plague of the death of the first born of every family in Egypt. God instructed Moses to have every Israelite family sacrifice an innocent lamb, spread its blood over their doorposts, and share a sacred meal of bread, wine, and the roasted flesh of the lamb. That night they would be passed over by the plague of death. God also commanded that the Israelites remember this original Passover event every year with a memorial meal. The original Passover foreshadows Christ's own sacrifice on the Cross. Jesus is the Lamb of God who offered His Body and Blood in the Eucharist at the Last Supper. His Sacrifice is the Passover of the New Covenant that freed us from slavery to sin and death.

Are there any questions you still have about the topics you learned last month? What steps can you take to find out the answers?

_____

_____

_____

_____

What questions do you have right now about the topics you will be learning about in this unit?

_____

_____

_____

_____

Angel of Death: In the tenth and final plague of the Exodus, God sent the Angel of Death upon Egypt to take the lives of all the first born children in Egypt. By sacrificing a lamb, spreading its blood on their doorposts, and eating its roasted flesh in a sacred meal of bread and wine, the Angel of Death passed over the Israelite homes and spared their first born.

Beatitude: Happiness or fulfillment. In the Sermon on the Mount Jesus gave the Beatitudes as the perfection of the Ten Commandments. They teach us how to be truly happy, or reach human perfection and fulfillment, which we ultimately find in Heaven.

Burning Bush: God spoke to Moses from a burning bush. He revealed His name to Moses and gave Him the mission of freeing the Israelites from slavery.

Eucharist: The Sacrament in which we receive the Body and Blood, Soul and Divinity of our Lord Jesus Christ under the appearances of bread and wine. The Eucharist is the source and summit of our Christian life. It is spiritual food for the soul. It is not merely a symbol, but is Jesus' true flesh and blood.

Exodus: Greek for "way or path for leaving." In the Old Testament, God called Moses to be His prophet and lead the Israelites, His Chosen People, out of slavery in Egypt to new life in the Promised Land.

Israelites: The descendants of Abraham, Isaac, and Jacob before they became the nation of Israel.

Lamb of God: Jesus is the Lamb of God whose sacrifice on the Cross freed us from sin and spiritual death. Just as the Israelites had to eat the flesh of the Paschal Lamb for the sacrifice to be complete, Jesus gave us His Body and Blood in the Eucharist at the Last Supper for us to receive the blessings of the Passover of the New Covenant.

Last Supper: The final meal Jesus shared with His Apostles. It was a Passover meal. Jesus, the Lamb of God, transformed the sacred meal into the Passover of the New Covenant by giving us His Body and Blood to eat in the Eucharist.

Liberator: See redeemer.

Memorial Feast: A sacred meal shared to remember, or make present again, an important event of the past. God commanded the Israelites to share a memorial feast each year to re-present the events of the Passover. Every Mass is a memorial feast that makes Christ's one sacrifice on the Cross present to us today.

Moses: "To draw out." The man God called to be His prophet and to whom He revealed His name. God gave Moses the mission of leading His people out of slavery in Egypt. God delivered the Ten Commandments and the whole of the Law to Moses to teach the Israelites how to love Him and how to love their neighbor.

Paschal Lamb: The lamb sacrificed by each Israelite family during the Passover. The blood of the lamb on the Israelite door posts was a sign for their homes to be passed over by the plague of death.

Passover: The central event of the Exodus. The final plague God sent upon Egypt was the plague of the death of the first born of every family in Egypt. By sacrificing a lamb, spreading its blood on their doorposts, and eating its roasted flesh in a sacred meal of bread and wine, the Israelite homes would be passed over by the plague of death. God also commanded that the Israelites remember this original Passover event every year with a memorial meal. The original Passover foreshadows Christ's own sacrifice on the Cross.

Plagues: Ten miraculous signs God sent upon Egypt during the Exodus as a sign of His power as the God of the universe. Examples of the plagues include turning the water of the Nile River to blood, sending large amounts of frogs to fill the land, darkness, and the final plague of the death of the first born in Egypt.

Redeemer: A person who saves or frees others from slavery or oppression. Moses was the redeemer of the Israelites from slavery in Egypt. He foreshadowed Jesus, our true Redeemer from sin.

Sacrifice: In ancient times, people offered the life of an animal to God as a way to praise God by, to give thanks to God, to honor a new beginning or to swear an oath, or as an expression of sorrow for sin. The original Passover required the sacrifice of a lamb. Jesus offered Himself as the supreme sacrifice to redeem all people from sin.

Signs and Wonders: The miracles that God worked in Egypt as signs of His power as the God of the universe. These miracles foreshadowed the miracles Jesus would later perform as signs of God's love and mercy and that He is truly the Son of God.

Slavery: When a person or group of people is controlled by someone or something else and is not free to what he or she wants. The Israelites were slaves in Egypt for many centuries before the Exodus.

Temptation: Something that attracts or lures a person to sin.

Ten Commandments: Laws of love God gave to Moses for the people of Israel to teach them how to love God and one another. They are an expression of the eternal law of God and help us to resist temptation and avoid sin. They are the foundation of the Christian moral life.

Theophany: A profound manifestation, or revelation, of God. God's revelation of His name to Moses in the burning bush was a great revelation of God that forever changed God's relationship with His Chosen People.

The Crossing of the Red Sea
BY UNKNOWN ARTIST (C. 1400-1410)

The J. Paul Getty Museum, Los Angeles.

The Crossing of the Red Sea

The Crossing of the Red Sea, *by unknown artist* (c. 1400-1410)

Directions: Take some time to quietly view and reflect on the art. Let yourself be inspired in any way that happens naturally. Then think about the questions below, and discuss them with your classmates.

Conversation Questions

1. Who are the people in this picture?

2. What is happening in this picture?

3. What else do you know about this event?

4. God is not directly shown in this picture, although God directly caused the events that are shown. What does this picture show us about God?

5. Read the Scripture passage below. How does this image illustrate the Scripture passage?

   The Lord preceded them, in the daytime by means of a column of cloud to show them the way, and at night by means of a column of fire to give them light. Thus they could travel both day and night.
   −EXODUS 13:21

6. How does a pillar of fire reveal God and at the same time conceal God?

7. God could have revealed Himself in any way that He wanted. Why do you think God chose to reveal Himself by first allowing the Israelites to be slaves and then miraculously freeing them?

The Exodus and the Lord's Prayer

Directions: Read the text of the Lord's Prayer, which is the most perfect prayer of the Church. Then, using the passages from the Book of Exodus on the next page, fill in the chart to match each passage from Exodus with a petition from the Lord's Prayer.

Our Father, who art in Heaven, hallowed be Thy name. Thy kingdom come, Thy will be done, on earth as it is in Heaven. Give us this day our daily bread, and forgive us our trespasses, as we forgive those who trespass against us. And lead us not into temptation, but deliver us from evil.

Petitions of the Lord's Prayer	Matching passage from Exodus
1. Our Father	
2. Who art in Heaven	
3. Hallowed be Thy name	
4. Thy Kingdom come	
5. Thy will be done, on earth as it is in Heaven.	
6. Give us this day our daily bread	
7. And forgive us our trespasses, as we forgive those who trespass against us	
8. And lead us not into temptation	
9. But deliver us from evil.	

Passages from the Book of Exodus

A   You will be to me a kingdom of priests, a holy nation. –EXODUS 19:6

B   The LORD said to Moses: "This is what you will say to the Israelites: You have seen for yourselves that I have spoken to you from heaven. You shall not make alongside of me gods of silver, nor shall you make for yourselves gods of gold."
–EXODUS 20:22-23

C   Now, if you obey me completely and keep my covenant, you will be my treasured possession among all peoples, though all the earth is mine.
–EXODUS 19:5

D   Then the Lord said to Moses: "I am going to rain down bread from heaven for you. Each day the people are to go out and gather their daily portion."
–EXODUS 16:4

E   So you will say to Pharaoh, "Thus says the LORD: Israel is my son, my firstborn. I said to you: Let my son go, that he may serve me."
–EXODUS 4:22-23

F   But Moses answered the people, "Do not fear! Stand your ground and see the victory the LORD will win for you today. For these Egyptians whom you see today you will never see again. The LORD will fight for you; you have only to keep still." –EXODUS 14:13-14

G   God replied to Moses: "I am who I am." Then He added: "This is what you will tell the Israelites: I AM has sent me to you." –EXODUS 3:14

H   Moses said to the people, "Remember this day on which you came out of Egypt, out of a house of slavery. For it was with a strong hand that the LORD brought you out from there." –EXODUS 13:3

I   So the LORD passed before him and proclaimed: "The LORD, the LORD, a God gracious and merciful, slow to anger and abounding in love and fidelity, continuing His love for a thousand generations, and forgiving wickedness, rebellion, and sin." –EXODUS 34:6-7

Matthew 6:9-13

This is how you are to pray: Our Father in heaven, hallowed be your name, your kingdom come, your will be done, on earth as in heaven. Give us today our daily bread; and forgive us our debts, as we forgive our debtors; and do not subject us to the final test, but deliver us from the evil one.

Exodus 3:14

God replied to Moses: "I am who I am."
Then he added: "This is what you will tell
the Israelites: I AM has sent me to you."

_____

_____

_____

_____

_____

_____

_____

_____

_____

Matthew 2:14-15

Joseph rose and took the child and his mother by night and departed for Egypt. He stayed there until the death of Herod, that what the Lord had said through the prophet might be fulfilled, "Out of Egypt I called my son."

_____

_____

_____

_____

_____

_____

_____

_____

_____

Exodus 12:14

This day will be a day of remembrance for you, which your future generations will celebrate with pilgrimage to the LORD; you will celebrate it as a statute forever.

Luke 22:15-16

He said to them, "I have eagerly desired to eat this Passover with you before I suffer, for, I tell you, I shall not eat it [again] until there is fulfillment in the kingdom of God."

Matthew 5:17

Do not think that I have come to abolish the law or the prophets. I have come not to abolish but to fulfill.

Deuteronomy 6:4-6

Hear, O Israel! The LORD is our God, the LORD alone! Therefore, you shall love the LORD, your God, with your whole heart, and with your whole being, and with your whole strength. Take to heart these words which I command you today.

Slaves in Egypt

Directions: Read about the enslaving of the Israelites, then answer the questions that follow in complete sentences.

At the beginning of the story of the Exodus, we learn that God's people have multiplied greatly. Jacob and his 12 sons and all of his family moved to Egypt at Joseph's request. There they settled in the best land of Egypt, the Land of Goshen, which was given to them by the Pharaoh. Over the years, Jacob's descendants, the Israelites, grew in number. Exodus 1:5-7 explains:

> The total number of Jacob's direct descendants was 70. Joseph was already in Egypt.

> Now Joseph and all his brothers and that whole generation died. But the Israelites were fruitful and prolific. They multiplied and became so very numerous that the land was filled with them.

The number of people who entered Egypt was between 70 and 75. When the Exodus began, there were about 600,000 men. When you add women and children to that number, there were about 2,000,000 people! They grew to this amount in approximately 400 years. It's no wonder the Bible tells us "the land was filled with them."

Eventually, there came a new king of Egypt, a pharaoh from a different line of kings. The book of Exodus tells us this new pharaoh "knew nothing of Joseph" (Exodus 1:8). This doesn't mean that the pharaoh didn't know who the Israelites or Joseph were. Rather, it means the new pharaoh chose not to uphold any agreements that were made by the old pharaoh with the Israelites. The new pharaoh became concerned that there were too many Israelites. He thought they might grow so numerous that they would be able to overthrow his rule. So the pharaoh forced the Israelites into "cruel slavery." We read about this in Exodus 1:11-14:

> Accordingly, they set supervisors over the Israelites to oppress them with forced labor. Thus they had to build for Pharaoh the garrison cities of Pithom and Raamses. Yet the more they were oppressed, the more they multiplied and spread, so that the Egyptians began to loathe the Israelites. So the Egyptians reduced the Israelites to cruel slavery, making life bitter for them with hard labor, at mortar and brick and all kinds of field work—cruelly oppressed in all their labor.

The more the Egyptians oppressed the people the more they grew in number and strength. The Egyptians responded by being even crueler to God's people. They made them work harder as slaves and made their lives very difficult.

The situation for the Israelites was miserable. But, it was about to get even worse. Pharaoh feared their numbers so much that he ordered all male children born to Israelite women to be killed:

Pharaoh then commanded all his people, "Throw into the Nile every boy that is born, but you may let all the girls live." (Exodus 1:22)

An entire generation of male Israelites would be killed. This would ensure there would be fewer Israelites in the future because there would be fewer men for the Israelite women to marry and therefore fewer children. By the end of the first chapter of the book of Exodus, things did not look good for God's Chosen People.

1. What do we learn about the descendants of Jacob at the beginning of the book of Exodus?

   God's people have multiplied greatly.

2. How many people entered Egypt? How many people left Egypt at the Exodus?

   70-75 entered   2m people +

3. What does the Bible tell us about the new pharaoh's relationship with "Joseph" and his descendants? What does this likely mean?

   "Knew nothing of Joseph" It means that the new Pharot chose not to uphold any agreements that were made by old Pharot

4. Why did the new Pharaoh fear the Israelites?

   He thought they might grow so numerous that they would be able to over know his rule

5. What did the pharaoh force the Israelites to do? How were they treated?

   He forced them into "cruel slavery"

6. The Israelites continued to grow in number. What drastic action did the pharaoh take to reduce their numbers?

   He ordered all male children born to Israelite women to be killed.

Reflection Questions

1. Describe a time when you felt mistreated by others. What did it feel like to be mistreated? What did you do? While your experience was probably very different from the experience of the Israelites, how do you think they felt when they were mistreated by the Egyptians?

I felt like I might not be her friend anymore. It was very different from Isereatles because she was not hurting me physicaly. They felt bad for what they have done.

2. There was a law in Old Testament times that slaves could be freed if someone paid for their freedom. The slaves were said to be ransomed or redeemed. Because Jesus ransomed us from slavery to sin by His death, we call Him our redeemer. Describe a time you volunteered to do something difficult or unpleasant for someone else. Why did you do it? How did you feel doing so? How do you think the other person felt?

In gym I partnered up with someone I did not like. I felt good dang it an the other person felt happy too, I did it because if I was in that position I would want someone to be my partner.

Peter Claver

Directions: Read the following excerpt from a letter written by St. Peter Claver, then answer the questions in complete sentences.

We laid aside our cloaks, therefore, and brought from a warehouse whatever was handy to build a platform. In that way we covered a space to which we at last transferred the sick, by forcing a passage through bands of slaves. Then we divided the sick into two groups: one group my companion approached with an interpreter, while I addressed the other group. There were two blacks, nearer death than life, already cold, whose pulse could scarcely be detected. With the help of a tile we pulled some live coals together and placed them in the middle near the dying men. Into this fire we tossed aromatics. Then, using our own cloaks, for they had nothing of the sort and to ask the owners for others would have been a waste of words, we provided for them a smoke treatment, by which they seemed to recover their warmth, and the breath of life. The joy in their eyes as they looked at us was something to see. This was how we spoke to them, not with words but with our hands and our actions. And in fact, convinced as they were that they had been brought here to be eaten, any other language would have proved utterly useless. Then we sat, or rather knelt, beside them and bathed their faces and bodies with wine. We made every effort to encourage them with friendly gestures and displayed in their presence the emotions which somehow naturally tend to hearten the sick.

–ST. PETER CLAVER

1. St. Peter Claver understood that service such as distributing medicine, food, or brandy to his black brothers and sisters was a very effective way to communicate the Word of God, much more than verbal preaching. Identify the sentence from above that Peter Claver often said that shows he lived in this way.

With the help of tile we pulled some live coals together and placed them in the middle near the dying men.

2. The Church celebrates feast days of saints throughout the year. This is one way the Church on earth (known as the Church Militant) shows she is united with all the holy men and women in Heaven (the Church Triumphant). St. Peter Claver's feast day is September 9. What are some special things you could do on this day (or any other day) to practice the Corporal and Spiritual Works of Mercy the way St. Peter Claver did?

Donate food to the hunger. or
I could donate some of the
cloths that I do not
wear.

3. Practicing acts of kindness while expecting nothing in return is life-giving. Think about the last time you went out of your way to be kind to someone. How did it make you feel? List ten acts of kindness you can do at home, at school, and in your community.

I recently donated a lot of
food, I felt blessed and sad at
same time.
1. donating 2. thankyou note, 3. hold door
4. find new friend 5. help mom 6. help dad
7. feed my dogs 8. clean the house
9. make dinner 10. call family

The Life of Moses

Directions: Read the listed Scripture passages from the book of Exodus about Moses' life. Next, write the chapter and verse on the line beside the correct event. Finally, number the events in the correct chronological order.

Scripture Verses from the Book of Exodus

Exodus 2:5-10   Exodus 2:1-4   Exodus 2:11-15   Exodus 7:1-6

Exodus 14:21-31   Exodus 5:1-2   Exodus 3:1-6

Order of Events	Events in the life of Moses
	1. The parting of the red sea; Exodus _____: _____
	2. The burning bush; Exodus _____: _____
	3. Found by Pharaoh's daughter; Exodus _____: _____
	4. Brought the ten plagues down on Egypt; Exodus _____: _____
	5. Put into a basket on the Nile River; Exodus _____: _____
	6. Asked Pharaoh to let the Israelites go; Exodus _____: _____
	7. Killed an Egyptian and fled; Exodus _____: _____

The Ten Plagues

Directions: After reading each passage, fill in the chart. The first one has been done for you. Once you have completed the chart, list three reasons the plagues are extraordinary, or brought on by God.

Exodus 7:19

The LORD then spoke to Moses: "Speak to Aaron: Take your staff and stretch out your hand over the waters of Egypt – its streams, its canals, its ponds, and all its supplies of water – that they may become blood. There will be blood throughout the land of Egypt, even in the wooden pails and stone jars."

Exodus 8:2

So Aaron stretched out his hand over the waters of Egypt, and the frogs came up and covered the land of Egypt.

Exodus 8:12-13

Thereupon the LORD spoke to Moses: "Speak to Aaron: Stretch out your staff and strike the dust of the earth, and it will turn into gnats throughout the land of Egypt. They did so. Aaron stretched out his hand with his staff and struck the dust of the earth, and gnats came upon human being and beast alike. All the dust of the earth turned into gnats throughout the land of Egypt."

Exodus 8:16-17

For if you do not let my people go, I will send swarms of flies upon you and your servants and your people and your houses. The houses of the Egyptians and the very ground on which they stand will be filled with swarms of flies. But on that day I will make an exception of the land of Goshen, where my people are, and no swarms of flies will be there, so that you may know that I the LORD am in the midst of the land.

Exodus 9:1-4

Then the LORD said to Moses: "Go to Pharaoh and tell him: Thus says the LORD, the God of the Hebrews: Let my people go to serve me. For if you refuse to let them go and persist in holding them, the hand of the LORD will strike your livestock in the field – your horses, donkeys, camels, herds and flocks – with a very severe pestilence. But the LORD will distinguish between the livestock of Israel and that of Egypt, so that nothing belonging to the Israelites will die."

Exodus 9:8-9

So the LORD said to Moses and Aaron: "Each of you take handfuls of soot from a kiln, and in the presence of Pharaoh let Moses scatter it toward the sky. It will turn into fine dust over the whole land of Egypt and cause festering boils on human being and beast alike throughout the land of Egypt."

Exodus 9:18

At this time tomorrow, therefore, I am going to rain down such fierce hail as there has never been in Egypt from the day it was founded up to the present.

Exodus 10:4-5

For if you refuse to let my people go, tomorrow I will bring locusts into your territory. They will cover the surface of the earth, so that the earth itself will not be visible. They will eat up the remnant you saved undamaged from the hail, as well as all the trees that are growing in your fields.

Exodus 10:21-23

Then the LORD said to Moses: "Stretch out your hand toward the sky, that over the land of Egypt there may be such darkness that one can feel it." So Moses stretched out his hand toward the sky, and there was dense darkness throughout the land of Egypt for three days. People could not see one another, nor could they get up from where they were, for three days. But all the Israelites had light where they lived.

Exodus 11:4-5

Moses then said, "Thus says the LORD: 'About midnight I will go forth through Egypt. Every firstborn in the land of Egypt will die, from the firstborn of Pharaoh who sits on his throne to the firstborn of the slave-girl who is at the handmill, as well as all the firstborn of the animals.'"

	Verse	Describe the plague	Who was affected? (Egyptians, Israelites, or both?)
1	Exodus 7:19	The water of the Nile River turned to blood.	Both
2	Exodus 8:2		
3	Exodus 8:12-13		
4	Exodus 8:16-17		

	Verse	Describe the plague	Who was affected? (Egyptians, Israelites, or both?)
5	Exodus 9:1-4		
6	Exodus 9:8-9		
7	Exodus 9:18		
8	Exodus 10:4-5		
9	Exodus 10:21-23		
10	Exodus 11:4-5		

In your opinion, what are three reasons the plagues are extraordinary events? Use the information you gathered in the chart to help you form your answer.

1. _____

2. _____

3. _____

Moses' Signs

Directions: Read the following passages from Exodus 4 to identify the three signs God gave Moses. Describe each sign in a complete sentence.

Exodus 4

"But," objected Moses, "suppose they do not believe me or listen to me? For they may say, 'The LORD did not appear to you.'" The LORD said to him: "What is in your hand?" "A staff," he answered. God said: "Throw it on the ground." So he threw it on the ground and it became a snake, and Moses backed away from it. Then the LORD said to Moses: "Now stretch out your hand and take hold of its tail." So he stretched out his hand and took hold of it, and it became a staff in his hand. That is so they will believe that the LORD, the God of their ancestors, the God of Abraham, the God of Isaac, and the God of Jacob, did appear to you. Again the LORD said to him: "Put your hand into the fold of your garment." So he put his hand into the fold of his garment, and when he drew it out, there was his hand covered with scales, like snowflakes. Then God said: "Put your hand back into the fold of your garment." So he put his hand back into the fold of his garment, and when he drew it out, there it was again like his own flesh. "If they do not believe you or pay attention to the message of the first sign, they should believe the message of the second sign. And if they do not believe even these two signs and do not listen to you, take some water from the Nile and pour it on the dry land. The water you take from the Nile will become blood on the dry land."

1. Sign in Exodus 4:2-5: _____

2. Sign in Exodus 4:6-8: _____

3. Sign in Exodus 4:9: _____

The serpent is a model of Satan. By turning the rod into a serpent big enough to frighten Moses and then having him pick it up by the tail (something no snake handler in his right mind would do, since it left the head free to come around and bite him), God was demonstrating his power over Satan, something only He has.

Throughout the Bible, leprosy is seen as a consequence for sin. The first miracle Matthew records in his Gospel is Jesus' healing a man of leprosy. Curing leprosy was symbolic of forgiving sins, something only God can do.

Blood is the symbol of life, something only God can give.

The signs God gave to Moses symbolize something only God has, something only He can do, and something only He can give. To the ancient person, these three things would have clearly identified God as the power behind Moses.

Now complete each of the following sentences:

4. Only God has power over _____

5. Only God can forgive _____

6. Only God can give _____

Moses Smashing the Tablets of the Law
BY REMBRANDT (C. 1659)

Gemäldegalerie, Berlin.

Moses' Birth Story

Directions: Read the story of the birth of Moses from Exodus 1:15-2:10, then answer the questions that following complete sentences.

Pharaoh then commanded all his people, "Throw into the Nile every boy that is born, but you may let all the girls live." Now a man of the house of Levi married a Levite woman, and the woman conceived and bore a son. Seeing what a fine child he was, she hid him for three months. But when she could no longer hide him, she took a papyrus basket, daubed it with bitumen and pitch, and putting the child in it, placed it among the reeds on the bank of the Nile. His sister stationed herself at a distance to find out what would happen to him. Then Pharaoh's daughter came down to bathe at the Nile, while her attendants walked along the bank of the Nile. Noticing the basket among the reeds, she sent her handmaid to fetch it. On opening it, she looked, and there was a baby boy crying! She was moved with pity for him and said, "It is one of the Hebrews' children." Then his sister asked Pharaoh's daughter, "Shall I go and summon a Hebrew woman to nurse the child for you?" Pharaoh's daughter answered her, "Go." So the young woman went and called the child's own mother. Pharaoh's daughter said to her, "Take this child and nurse him for me, and I will pay your wages." So the woman took the child and nursed him. When the child grew, she brought him to Pharaoh's daughter, and he became her son. She named him Moses; for she said, "I drew him out of the water."

1.   What did Pharaoh command his people to do to the Israelites?

    _____

2.   What did Moses' mother do after she could no longer hide him?

    _____

3.   Who watched the basket to see what would happen to Moses? _____

4.   Who found the basket? _____

5.   Who was brought to nurse the child? _____

6.   What happened when Moses grew? _____

7.   The name Moses means "to draw out." Why was he named Moses?

    _____

    _____

8. Who ordered the newborn baby boys to be killed? _____

9. Why did he give this order?

    _____

    _____

10. How did Moses survive?

    _____

    _____

Jesus' Escape to Egypt

Directions: Read the story of the birth of Moses and then answer the focus questions in complete sentences. Wait for more instructions to complete the Venn diagram.

Matthew 2:13-23

When they had departed, behold, the angel of the Lord appeared to Joseph in a dream and said, "Rise, take the child and his mother, flee to Egypt, and stay there until I tell you. Herod is going to search for the child to destroy him." Joseph rose and took the child and his mother by night and departed for Egypt. He stayed there until the death of Herod, that what the Lord had said through the prophet might be fulfilled, "Out of Egypt I called my son." When Herod realized that he had been deceived by the magi, he became furious. He ordered the massacre of all the boys in Bethlehem and its vicinity two years old and under, in accordance with the time he had ascertained from the magi. Then was fulfilled what had been said through Jeremiah the prophet: "A voice was heard in Ramah, sobbing and loud lamentation; Rachel weeping for her children, and she would not be consoled, since they were no more." When Herod had died, behold, the angel of the Lord appeared in a dream to Joseph in Egypt and said, "Rise, take the child and his mother and go to the land of Israel, for those who sought the child's life are dead." He rose, took the child and his mother, and went to the land of Israel. But when he heard that Archelaus was ruling over Judea in place of his father Herod, he was afraid to go back there. And because he had been warned in a dream, he departed for the region of Galilee. He went and dwelt in a town called Nazareth, so that what had been spoken through the prophets might be fulfilled, "He shall be called a Nazorean."

1. Who appeared to Joseph in a dream? What message did this person give to him?

    _____

    _____

2. How long did Joseph and his family stay in Egypt? _____

3. What prophecy was fulfilled by Joseph taking his family to Egypt?

    _____

    _____

4. What did Herod do when he discovered that the Magi had deceived him (by not returning to him and telling him where the infant Jesus was so that he could kill Him)?

_____

_____

_____

5. After Herod had died, what message was given to Joseph in a dream?

_____

_____

6. Where did Joseph take his family? _____

7. What prophecy was fulfilled by this?

_____

_____

8. Who ordered the newborn baby boys to be killed? _____

9. Why did he give this order?

_____

_____

10. How did Jesus survive?

_____

_____

Venn Diagram

Directions: Complete the diagram below by noting the unique characteristics of Moses' birth story and Jesus' escape to Egypt in the circles as well as the similarities between the two stories.

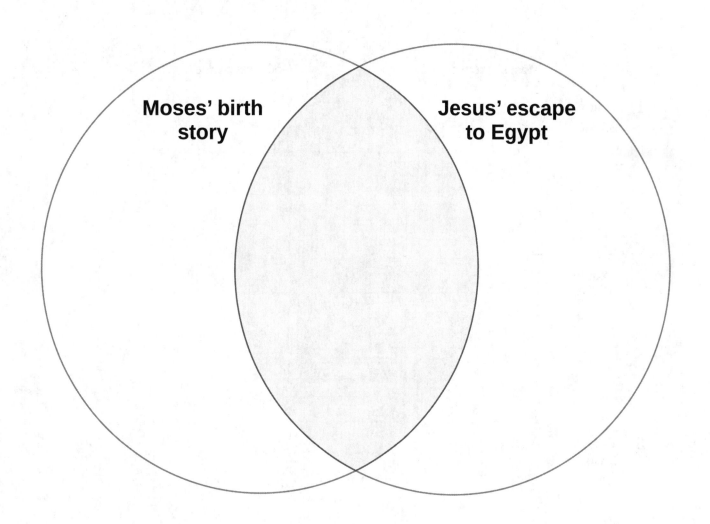

God's Call to Moses Graphic Organizer

Directions: The story of Moses gives us the opportunity to think about how God calls each of us in our own lives. God chose Moses to lead the people of Israel out of slavery in Egypt. Moses was a sinner (a murderer!) and was at first unwilling to accept his call. God, however, always answered Moses' excuses.

Read the verses given below and complete the chart. List all of the ways Moses tries to convince God that he would not be able to free Israel, and then, for each excuse, list God's response. Finally, answer the reflection questions.

		Moses' excuse	God's response
1	Exodus 3:11-12		
2	Exodus 3:13-15		
3	Exodus 4:1-9		

		Moses' excuse	God's response
4	Exodus 4:10-12		
5	Exodus 4:13-17		

Reflection Questions

1. Why do you think Moses at first did not want to accept God's call?

   _____

   _____

   _____

2. What do God's responses to Moses' excuses tell us about God's call to each of us?

   _____

   _____

   _____

God's Name

Directions: Read about God's revelation of His name to Moses in the burning bush, then complete the graphic organizer.

When God spoke to Moses from the burning bush, the human race's relationship with God changed forever. Before God spoke to Moses in the burning bush, the human race did not know God's name. Human beings, like Abraham and his descendants, knew there was a God, but He was not yet a personal God. He was not yet knowable. But everything changed when God spoke to Moses in the burning bush. God revealed His name to Moses – "I am who I am" (Exodus 3:14) or "Yahweh" in Hebrew. "I am" means "I exist." God's name reveals His existence and His constant presence to His people. He was in the beginning, is with them now in their suffering, and will be when all is finished.

In the ancient world, names represented a person's essence, his or her identity deep inside. In fact, to have a name means that you are not *something*, but *someone*. You are not an object, but a person, not anonymous, but knowable. Then, to tell someone else your name is to invite that person to know you.

Imagine that you were standing in a crowd of people and you did not know anyone's name. They would all be unknown to you and anonymous. Then imagine that you needed to get the attention of one of those people in the crowd. How would you do it? How could you call the person without knowing his name? Now, imagine that the person you're trying to reach comes to you and introduces himself to you. Imagine that he gives you his name. Now

you know something about that person. He is no longer an unknown person in a crowd of unknowns. And now that you know his name, you can call upon him. He has become accessible to you.

There is power in knowing someone's name. This is true of God as well. The *Catechism of the Catholic Church* nos. 203 and 204 describe this reality well:

> God revealed himself to his people Israel by making his name known to them. A name expresses a person's essence and identity and the meaning of this person's life. God has a name; he is not an anonymous force. To disclose one's name is to make oneself known to others; in a way it is to hand oneself over by becoming accessible, capable of being known more intimately and addressed personally.

> God revealed himself progressively and under different names to his people, but the revelation that proved to be the fundamental one for both the Old and the New Covenants was the revelation of the divine name to Moses in the theophany of the burning bush, on the threshold of the Exodus and of the covenant on Sinai.

When God revealed His name to Moses (and then to Pharaoh and all of the Israelites), He went from being an unknown, anonymous force to being known and able to be called upon. He became someone, not something.

He is not an anonymous force. By revealing His name, God invited us to know Him personally and intimately. This moment is called a theophany – a profound manifestation of God. Salvation History is marked with theophanies, but none, perhaps, were as meaningful and important as God's revelation to Moses. Everything changed for man's relationship with God after the burning bush. Nothing would ever be the same again.

	The meaning of a name	God's name
1	What does a person's name express?	What does God's name, "I AM," mean?
2	What does it mean to have a name?	What does the fact that God has a name reveal about Him?
3	What is the meaning of telling someone your name?	How did God reveal Himself to His people Israel? What did this revelation mean for man's relationship with God?

The Sacrificial Lamb

BY JOSEFA DE AYALA

Walters Art Museum, Baltimore, Maryland.

The Passover

Directions: Read the story of the Passover from Exodus 12:1-14, then answer the questions.

The LORD said to Moses and Aaron in the land of Egypt:" This month will stand at the head of your calendar; you will reckon it the first month of the year. Tell the whole community of Israel: On the tenth of this month every family must procure for itself a lamb, one apiece for each household. If a household is too small for a lamb, it along with its nearest neighbor will procure one, and apportion the lamb's cost in proportion to the number of persons, according to what each household consumes. Your lamb must be a year-old male and without blemish. You may take it from either the sheep or the goats. You will keep it until the fourteenth day of this month, and then, with the whole community of Israel assembled, it will be slaughtered during the evening twilight. They will take some of its blood and apply it to the two doorposts and the lintel of the houses in which they eat it. They will consume its meat that same night, eating it roasted with unleavened bread and bitter herbs. Do not eat any of it raw or even boiled in water, but roasted, with its head and shanks and inner organs. You must not keep any of it beyond the morning; whatever is left over in the morning must be burned up. This is how you are to eat it: with your loins girt, sandals on your feet and your staff in hand, you will eat it in a hurry. It is the LORD's Passover. For on this same night I will go through Egypt, striking down every firstborn in the land, human being and beast alike, and executing judgment on all the gods of Egypt—I, the LORD! But for you the blood will mark the houses where you are. Seeing the blood, I will pass over you; thereby, when I strike the land of Egypt, no destructive blow will come upon you. This day will be a day of remembrance for you, which your future generations will celebrate with pilgrimage to the LORD; you will celebrate it as a statute forever."

1. Who were the two leaders of the Israelites? _Moses, Aaron_

2. In what land were the Israelites enslaved? _Egypt_

3. What type of animal was to be sacrificed? _lamb_

4. What was the age and sex of the animal to be sacrificed? _a year old, without blemish_

5. On what day was the animal to be killed? _14 day of this month_

6. What were the Israelites to do with the animal's blood? _Apply it to the two door post and the lintel of the houses wich will eat it._

7. How were the Israelites to cook the animal? _Roasting it with unleaved butter and bitter harbs_

8. What were the Israelites to do with the meat of the animal?

with your loins girt, sandals on, staff in hand, in a hurry.

9. What type of bread were the Israelites to eat? unleavened bred

10. What type of herbs were the Israelites to eat? bitter herbs

11. What was the meal was called? Lord's passover

12. Whom would the Lord strike down? First born in Egypt +

13. What was the sign to be placed on the Israelite houses? Why?

The lord would not strike them down.

14. What type of day was this day always to be? Memorial Feast

15. Why do you think "Passover" is a good name for this event?

Because God will pass over the hoses with blood

Old Testament Sacrifices

Directions: Read the following Scripture passages about sacrifice in the Old Testament. Then, on the lines provided, describe the sacrifice that occurred and why you think each sacrifice was made.

1. Genesis 4:3-5

In the course of time Cain brought an offering to the LORD from the fruit of the ground, while Abel, for his part, brought the fatty portion of the firstlings of his flock. The LORD looked with favor on Abel and his offering, but on Cain and his offering he did not look with favor.

Cain, just brought fruit from the ground. Abel, searched for a good sheep to give to the lord. Abel took more time and thought into it.

2. Genesis 8:20

Then Noah built an altar to the LORD, and choosing from every clean animal and every clean bird, he offered burnt offerings on the altar.

Noah not only built the altar, he also made sure the burnt offerings were all from clean animals.

3. Genesis 22:1-2, 9-13

Sometime afterward, God put Abraham to the test and said to him: "Abraham!" "Here I am!" he replied. Then God said: "Take your son Isaac, your only one, whom you love, and go to the land of Moriah. There offer him up as a burnt offering on one of the heights that I will point out to you." ...When they came to the place of which God had told him, Abraham built an altar there and arranged the wood on it. Next he bound his son Isaac, and put him on top of the wood on the altar. Then Abraham reached out and took the knife to slaughter his son. But the angel of the LORD called to him from heaven, "Abraham, Abraham!" "Here I am," he answered. "Do not lay your hand on the boy," said the angel. "Do not do the least thing to him. For now I know that you fear God, since you did not withhold from me your son, your only one."

Abraham looked up and saw a single ram caught by its horns in the thicket. So Abraham went and took the ram and offered it up as a burnt offering in place of his son.

Abraham sacrifised his son to be a burnt offering. He did not want to. Because of this kindness that Abraham was showing God did not kill his son.

4. Exodus 12:3, 6-7

Tell the whole community of Israel: On the tenth of this month every family must procure for itself a lamb, one apiece for each household. ...You will keep it until the fourteenth day of this month, and then, with the whole community of Israel assembled, it will be slaughtered during the evening twilight. They will take some of its blood and apply it to the two doorposts and the lintel of the houses in which they eat it.

The sacrifice that occured was that they had to put their food on their door step so that your house will not be slaughtered.

Reasons to Sacrifice

Directions: Read about the reasons people offered sacrifice, then answer the questions.

People from many ancient cultures frequently offered animal sacrifices to God. An animal sacrifice involved killing the sacrificial animal and offering its life to God. This sometimes involved cooking and eating part of the animal. Other times it involved burning the remains of the animal as a burnt offering. As the fire consumed the animal, the smoke would rise to the heavens, where God would receive the sacrifice.

All sorts of animals would be sacrificed, from large animals, such as bulls and cows, to small animals, such as birds. One of the most common sacrificial animals was the lamb. Lambs provided many things that ancient people needed: wool, meat, and later, milk. Lambs also willingly follow and are obedient to their shepherd. Therefore, lambs came to symbolize obedience and innocence to ancient people and were a true sacrifice.

There are four main reasons for offering animal sacrifice:

1. To praise God joyfully for His glory and rule over creation: the sacrifice was an act of giving back to God what was His.

2. To give thanks to God: people understood that God gave them all that they had. Therefore, in thanksgiving, they could give to God only what they had already been given.

3. To honor a new beginning by swearing an oath: although maybe strange by today's standards, the sacrificed animal sealed the oath in blood. In other words, the persons entering the new relationship agreed that their blood would be spilled if they failed their part of the bargain.

4. To express sorrow for sins: this was the most common form of sacrifice. The consequence for sin is death, but it is a price too high for anyone to pay. Therefore, the sacrifice of an animal was made to pay a small piece of the price that could never be fully paid.

The practice of sacrifice was a tradition that people participated in to symbolize important moments in their lives and to bring about God's blessing. Offering sacrifice was not a small matter and was not done thoughtlessly. The sacrifice of the animal carried a lot of meaning and importance.

God did not require animal sacrifice, however. He allowed human beings to make animal sacrifices as a step in the right direction. Instead of sacrifice, God desired that we love and obey Him. Love and obedience, of course, require a different kind of sacrifice. In order to love someone and be obedient to that person, we have to sacrifice our will and desires and place the other person before ourselves. True love, of God and neighbor, requires sacrificing ourselves.

Even though God did not require animal sacrifice, the matter of the penalty for sin remained. How could a price we could not afford be paid? Imagine that you owed a debt of 100 billion dollars to someone. How could you possibly afford that? For most of us, even if we worked every moment of our entire lives, we'd never be able to pay that back. Now, imagine that someone came to you and offered to pay your debt for you, and give you 100 billion dollars on top of it. To pay the price for our sin, God sent His only Son into the world to die for us. On the third day, He rose from the dead and defeated death and sin forever. He came not to condemn us for our sins, but to give us life so that we can live more abundantly. Christ's sacrifice on the Cross was the final sacrifice, made once and for all, and fully paid the debt for sin, and then some. No animal sacrifice would be needed ever again.

Even though we do not offer animal sacrifices anymore, our human experiences are similar to those of our ancient ancestors. And we continue to use symbols and traditions to mark the important moments of our lives.

1. What was involved in offering an animal as a sacrifice?

   Killing it and offering it's life to God.

2. Why was the lamb a common sacrificial animal?

   They provided: wool, meat, and later, milk

3. Why would ancient people offer sacrifice to praise God joyfully?

   It was an act of giving back what was His.

4. Why would ancient people offer sacrifice to thank God?

   They understood that God gave them all that they have.

5. Why would ancient people offer sacrifice to mark new beginnings and swear oaths?

   When people were in a new relationship they agreed that their blood would be spilled if they failed there part

6. Why would ancient people offer sacrifice in sorrow for sin?

   The consequence of sin+death, but it is a price too high for anyone to pay.

7. How did God pay the debt for our sin?

   God's desire was that we love and obey him, Christ comes

Reflection Question

If our experiences are similar to those of our ancient ancestors, what are some ways today that we use symbols and traditions to mark the important moments of our lives?

Today we mark the important moments by the following. We joural, and talk to people about it.

The New Passover

Part 1

Directions: Read Luke 22:14-20, then answer the focus questions.

When the hour came, He took his place at table with the Apostles. He said to them, "I have eagerly desired to eat this Passover with you before I suffer, for, I tell you, I shall not eat it [again] until there is fulfillment in the kingdom of God." Then He took a cup, gave thanks, and said, "Take this and share it among yourselves; for I tell you [that] from this time on I shall not drink of the fruit of the vine until the kingdom of God comes." Then He took the bread, said the blessing, broke it, and gave it to them, saying, "This is my body, which will be given for you; do this in memory of me." And likewise the cup after they had eaten, saying, "This cup is the new covenant in my blood, which will be shed for you."

1. What is this Scripture passage the story of?

    _____

2. What special meal were Jesus and His Apostles celebrating? How do you know?

    _____

    _____

3. When does Jesus say He will drink of the fruit of the vine again?

    _____

4. What does Jesus say to His Apostles when He breaks the bread and gives it to His Apostles?

    _____

5. What does Jesus say to His Apostles when He gives them the cup of wine after they have eaten?

    _____

6. Notice that while there is bread and wine, there is no lamb mentioned at this Passover meal. Why do you think that is?

    _____

7. Just as in the original Passover, Jesus asked His Apostles to remember this event, to "do this in memory" of Him. How are the Last Supper and Jesus' sacrifice made present to us today?

_____

_____

8. What similarities do you see between this account of the Last Supper and the Passover that we studied in the last lesson?

_____

_____

Part 2

Directions: After watching the Sophia Sketchpad video on the Eucharist, answer the following focus questions.

1. What did Jesus claim in John 6?

_____

2. How did the crowd respond to Jesus' claims?

_____

_____

3. What did Jesus do in response to the crowd?

_____

_____

4. What did Jesus claim about eating the flesh of the Son of Man and drinking His blood?

_____

_____

5. Ultimately, what did many of the people in the crowd do?

_____

_____

6. When was the very first Mass celebrated? By whom?

_____

7. What did Jesus make the Apostles at the Last Supper?

_____

8. Was Jesus being literal when offered His Body and Blood to eat and drink?

_____

9. Why do you think it is hard for some people to believe the bread and wine at Mass become the Body and Blood of Jesus?

_____

_____

10. What do we have to do sometimes with things that are hard to believe?

_____

_____

Moses Parts the Red Sea

Directions: Read Exodus 14 about how Moses parted the Red Sea and the Israelites escaped slavery in Egypt, then answer the questions that follow for each section.

Read Exodus 14:1-9, then answer:

1. What did God tell Moses to have the Israelites do by the sea?

    _____

    _____

2. What change of heart did Pharaoh and the Egyptians have? What did Pharaoh then do? What did he take with him? What did Pharaoh do?

    _____

    _____

    _____

Read Exodus 14:10-22, then answer:

3. How did the Israelites feel when they realized Pharaoh had caught up to them? What did the Israelites then do?

    _____

    _____

    _____

4. Whom did the Israelites blame for their dire situation? _____

5. What did Moses say in response to the Israelites' accusations?

    _____

    _____

6. What did God instruct Moses to do?

_____

_____

_____

_____

7. What moved behind the Israelites? What did it look like in the day? What did it look like in the night?

_____

_____

_____

8. As the Israelites passed through the sea on dry land, what appeared to their right and their left?

_____

Read Exodus 14:23-31, then answer:

9. What happened when Pharaoh's chariots followed the Israelites into the parted waters of the sea?

_____

10. What did God tell Moses to do? What happened to Pharaoh's armies when Moses did as the Lord instructed?

_____

_____

_____

11. How did the Israelites respond to all that they had just witnessed the Lord do?

_____

_____

_____

Reflection Question

Think about how the Israelites reacted to all that they had witnessed as they fled Egypt and crossed the Red Sea (as well as all that they had witnessed before their flight from Egypt). How are we sometimes like the Israelites? Is our response to God in our lives more or less like the Israelites' response to God? Why do you think so?

_____

_____

_____

_____

_____

_____

_____

_____

_____

_____

_____

The Ten Commandments

Harper Leutsky

Directions: Look up and write, in the first column, each of the Ten Commandments from Exodus 20. Then discuss each Commandment with your partner or group and, in the second column, write what each Commandment teaches us about how to love God or our neighbor. Finally, in the third column, make a list of ways the modern world poses challenges to living each of the Commandments.

Commandments	What does this Commandment teach us about how to love God or our neighbor?	What challenges to living this Commandment are posed by the world today?
1. Exodus 20:2-3 You shall have no other gods before me	Shows us how to love god by making him a priority.	If the people you know worship other Gods you might want to too.
2. Exodus 20:7 You shall not take the name of the Lord god in vain	Shows us how to love God by saying his name respectfully.	If you get mad maybe you might want to say
3. Exodus 20:8 Remember the Sabbath day	Shows how to love God and make him happy	If you have plans you may be tempted
4. Exodus 20:12 Honor your father and your mother	Shows that God wants you to love your Neighbor	If you get mad at them

Commandments	What does this Commandment teach us about how to love God or our neighbor?	What challenges to living this Commandment are posed by the world today?
5. Exodus 20:13 You shall not kill	A little bit of both Is Neighbor Is respectfulness	Here and mask y... p... were a mess
6. Exodus 20:14 You shall not commit adultery	Neighbors because the commandment is based off of people	Cut over all your norms
7. Exodus 20:15 You shall not steal	Neighbors becaus you can not steal from God	If you want something bad, but you do not have the money
8. Exodus 20:16 You shall not bear false witness against your neighbor	Neighbor? God because they both conected to	You do not want to get in trouble
9. Exodus 20:17a You shall not covet your neighbors wife	Neighbors because God does not have a living wife	If good not want them together
10. Exodus 20:17b you shall not covet your neighbors wife and goods	Neighbors because God goods are also yours	You are jealous

jealousy

Why the Beatitudes Still Matter

Directions: Give five reasons why the Beatitudes, spoken by Christ over 2,000 years ago, still matter today. Review the Ten Commandments and the Beatitudes and what they teach us about love, goodness, sin, temptation, and happiness.

1. _____

_____

2. _____

_____

3. _____

_____

4. _____

_____

5. _____

_____

UNIT 6

The Royal Kingdom, Exile, and the Prophets

In this unit, you will learn about...

> Joshua leading the Israelites into the Promised Land and fulfilling the covenant.

> The judges and Samuel.

> Saul, the first king of Israel.

> King David and the final covenant of the Old Testament.

> The exile of Israel and the Prophets.

Introduction

After reaching the Promised Land, it took some time for the people of Israel to become the kingdom God promised them. Joshua took over as leader of the Israelites after the death of Moses and led the people into the Land of Canaan, fulfilling what was incomplete in God's covenant with Moses. Over the next period of centuries, God raised up temporary leaders for Israel when they were needed. These men and women were known as judges and won military victories against foreign invaders, settled disputes between tribes, and called the people to right worship and relationship with God.

Eventually the people demanded that Samuel, the last of the judges, give them a king. A man named Saul was chosen to be the first king of Israel, but he proved to be a poor king. He failed to unify the people and selfishly disobeyed God. God withdraw Saul's dynasty and kingship from him and led Samuel to anoint a new king, David, who was "a man after God's own heart." Though David was flawed, he sought to be faithful to God and His commands and keep his people faithful to God. God entered into a new covenant with David, the last covenant of the Old Testament. God promised David that he would be the first in an everlasting line of kings and that David's son would build a dwelling place for God among the people. This promise was ultimately fulfilled by Jesus Christ.

Over the next millennia until the coming of Christ, the people of Israel suffered many ups and downs in their relationship with God. Eventually the kingdom was conquered by foreign powers and the people were exiled from their homeland. Throughout this time God called many men to be His prophets. They called the people back to right worship of God and warned of doom and consequences if they did not change their ways. They delivered a message of hope and told of the coming of the Messiah who would fulfill God's promise of salvation. The prophets prepared the way for the coming of Christ and the salvation from sin He would win by His sacrifice on the Cross.

Are there any questions you still have about the topics you learned last month? What steps can you take to find out the answers?

_____

_____

_____

_____

What questions do you have right now about the topics you will be learning about in this unit?

_____

_____

_____

_____

Unit 6 Vocabulary

Call Narrative: The story or pattern for God's calling of all of the prophets. The pattern follows the story of the calling of Moses, the first prophet. The five parts of the call narrative of a prophet are: the setting is one of mystery and awe, God calls the prophet to action, the prophet feels unworthy and objects, God reassures the prophet, and then God sends the prophet forth and offers a sign.

Characteristics of the Davidic Covenant: There are six important features of God's covenant with David. They are: God will make David the founder of a dynasty, God will make David's descendants kings, God will have a father-son relationship with David's descendants, David's son will build a Temple as a dwelling place for God among His people, God will never withdraw His favor from David or his descendants, and David's kingdom and dynasty will never end. Each of these features of the covenant are fulfilled by Jesus Christ.

Christ: The Greek word for "anointed one." See Messiah.

Davidic Covenant: The covenant God entered into with David.

Ish Elohim: Hebrew for "men of the spirit," or "one called by God to speak for Him." Used to describe the prophets of the Old Testament.

Judge (shofet): A temporary military leader appointed by God to govern the Israelites and return them to right worship. They also won military victories against foreign invaders and settled disputes between tribes.

Messiah: The Hebrew word for "anointed one." All of the kings descended from David were anointed as a sign of their kingship. This made all of the kings in the line of David "messiahs." God promised the Chosen People that He would send the Messiah to free them from sin. Jesus is the Son of David and God's promised Messiah and Savior. (453)

Prophetes: Greek for "one who speaks for another." The word "prophet" comes from this word.

Ro eh: Hebrew for "to see beneath the surface," or "to possess vision." Used to describe the prophets of the Old Testament.

Scepter: A staff or baton held by a king that represents kingly authority.

King David

BY GIOVANNI FRANCESCO BARBIERI (C. 1651)

Musée des Beaux-Arts de Rouen, France.

King David

King David, *by Giovanni Francesco Barbieri (c. 1651)*

Directions: Take some time to quietly view and reflect on the art. Let yourself be inspired in any way that happens naturally. Then think about the questions below, and discuss them with your classmates.

Conversation Questions

1. This is a painting of Kind David from the Old Testament. What in this painting shows that he is a king?

2. Does David look old or young in this painting? What do you think his age tells us about the kind of king David was at the moment depicted in this painting?

3. David is holding a scepter in this painting. A scepter represents the authority of a king. Why do you think the artist chose to depict David holding a scepter?

4. David is wearing a red robe in this painting. Red is the color of blood and represents life. It is also the color of sacrifice. Why do you think the artist chose to depict David wearing a red robe?

5. David is seated upon a throne in this painting. A throne is a symbol of kingship. Why do you think the artist chose to depict David seated upon a throne?

6. David is wearing sandals in this painting. In the ancient world, bare or sandaled feet were a sign of humility. Why do you think the artist chose to depict David wearing sandals?

7. David is wearing a crown in this painting. A crown is a symbol of honor, power. Why do you think the artist chose to depict David wearing a crown?

8. Why do you think Jesus is often depicted in art with many of the same elements that David is depicted with: a crown, a red robe, barefoot or sandaled, and holding a scepter?

Psalm 86

Directions: In the painting, *King David*, by Giovanni Francesco Barbieri, David is holding a tablet with the Latin words "gloriosa dicta sunt de te civitas Dei" from Psalm 86:3. In English, this phrase is translated as "be gracious to me, Lord; to you I call all the day." Read the rest of Psalm 86 in your Bible, and then answer the following reflection questions.

1. Psalm 86 is considered to be a psalm written by David himself. It is a personal prayer of David to God. In part I of the psalm, what does David ask of God? Why does He ask for this?

   _____

   _____

2. What does part II tell us about who David understands God to be?

   _____

   _____

3. What does David ask of God at the beginning of Part III?

   _____

   _____

4. How does David describe God in Part III?

   _____

   _____

5. What does David want from God in Part III?

   _____

   _____

6. After reading Psalm 86 and reflecting on the painting of David, what kind of king do you think David wanted to be?

   _____

   _____

Psalm 86:3

Be gracious to me, Lord; to you I call all the day.

Psalm 29:10

The LORD sits enthroned above the flood!
The LORD reigns as king forever!

Judges 21:24-25

In those days there was no king in Israel; everyone did what was right in their own sight.

1 Timothy 6:15

The blessed and only ruler will make manifest [his appearance] at the proper time, the King of kings and Lord of lords.

1 Samuel 13:14

The Lord has sought out a man after His own heart to appoint as ruler over His people.

Matthew 17:20

If you have faith the size of a mustard seed, you will say to this mountain, 'Move from here to there,' and it will move. Nothing will be impossible for you.

Luke 24:25-27

And he said to them, "Oh, how foolish you are! How slow of heart to believe all that the prophets spoke! Was it not necessary that the Messiah should suffer these things and enter into his glory?" Then beginning with Moses and all the prophets, he interpreted to them what referred to him in all the scriptures.

Exodus 4:11-12

The LORD said to him: Who gives one person speech? Who makes another mute or deaf, seeing or blind? Is it not I, the LORD? Now go, I will assist you in speaking and teach you what you are to say."

The Fall of Jericho

Directions: Read each of the passages, then answer the questions that follow.

Read Joshua 6:1-2, then answer:

1.   Why was the city of Jericho in a state of siege?

   _____

2.   How did Jericho come under the power of the Israelites?

   _____

Read Joshua 6:3-5, then answer:

3.   Summarize in your own words the instructions God gave to Joshua.

   _____

   _____

Read Joshua 6:6-19, then answer:

4.   What did the Israelites do for the next seven days?

   _____

   _____

5.   What warning did Joshua give the Israelites on the seventh day?

   _____

   _____

6.   Recall the use and significance of the number seven in previous stories in Scripture.
     How is the number seven used in the story of the fall of Jericho? Why do you think this is
     important?

   _____

   _____

   _____

Read Joshua 6:20-21, then answer:

7. What did the people do when horns were blown? What happened as a result of this?

    _____

    _____

8. What did the Israelites observe, and how did they do so?

    _____

    _____

Read Joshua 6:22-25, then answer:

9. What did the two men who had spied out the land do? Why did they do so?

    _____

    _____

10. Read the footnote in the New American Bible that corresponds to Joshua 6:25. Who was Rahab, and why is she an important biblical figure?

    _____

    _____

Read Joshua 6:26-27, then answer:

11. What was the curse Joshua placed upon Jericho?

    _____

    _____

12. What was the result of the siege of Jericho for Joshua?

    _____

    _____

The Judges

Directions: Read the story of your assigned judge, following the given Scripture passages below. Then answer the questions below about your assigned judge in the space provided. Lastly, on a separate piece of paper, create a "campaign" poster for your judge (or judges) that creatively presents information about the accomplishments of the judge during his or her time of leadership.

Othniel and Ehud:	Judges 3:7-11 (Othniel) and Judges 3:12-30 (Ehud)
Deborah:	Judges 4:1-24
Gideon:	Judges 6:1-16, 24-35; Judges 7:1-9, 16-22; Judges 8:22-23, 28
Jephthah:	Judges 10:6-10, 15-18; Judges 11:1-11, 20-22; Judges 12:7
Samson:	Judges 13:1-5, 24; Judges 15:9-20; Judges 16:15-31

Who is (are) your assigned judge(s)? _____

1. What were the reasons your assigned judge was called by God to be a judge?

   _____

   _____

2. Who were the oppressors of Israel during the time of your assigned judge? How many years was Israel oppressed before your judge was appointed? How many years of peace came during his or her leadership?

   _____

   _____

3. What did your assigned judge accomplish during his or her time of leadership of Israel?

   _____

   _____

4. What other unique information did you learn about your assigned judge?

   _____

   _____

Saul's Mistakes as King

Directions: Read the accounts from Scripture of Saul's two mistakes that end up costing him his kingship and dynasty, then respond to the questions for each selection.

Saul's First Mistake: 1 Samuel 13:2-14

1. How many people of Israel did Saul choose to be part of his army? _3,000_

2. Which fierce and persistent enemy of Israel did Saul attack? _Philistenes_

3. Why did Saul's army hide or run away?
   They are in trouble because they are out-numbered

4. Why did Saul wait for seven days?
   He waited for Samuel to come

5. What did Saul do (that he was not supposed to do) at the end of seven days?
   He offered a burnt offering without
   ↳ sacrificed   Samuel

6. Which verses indicate that Saul acted to manipulate God into doing what he wanted Him to do? Write the verse numbers of the applicable passage(s).
   Verse 11-12

7. What is the consequence or punishment for Saul's actions?
   His dynasty is over/he will not have a dynasty

Saul's Second Mistake: 1 Samuel 15:2-31

8. What did God command Saul to do when he attacked the Amalekites?
   God said go strike Amalect and destroy what they have and everyone

9. Which verses indicate that Saul did not follow God's orders after attacking and defeating the Amalekites? Write the verse numbers of the applicable passage(s).
   Verse 8-9

10. Why did God "regret" making Saul king?

Because Saul disobeys God's commands

11. Which verses indicate that Saul knowingly lied to Samuel about following God's commands? Write the verse numbers of the applicable passage(s).

Verse 13

12. What did Saul explain he intended to do with the spoils of the battle with the Amalekites?

He explained that he attended to sacrifice them to God! False

13. What does Samuel say is better than sacrifice?

Saul says obey is better than sacrifice!
obedience

14. How does Saul's tearing of Samuel's garment represent Saul's punishment?

It represents Saul's kingship (he has no kingdom!)

Joshua, Judges, Samuel, and Saul Quiz

Directions: Follow the given directions for each section of the quiz.

Multiple Choice

Circle the correct answer to each question.

1. The successor of Moses was:

   a. Samuel

   b. Caleb

   c. Joshua

   d. Saul

2. Samuel was the last of the:

   a. Kings

   b. Prophets

   c. Priests

   d. Judges

3. What did Saul lose for his first offense against God?

   a. His kingdom

   b. His army

   c. His spoils of war

   d. His dynasty

4. What did Saul lose for his second offense against God?

   a. His life

   b. His kingship

   c. His army

   d. His dynasty

5. What was the root of Saul's big mistakes?

   a. He did not pay attention to the people.

   b. He tried to "buy off" God with sacrifices so that he could do things his own way.

   c. He did not respect other people's feelings and instead selfishly listened only to the advice of Samuel.

   d. He allowed the Philistines to take over part of Canaan.

True or False

Write "True" if the statement is true and "False" if the statement if false.

6. _____ The judges were temporary soldier-prophets.

7. _____ When the people demanded a king, they were ultimately showing their displeasure with Samuel.

8. _____ Saul's main qualification to be king was that he was tall and handsome.

Identification

On the line provided, write the name of the person described in each statement.

9. _____ A blood relative of Jesus who protected Israelite spies from the soldiers of Jericho.

10. _____ Led the Israelites as a judge into his old age. The Israelites begged him for a king.

11. _____ Had superhuman strength because of his long hair. Defeated the Philistines by causing a temple to collapse where their leaders had gathered.

12. _____ Offered sacrifice to God not out of love for Him, but rather because he wanted God to do something for him.

13. _____ The only female judge who led Israel into battle.

14. _____ Destroyed the town altar to the pagan god Baal and gathered an Israelite army that God deemed too large and had to be reduced to 300 by separating out those who drank water from a stream like a dog from those who drank using cupped hands.

15. _____ Circumcised the Israelites for a second time before entering the Promised Land.

David and Goliath Reading Guide

Directions: Read the story of David and Goliath in 1 Samuel 17. For each section of the story, answer the corresponding questions.

Read 1 Samuel 17:38-40, then answer:

1. How did Saul dress David for his battle with Goliath? Why did David end up taking off this battle dress?

_____

_____

2. What weapon did David choose to use to battle Goliath? What did he select from the wadi (a dry riverbed)?

_____

_____

Read 1 Samuel 17:41-44, then answer:

3. Why did Goliath "deride" (ridicule and laugh at) David?

_____

4. With what insult did Goliath taunt David?

_____

Read 1 Samuel 17:45-47, then answer:

5. What was David's response to Goliath's taunts?

_____

6. With what weapons was Goliath armed?

_____

7. What did David proclaim to Goliath would help him "deliver" Goliath "into his hand"?

_____

_____

8. How would the whole land learn that Israel has a God?

_____

_____

_____

Read 1 Samuel 17:48-51, then answer:

9. With what weapon did David defeat Goliath? _____

10. What did David do to Goliath after he defeated him?

_____

_____

Goliath Worksheet

Directions: For each given category, identify an obstacle or "Goliath" that prevents or stands in the way of the success of that topic. Then identify three "stones" or actions you can take to overcome this "Goliath." Try to think practically and consider actions or steps that are within your power to take.

Relationship with God

What is an obstacle or "Goliath" that prevents our relationship with God from becoming the best it can be? What are some "stones" or actions that you can take to overcome this "Goliath"? What do you hope God will do with this "stone" once you "throw" it? How do you hope God will turn your effort into something greater?

Goliath: _____

Stone 1: _____

_____

Stone 2: _____

_____

Stone 3: _____

_____

Friendships

What is an obstacle or "Goliath" that prevents our friendships from becoming the best they can be? What are some "stones" or actions that you can take to overcome this "Goliath"? What do you hope God will do with this "stone" once you "throw" it? How do you hope God will turn your effort into something greater?

Goliath: _____

Stone 1: _____

_____

Stone 2: _____

_____

Stone 3: _____

_____

School Success

What is an obstacle or "Goliath" that you face in your own school success? What are some "stones" or actions that you can take to overcome this "Goliath"? What do you hope God will do with this "stone" once you "throw" it? How do you hope God will turn your effort into something greater?

Goliath: _____

Stone 1: _____

_____

Stone 2: _____

_____

Stone 3: _____

_____

Your School Community

What is an obstacle or "Goliath" that prevents your school community from becoming the best it can be? What are some "stones" or actions that you can take to overcome this "Goliath"? What do you hope God will do with this "stone" once you "throw" it? How do you hope God will turn your effort into something greater?

Goliath: _____

Stone 1: _____

_____

Stone 2: _____

_____

Stone 3: _____

_____

Society

What is an obstacle or "Goliath" that prevents our society/culture from becoming the best it can be? What are some "stones" or actions that you can take to overcome this "Goliath"? What do you hope God will do with this "stone" once you "throw" it? How do you hope God will turn your effort into something greater?

Goliath: _____

Stone 1: _____

_____

Stone 2: _____

_____

Stone 3: _____

_____

The Davidic Covenant

Harper Levitsky

100%

Directions: Read 2 Samuel 7:11-16 about God's covenant with David, then answer the questions below.

1. Write the text that indicates that God will make David the founder of a dynasty.
(Hint: Sometimes the word *house* can refer to one's family or a dynasty of kings.)

   Morever, the Lord declares to you that the Lord will make you a house. Verse 11

2. Write the text that indicates that God will make David's descendants kings.

   Who shall come forth from your body, and I will establish, his kingdom Verse 12

3. Write the text that indicates that David's descendants will have a father-son relationship with God.

   I will be his father and he will be my son Verse 14

4. Write the text that indicates that a descendant of David's will build a Temple, or dwelling place, for God.

   He shall build a house for my name and I will establish a throne forever. Verse 13

5. Write the text that indicates that God will never withdraw His favor from David or his descendants as He did with Saul.

   But I will not take my merictul love from him, as I took it from Saul. Verse 15

6. Write the text that indicates that David's kingdom and dynasty will never end.

   Your house and your kingdom shall be made sure for ever before me. Verse 16

Characteristics of the Davidic Covenant Scripture Hunt

Directions: Look up the Scripture passages listed below. Determine which of the characteristics of the Davidic covenant each passage refers to and mark the letter next to the passage. There are two passages for each feature – one referring to God's covenant with David and one referring to its fulfillment in the New Covenant in Christ.

Characteristics of the Davidic Covenant

A. Kingdom

B. Dynasty

C. Father-son relationship

D. God will not withdraw His favor

E. Temple

F. Everlasting

1. _____Revelations 21:22

2. _____1 Kings 6:13

3. _____Jeremiah 33:17

4. _____2 Samuel 7:19

5. _____Psalm 89:27

6. _____Romans 11:29

7. _____Revelations 5:13

8. _____Isaiah 32:1

9. _____Matthew 3:16-17

10. _____Acts 13:22-23

11. _____Mark 1:14-15

12. _____John 2:19

Davidic Kingdom Flag

Directions: Create a flag that represents the Kingdom of David (the Davidic Kingdom) by choosing one of the characteristics of God's covenant with David and creatively representing it on the flag. Then write a two- or three-sentence explanation of the covenant characteristic represented on your flag.

The clouds and man represent Father-son relationship. Crown represents Kingdom. The infinity sign represents Everlasting.

THE END

Great Deesis with Prophets

16TH CENTURY ICON

Walters Art Museum, Baltimore, Maryland.

The Prophets

Directions: Read the essay, then complete the fill-in-the-blank activity that follows.

The prophets were men and women who were called by God to experience deeply God's saving presence in the historical situation of their times and who were given a mission to make known the message of God's saving power. They were involved in the renewal and reform of the Israelite community. The prophets were God's spokespersons – making known God's message to His people. The word prophet comes from the Greek *prophetes*, meaning "one who speaks for another," and from the Hebrew words *navi*, which means "to call or announce," *ro eh*, which means "to see beneath the surface" or "to possess vision," and *Ish Elohim* which means "men of the Spirit" or "one called by God to speak for Him." Prophets are often associated with what will happen in the future. The biblical prophets, however, spoke not only of what would happen in the future but also of what was happening in the present. The prophets served as the conscience of the People of God and called them back to right worship of God. They kept alive the faith in God and the hope in His promise to send a Savior.

The prophets responded to God's commission and became His spokespersons without worrying about money or personal gain. They were not motivated by success or failure but by fidelity to God and His truth. They suffered both physically and spiritually because of their proclamation of the Word of God. The prophets interacted with kings and directly with the people of Israel. Sometimes, their message was one of doom and condemnation, and other times it was one of hope and peace.

The prophets appeared throughout a long period of time in Israel's history. Moses is considered to be the first and prototype of the prophets. He was the prophet whom all the others aspired to be like. The rest of the prophets appeared from after the time of Moses to the end of the Exile, which spans more than a thousand years. The majority of those we typically think of as "the prophets" of the Old Testament appeared throughout the time of the royal kingdoms of Israel and Judah, and throughout the conquering, deportation, exile, and return of the Hebrew people.

Most of the prophets called by God followed a fivefold pattern, after Moses' own call. First, the prophet was overwhelmed by the mystery and awe of God's presence and power. Second, God took the initiative and called the prophet to action. Third, the prophet felt within himself a deep sense of unworthiness in the presence of God and objected to the call. Fourth, God reassured the prophet and promised that He would be with him. Fifth and finally, God commissioned the prophet and sent him forth, often accompanied by a sign, to speak His Word to the people.

Fill-in-the-Blanks

1. The prophets were men and women who were called by __God__ to experience deeply God's __saving presence__ in the __historical__ situation of their own times.

2. The prophets were given a mission to __make known__ the message of God's __saving power__.

3. The prophets were involved in the __renewal__ and __reform__ of the Israelite community.

4. The prophets were God's __spokepersons__ – making known God's __message__ to His people.

5. The Greek word __prophetis__ means "one who speaks for another."

6. The Hebrew word *navi* means __to call or anounce__, and the Hebrew word *ro eh* means to __see beneath the surface__.

7. The Hebrew word __Ish Elohim__ means "men of the Spirit" or __one called by God to speak for him__.

8. The prophets spoke not only of the future but also of what was happening in __the present__.

9. The prophets served as the __consience__ of the People of God and called the people back to __right worship__ of God.

10. They kept alive the faith in God and the hope in His promise to __send a Savior__.

11. The prophets responded to __God's commision__ and became God's __spokeperson__ without worrying about __money__ or __personal gain__.

12. They were motivated by __fidelity__ to God and His __truth__.

13. They suffered both _____physically_____ and _____spiritually_____ because of their proclamation of ___the word of God___

14. Sometimes, the message of the prophets was one of _____doom_____ and condemnation; at other times it was one of _____hope_____ and peace.

15. _____Moses_____ is considered to be the first and prototype of the prophets.

16. The prophets appeared over a longer period of Israel's history that stretched from after the time of _____Moses_____ to the end of the _____Exile_____, which spans more than _____thousands_____ years.

17. Every prophet followed a fivefold pattern for his _____own call_____.

18. First, the prophet was overwhelmed by the _____mistery_____ and _____awl_____ of God's _____presence_____ and _____power_____.

19. Second, God took the initiative and ___called the prophet to action___

20. Third, the prophet felt a deep sense of ___unworthlessnes___ and objected to the call.

21. Fourth, God _____reassured_____ the prophet and promised ___he would be with him___

22. Fifth and finally, God _____commisioned_____ the prophet and ___sent him fourth___, often accompanied by a _____sign_____, to speak His Word to the people.

The Call Narrative of the Prophets

Directions: Moses was the first of the prophets. The story of his calling to be a prophet is the model for the call of all of the other prophets. Read the following Scripture passages, and for each prophet, match the Scripture passage with the correct part of the call narrative. (*Hint: For Moses, one part of the call narrative applies to multiple passages.*)

Parts of the Call Narrative of a Prophet

A. Setting of mystery and awe.

B. God calls the prophet to action.

C. The prophet feels unworthy and objects.

D. God reassures the prophet.

E. God sends the prophet forth and offers a sign.

Moses

___B___ 1. Exodus 3:9–10

___C___ 2. Exodus 4:1

___C___ 3. Exodus 4:10

___D___ 4. Exodus 3:12

___A___ 5. Exodus 3:1–6

___E___ 6. Exodus 3:11

___B___ 7. Exodus 3:14

___B___ 8. Exodus 4:19–23

___A___ 9. Exodus 4:2–9

___B___ 10. Exodus 4:14–16

Jeremiah

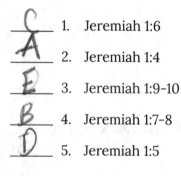

___C___ 1. Jeremiah 1:6

___A___ 2. Jeremiah 1:4

___E___ 3. Jeremiah 1:9–10

___B___ 4. Jeremiah 1:7–8

___D___ 5. Jeremiah 1:5

Jonah

_____ 1. Jonah 3:1–3

_____ 2. Jonah 1:3

_____ 3. Jonah 1:2

_____ 4. Jonah 1:4, 10–12, 15; 2:1–2, 11

_____ 5. Jonah 1:1

Old Testament Prophecy of the Messiah

Directions: Look up each of the given Old Testament prophecies of the coming Messiah and then, in the space provided, describe in your own words what is being prophesied about the Messiah.

Old Testament Prophecy	Description of the Prophecy
1 Deuteronomy 18:15	
2 Isaiah 7:14	
3 Isaiah 35:4–6	
4 Isaiah 53:5–7	
5 Isaiah 60:6	
6 Isaiah 61:1	

Old Testament Prophecy	Description of the Prophecy
7 Daniel 7:13-14	
8 Micah 5:2	
9 Zechariah 9:9	
10 Zechariah 11:12-13	
11 Ezekiel 34:11-16	
12 Malachi 3:1	
13 Jonah 1:17	

UNIT 7

Jesus and the New Testament

In this unit, you will learn about...

> The New Testament's account of God's saving actions.

> Jesus the Messiah.

> How Jesus fulfills the Old Testament roles of priest, prophet, and king.

> The Paschal Mystery – Christ's Passion, Death, and Resurrection which saved us from sin.

> The New Covenant.

Introduction

The moment had come for God to complete all He had done to prepare His people for the coming of Christ. In what we call "the fullness of time," the Word of God became flesh by the power of the Holy Spirit—a baby in the Virgin Mary's womb. As Isaiah had prophesied, the Father gave the world Emmanuel, "God with us." From the very beginning, after the first sin of Adam and Eve, God had promised a savior. Because He loves us so much, He sent His only Son into the world to free us from sin and spiritual death.

Jesus is the promised and awaited Messiah who fulfills the Old Testament roles of priest, prophet, and king. He established God's Kingdom here on earth during His earthly life and founded the Catholic Church as the means of drawing all people to the Kingdom. Jesus' Passion, Death, and Resurrection are the Paschal Mystery, the Passover of the New Covenant. Jesus is the Lamb of God who offered Himself as sacrifice on the Cross and paid the price for our sins that we could not. He freed us from sin and death and invites us to receive the grace of salvation and become sons and daughters of God again.

We participate in Christ's saving sacrifice when we receive the Eucharist at Mass. And we experience the Paschal Mystery in our daily lives. Christ's Resurrection teaches us that our life is not only sin, suffering, and death. There is a new, greater life beyond these. We are called to receive God's mercy and salvation in the New Covenant in Christ. We are called to be His hands and feet throughout the world, to share the Good News of salvation, and make God's mercy and love known to all.

Are there any questions you still have about the topics you learned last month? What steps can you take to find out the answers?

_____

_____

_____

What questions do you have right now about the topics you will be learning about in this unit?

_____

_____

_____

Baptism: The first Sacrament we receive. Baptism makes us members of the Church, forgives our sins, and gives us new life in Christ. It is necessary for salvation. The celebration of Baptism involves being immersed in water or having water poured over one's head in the name of the Holy Trinity.

Corporal Works of Mercy: Jesus taught us that we must love our neighbor by performing Corporal (and Spiritual) Works of Mercy. Corporal means "body." The corporal works of mercy help us meet a person's physical needs. They are: feed the hungry, give drink to the thirsty, clothe the naked, shelter the homeless, visit the sick, ransom the captive, and bury the dead.

Divine Nature: That which makes God who and what He is, God. Jesus possesses both a divine nature and a human nature. He is 100% fully God and 100% fully human.

Forgive: To stop feeling anger toward someone who has harmed you. Forgiveness involves wishing well for your enemy. Jesus taught us to forgive our enemies. Jesus forgives our sins in the Sacrament of Confession.

Gifts of the Holy Spirit: Wisdom, knowledge, understanding, counsel, fortitude, piety, and fear of the Lord. The anointing in the Sacraments of Baptism and Confirmation are a sign of receiving these gifts.

Good Shepherd: A title for Jesus taken from the parable of the lost sheep (Luke 15:1-7). We are like the sheep in the parable. Sin has caused us to go astray and become lost. But Jesus, who is like the shepherd, comes to us sinners. He seeks us out and invites us to receive salvation and be restored to God's family.

Holy Orders: The Sacrament through which the mission entrusted by Christ to His Apostles continues to be carried out in the Church until the end of time. This Sacrament ordains men to the priesthood of the Catholic Church and bestows upon them the power to administer the Sacraments.

Human Nature: That which makes human beings human. Jesus possesses both a divine nature and a human nature. He is 100% fully God and 100% fully human.

***In Persona Christi Capitas*:** In the Person of Christ the Head. When an ordained priest performs his priestly function—for example, when consecrating the Eucharist—he is no longer working as himself, but rather, "in the person of Christ the Head." When we say "the Head," we mean the Head of the Church. It is not the priest who transforms the bread and wine into the Body and Blood of Christ, but rather, Jesus Himself, working in and through the priest.

Incarnation: The Christian belief that the second Person of the Holy Trinity, the Son of God, assumed a human nature and became man in the Person of Jesus Christ.

King: In the Old Testament, kings were to rule justly according to the law of God. They were to lead His people into relationship with God and right worship of Him. Jesus fulfills this role by establishing the Kingdom of God on earth and by teaching the law of God by which all will be judged. Jesus taught us to love God and to love our neighbor, He gave us the Beatitudes to teach us how to be happy or fulfilled in the Kingdom, and He taught us the works of mercy as the way to live out the law of God in His Kingdom.

Melchizedek: A priest and king of Salem whom Abraham meets in the Old Testament. He offers Abraham a sacrificial blessing in the form of a sacred meal of bread and wine. This sacrifice will later become the foundation of the thank offering in the Temple of Solomon and the sacrifice of Christ offered at the Last Supper and which we receive today at every Mass.

Mercy: Compassion, kindness, and forgiveness shown to others. God has infinite mercy for us. Jesus taught us to show mercy to others.

Mysterion: Greek for "mystery." In Greek, the word was interchangeable with *sacramentum*, from which we derive the word "sacrament." Both mean the same thing: a visible sign of God's grace.

Mystery of Faith: The proclamation of the Paschal Mystery in prayer at every Mass.

New Covenant: The new and everlasting covenant won for us by Christ's Paschal Mystery. In this covenant is the fulfillment of centuries of prophecies and all of God's promises for the forgiveness of sins. We are made members of the New Covenant by our Baptism and we renew and participate in the covenant every time we receive the Eucharist. All people are invited to be members of the New Covenant.

Old Covenant: All the ways that God revealed Himself to us in Salvation History in order to prepare us for salvation. The story of the Old Covenant is found in the Old Testament.

Paschal: Of or having to do with the Passover. Christ's Passion, Death, and Resurrection are the Passover of the New Covenant.

Paschal Mystery: Christ's Passion, Death, and Resurrection which saved us from sin and death for new life as sons and daughters of God.

Priest: In the Old Testament, the primary task of a priest was to offer sacrifice to God on behalf of the people for their sins. Jesus fulfills this role by offering Himself as a sacrifice on the Cross for the sins of all.

Prophet: In the Old Testament, the prophets were God's spokespersons who made known God's message to His people. They proclaimed hope and salvation to the people if they would repent and worship God. Jesus fulfills this role not by speaking for God, but because He is God. He did God's will throughout His life and spoke God's truth to the people. He revealed God to the people and taught about God's law and love.

Sacrament: A sign of God's grace that gives the grace that it signifies. Jesus founded seven Sacraments: Baptism, Confirmation, Holy Eucharist, Penance and Reconciliation, Anointing of the Sick, Holy Orders, and Holy Matrimony.

Sermon on the Mount: The central teaching of Christ's public ministry. During this teaching on a wide variety of topics, Jesus delivers the Beatitudes and the Lord's Prayer. He also spends time talking about the teachings of the Old Law (the law of the Old Testament, or the Law of Moses). While He makes it clear that the Old Law is still in effect, He delivers new teachings or laws that deepen the requirements of His followers and challenge us to go beyond just what the law tells us not to do.

Spiritual Works of Mercy: Jesus taught us that we must love our neighbor by performing Spiritual (and Corporal) Works of Mercy. The spiritual works of mercy help us meet a person's spiritual needs. They are: instruct the ignorant, counsel the doubtful, admonish sinners, bear wrongs patiently, forgive offenses willingly, comfort the afflicted, and pray for the living and the dead.

Suffering Servant: In the Old Testament, Isaiah prophesied, or foretold, of a person who comes to voluntarily suffer in atonement for the sins of the people. His suffering would save the people from just punishment at the hands of God. Jesus perfectly fulfills this prophecy by His suffering and death on the Cross.

Christ, the Great Hierophant
BY BROTHER NICHOLAS (C. 17TH CENTURY)

Greek Institute of Venice, Italy.

Christ, the Great Hierophant

Christ, the Great Hierophant *by Brother Nicholas*

Directions: Take some time to quietly view and reflect on the art. Let yourself be inspired in any way that happens naturally. Then think about the questions below, and discuss them with your classmates.

Conversation Questions

1. Who is the man in this picture?

2. What is the white cloth He is wearing around His neck?

3. What is He sitting on? What is on His head? What is He holding?

4. A priest is a man specially called by God to offer sacrifice and to acknowledge God's greatness. A priest mediates between God and His people. Read John 17:1-5, 15:

   > When Jesus had said this, he raised his eyes to Heaven and said, "Father, the hour has come. Give glory to your son, so that your son may glorify you, just as you gave him authority over all people, so that he may give eternal life to all you gave him. Now this is eternal life, that they should know you, the only true God, and the one whom you sent, Jesus Christ. I glorified you on earth by accomplishing the work that you gave me to do. Now glorify me, Father, with you, with the glory that I had with you before the world began. I do not ask that you take them out of the world but that you keep them from the evil one.

   How is Jesus acting in His role as priest?

5. A prophet is one who speaks for God to make known God's will to the people. Read John 18:37:

   > For this I was born and for this I came into the world, to testify to the truth. Everyone who belongs to the truth listens to my voice.

   How is Jesus acting in His role as prophet?

6. A king is a man who is the chief authority and ruler of his kingdom. His greatest responsibility is to ensure that his subjects live virtuously. Read Matthew 10:5, 7-8:

   > Jesus sent out these twelve after instructing them thus, "As you go, make this proclamation: 'The kingdom of Heaven is at hand.' Cure the sick, raise the dead, cleanse lepers, drive out demons."

   How is Jesus acting in His role as king?

7. The *Catechism of the Catholic Church* no. 783 tells us, "Jesus Christ is the one whom the Father anointed with the Holy Spirit and established as priest, prophet, and king." How does the icon depict Jesus in the roles of priest, prophet, and king?

John 18:37

For this I was born and for this I came into the world, to testify to the truth. Everyone who belongs to the truth listens to my voice.

Luke 19:10

For the son of man has come to seek and to save what was lost.

Matthew 16:15-17

He said to them, "But who do you say that I am?" Simon Peter said in reply, "You are the Messiah, the Son of the living God." Jesus said to him in reply, "Blessed are you, Simon son of Jonah. For flesh and blood has not revealed this to you, but my Heavenly Father."

Isaiah 61:1

The spirit of the Lord GOD is upon me, because the LORD has anointed me; He has sent me to bring good news to the afflicted, to bind up the brokenhearted, to proclaim liberty to the captives, release to the prisoners.

Hebrews 5:1

Every high priest is taken from among men and made their representative before God, to offer gifts and sacrifices for sins.

Deuteronomy 18:15

A prophet like me will the LORD, your God, raise up for you from among your own kindred; that is the one to whom you shall listen.

John 18:37

You say I am a king. For this I was born and for this I came into the world, to testify to the truth. Everyone who belongs to the truth listens to my voice.

John 11:25

Jesus told her, "I am the resurrection and the life; whoever believes in me, even if he dies, will live."

Jeremiah 31:31

See, days are coming—oracle of the LORD—when I will make a new covenant with the house of Israel and the house of Judah.

Luke 24:46-47

Thus it is written that the Messiah would suffer and rise from the dead on the third day and that repentance, for the forgiveness of sins, would be preached in his name to all the nations, beginning from Jerusalem.

The Parable of the Unforgiving Servant

Directions: Read Matthew 18:21-35, the parable of the unforgiving servant, then answer the questions that follow.

Then Peter approaching asked him, "Lord, if my brother sins against me, how often must I forgive him? As many as seven times?" Jesus answered, "I say to you, not seven times but seventy-seven times. That is why the kingdom of Heaven may be likened to a king who decided to settle accounts with his servants. When he began the accounting, a debtor was brought before him who owed him a huge amount. Since he had no way of paying it back, his master ordered him to be sold, along with his wife, his children, and all his property, in payment of the debt. At that, the servant fell down, did him homage, and said, 'Be patient with me, and I will pay you back in full.' Moved with compassion the master of that servant let him go and forgave him the loan. When that servant had left, he found one of his fellow servants who owed him a much smaller amount. He seized him and started to choke him, demanding, 'Pay back what you owe.' Falling to his knees, his fellow servant begged him, 'Be patient with me, and I will pay you back.' But he refused. Instead, he had him put in prison until he paid back the debt. Now when his fellow servants saw what had happened, they were deeply disturbed, and went to their master and reported the whole affair. His master summoned him and said to him, 'You wicked servant! I forgave you your entire debt because you begged me to. Should you not have had pity on your fellow servant, as I had pity on you?' Then in anger his master handed him over to the torturers until he should pay back the whole debt. So will my Heavenly Father do to you, unless each of you forgives his brother from his heart."

1. At the beginning of this parable, what did the king decide to do? What do you think this means?

    _____

    _____

2. What problem did the first servant encounter? _____

3. What did the king command to be done with the servant?

    _____

4. What did this servant ask of the king? _____

5. What did the king do for the servant? _____

6. What did the servant do to his fellow servant?

_____

7. What did the king do to the unforgiving servant?

_____

8. Was the servant thankful to his king? Why or why not?

_____

_____

Reflection Questions

1. Peter asked Jesus, "Lord, if my brother sins against me, how often must I forgive him? As many as seven times?" Jesus answered, "I say to you, not seven times but seventy-seven times." What do these words mean to you? In Jewish culture, the number seven represented perfection, completeness, or wholeness. It was also a number that represented covenant, the unbreakable bond of family relationship. Given this understanding, what do Jesus' words to Peter mean to you? What attitude toward forgiveness of others should we have?

_____

_____

_____

_____

_____

2. What does this parable teach us about how we should treat those who wrong us? Hint: think of the Beatitudes and the Lord's Prayer for some ideas.

_____

_____

_____

_____

_____

3. Describe a time when you had to forgive someone. How did you feel before you forgave that person? How did you feel afterward? Was it difficult to forgive the person? Why or why not?

_____

_____

_____

_____

_____

4. How are we like Jesus when we forgive another person, especially when that person has not asked for forgiveness?

_____

_____

_____

_____

_____

314

Jesus Washing Peter's Feet

BY FORD MADOX BROWN (C. 1856)

City of Manchester Art Galleries, Manchester, UK.

Jesus Washing Peter's Feet

Jesus Washing Peter's Feet, *by Ford Madox Brown (c. 1856)*

Directions: Take some time to quietly view and reflect on the art. Let yourself be inspired in any way that happens naturally. Then think about the questions below, and discuss them with your classmates.

Conversation Questions

1. Who are the two people in the front of the painting? Who are the others in the background?

2. What is happening in this painting?

3. Read John 13:1-20. How does this painting illustrate this story from Scripture?

4. Why do you think Peter reacted the way he did in this story? How is this shown in the painting?

5. In John 13:14-15, Jesus tells His disciples "If I, therefore, the master and teacher, have washed your feet, you ought to wash one another's feet. I have given you a model to follow, so that as I have done for you, you should also do." What do you think Jesus is commanding His disciples, and us, to do? Why is this command important for living a Christian life?

Foot Washing

Directions: Look at the image and answer the questions below.

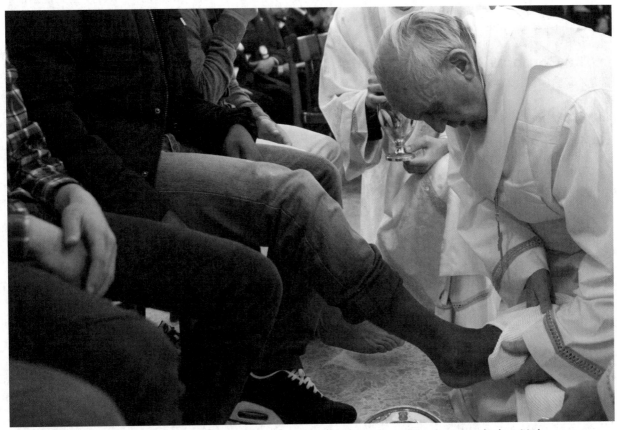

*This photo is of Pope Francis washing the feet of a prison inmate during Holy
Thursday Mass in 2013. (Photo courtesy L'Osservatore Romano.)*

Choose from one of the following Bible verses below and write a short reflection in response:
Deuteronomy 15:11, Matthew 25:40, or Acts 25:40.

_____

_____

_____

_____

The Corporal and Spiritual Works of Mercy

Directions: Read the works of mercy, looking up any words you don't know. Then write them out on the lines provided. Finally, answer the questions that follow.

The Corporal Works of Mercy are	Write the Corporal Works of Mercy
Feed the hungry.	_____
Give drink to the thirsty.	_____
Clothe the naked.	_____
Shelter the homeless.	_____
Visit the sick.	_____
Visit the imprisoned.	_____
Bury the dead.	_____

The Spiritual Works of Mercy are	Write the Spiritual Works of Mercy
Instruct the ignorant.	_____
Counsel the doubtful.	_____
Admonish the sinner.	_____
Bear wrongs patiently.	_____
Forgive offenses willingly.	_____
Comfort the afflicted.	_____
Pray for the living and the dead.	_____

"The works of mercy are not optional but are absolutely essential to living the Christian life of holiness and goodness."

CCC 2447

1. The word "corporal" means "body." The corporal works of mercy help us meet a person's physical needs. Why do you think it is important to help meet the physical needs of others?

   _____

   _____

2. The spiritual works of mercy help us meet a person's spiritual needs. Why do you think it is important to help meet the spiritual needs of others?

   _____

   _____

Reflection Question

Both the Corporal and the Spiritual Works of Mercy are essential to the Christian Life. Which do you think are more important, the Corporal Works of Mercy or the Spiritual Works of Mercy? Explain.

_____

_____

_____

_____

_____

_____

Gifts of the Holy Spirit

Directions: Read about your assigned gift of the Holy Spirit, then answer the questions that follow.

Wisdom	Wisdom allows us to know the purpose and plan of God and value it above all else. God's wisdom is His truth. God gives us a share in His Wisdom to allow us to recognize the truth and see things from His point of view.
Understanding	Understanding empowers human intelligence to know and comprehend the truths of the Catholic Faith that go beyond simple human abilities. It allows us to discover God's will in everything through prayer, reading Scripture, and receiving the Sacraments.
Counsel	Counsel helps us to know right from wrong and to avoid sin. It allows us to make the right decisions in the face of temptation and evil, to live a moral life, and to attain salvation.
Fortitude	Fortitude emboldens us to stand up for and defend the Catholic Faith in the face of persecution, even to the point of physical harm or death. This gift strengthens us to do God's will, and helps us overcome fear.
Knowledge	Knowledge allows us to be aware of God's plan in our lives and to apply it and take action upon it. Knowledge sheds light on our weaknesses, sins, and failures and helps us strive to overcome them with the grace of God.
Piety	Piety moves us to serve God in humility and love. It allows us to worship God rightly, not because we feel a responsibility or duty, but because we love Him and desire to worship Him.
Fear of the Lord	Fear of the Lord allows to recognize that God is God and we are not. By this gift, we rightly know our relationship to God and His glory and greatness. We fear displeasing God by our sin and desire to be close to Him.

What is your assigned gift of the Holy Spirit? _____

Rewrite the definition of your assigned gift of the Holy Spirit in your own words.

_____

_____

_____

_____

Give three specific examples of how your assigned gift of the Holy Spirit can help you announce the Good News of Jesus Christ to others. (For example, how can the gift of knowledge help you tell others about Jesus, salvation, and the Church?)

1. _____

   _____

2. _____

   _____

3. _____

   _____

Jesus' Two Natures: God and Man Crossword Puzzle

Directions: Complete the crossword puzzle using your Bible. Find and read each verse, then fill in the missing word. The words are found in the Word bank.

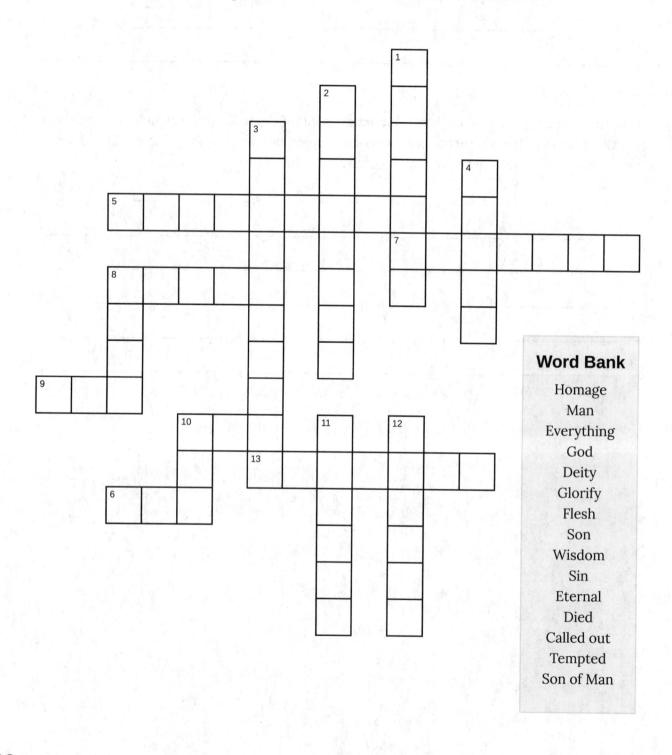

Word Bank

Homage
Man
Everything
God
Deity
Glorify
Flesh
Son
Wisdom
Sin
Eternal
Died
Called out
Tempted
Son of Man

Down

1. **Matthew 4:1:** Then Jesus was led by the Spirit into the desert to be _____ by the devil.

2. **John 9:35-36:** When Jesus heard that they had thrown him out, he found him and said, "Do you believe in the _____ _____ _____ ?" He answered and said, "Who is he, sir, that I may believe in him?"

3. **John 21:17:** He said to him the third time, "Simon, son of John, do you love me?" Peter was distressed that he had said to him a third time, "Do you love me?" and he said to him, "Lord, you know _____; you know that I love you." [Jesus] said to him, "Feed my sheep."

4. **Luke 24:39:** Look at my hands and my feet, that it is I myself. Touch me and see, because a ghost does not have _____ and bones as you can see I have.

8. **Romans 5:8:** But God proves his love for us in that while we were still sinners Christ _____ for us.

10. **Mark 1:1:** The beginning of the gospel of Jesus Christ [the _____ of God].

11. **Matthew 2:2:** Where is the newborn king of the Jews? We saw his star at its rising and have come to do him _____.

12. **Luke 2:52:** And Jesus advanced [in] _____ and age and favor before God and man.

Across

5. **Acts 7:59:** As they were stoning Stephen, he _____ _____, "Lord Jesus, receive my spirit."

6. **Mark 15:39:** When the centurion who stood facing him saw how he breathed his last he said, "Truly this _____ was the Son of God!"

7. **John 10:28:** I give them _____ life, and they shall never perish. No one can take them out of my hand.

8. **Colossians 2:9-10:** For in him dwells the whole fullness of the _____ bodily, and you share in this fullness in him, who is the head of every principality and power.

9. **John 20:28:** Thomas answered and said to him, "My Lord and my _____!"

10. **1 Peter 2:22:** He committed no _____, and no deceit was found in his mouth.

13. **John 17:1:** When Jesus had said this, he raised his eyes to heaven and said, "Father, the hour has come. Give glory to your son, so that your son may _____ you."

Bible Verse Sort

Directions: Reread each Bible verse from the crossword puzzle and decide whether it tells us something about Jesus' humanity or Jesus' divinity. Then list the Scripture reference under the correct column on the chart and write a brief summary of what the passage tells us about Jesus' humanity or divinity. The first two have been completed for you. Lastly, answer the reflection questions.

The Son of God/ Jesus is man	God the Son/ Jesus is God
John 17:1: Jesus worshiped the Father.	Matthew 2:2: Jesus is worshiped.

1. Describe in your own words what it means that Jesus is fully God and fully man.

    _____

    _____

    _____

    _____

    _____

    _____

2. We have special encounters with Jesus in all the Sacraments, and espeically the Eucharist. In the Eucharist, Jesus is really present: His Body, Blood, Soul, and Divinity. One very special form of prayer is called Eucharistic adoration. In this type of prayer, we kneel before a consecrated host in a monstrance, and contemplate the mystery of God with us. When we visit Jesus in adoration, Christians create a community of love. Does your parish offer regular adoration times, or even perpetual adoration? If you don't know, how can you find out?

    _____

    _____

The Transfiguration

BY BL. FRA ANGELICO (C. 1440-1442)

Convento di San Marco, Florence, Italy.

The Incarnation

Directions: First, read the following passage from St. Augustine about the Incarnation and highlight or underline all of the names for Jesus mentioned in the passage. Then read about the four reasons for the Incarnation according to the *Catechism of the Catholic Church*. Finally, answer the questions.

St. Augustine's Sermon 191

The word of the Father by whom all time was created was made flesh and born in time for us. He without whose divine permission no day completes its course, wished to have one of those days for His human birth. In the bosom of His Father He existed before all the cycles of the ages. Born of an earthly mother, He entered on the course of the years on that very day. The maker of man became man that He, ruler of the stars, might be nourished at the breast; that He, the bread, might be hungry; that He, the fountain, might thirst; that He, the light, might sleep; that He, the way, might be wearied in the journey; that He, the truth, might be accused by false witnesses; that He, the judge of the living and the dead, might be brought to trial by a mortal judge; that He, justice itself, might be condemned by the unjust; that He, discipline personified, might be scourged with a whip; that He, the foundation, might be suspended on a Cross; that He, courage incarnate, might be weak and He, security itself, might be wounded, and He, life itself, might die.

Four reasons for the Incarnation

The *Catechism of the Catholic Church* gives us four reasons for the Incarnation in paragraphs 456-460. The first reason for the Incarnation is to save us from sin. Christ's sacrifice on the Cross paid the penalty for sin that we could not. Out of sheer gratuitous love for us, Jesus laid down His life so that we might live.

The second reason for the Incarnation is so we might know God's love. The very act of God becoming one of His own creatures while remaining truly God shows how much He loves us. And then, He demonstrated His perfect self-giving love by sacrificing Himself on the Cross.

The third reason for the Incarnation is to be our model of holiness. Christ's public ministry taught us what it means to be holy and how to be loved by God and to love Him in return.

The fourth reason for the Incarnation is to make us sharers in God's divine nature. St. Thomas Aquinas wrote, "The only-begotten Son of God, wanting to make us sharers in his divinity, assumed our human nature, so that he, made man, might make men gods."

1. According to St. Augustine, what was made flesh, and what did He do?

_____

_____

2. What day (that we continue to celebrate today) is St. Augustine talking about in his homily?

_____

3. After reading through all of the various titles St. Augustine used for Christ, what can we say St. Augustine believed about the purpose of the Incarnation?

_____

_____

_____

4. According to the *Catechism*, what are the four reasons for the Incarnation?

_____

_____

_____

_____

5. How did Jesus save us from sin?

_____

_____

6. How does Jesus show us God's love for us?

_____

_____

7. How is Jesus our model of holiness?

_____

_____

8. How does Jesus make us sharers in God's divine nature?

_____

_____

Reflection Question

We can summarize all of the various reasons for the Incarnation by simply saying that the Son of God assumed a human nature because He loves us. Describe a time in your life when you knew confidently that God loved you. How did you know? What did you do in response to God's love?

_____

_____

_____

_____

_____

_____

Priest, Prophet, and King

Directions: Read about the roles of priest, prophet, and king as they applied to Adam at the beginning of Creation to help you understand how Jesus is priest, prophet, and king. Then answer the questions that follow.

In the beginning, God gave Adam three roles: priest, prophet, and king. In ancient times, the most important job of a priest was to offer sacrifice to God on behalf of the people. This made the priest a mediator, or someone who communicates to God for others. The sacrifices a priest offered were meant to ensure the life of the people.

Prophets in the ancient world spoke on God's behalf. They communicated to the people the message of repentance and salvation and told the world of God's love. Prophets also taught the people about God and His law.

Kings in ancient times and even today rule their kingdoms. They have dominion over their land and all of their subjects. Dominion means power or authority over something. A king governs by creating the laws of his kingdom, enforcing the laws, and judging his subjects based on those laws. A good king will create, enforce, and judge his kingdom so that it and everyone in it can be the best he or she can be. Throughout history there have been bad kings who ruled with cruelty and selfishness and there have been good kings who ruled with kindness and generosity.

Adam was the first priest, prophet, and king. God gave Adam the job of being the mediator between all of Creation and God.

Adam was to offer all of Creation back to God in thanksgiving for all He had made. This made him the first priest. Adam was also given the task of naming all of the animals. Normally, the one who creates something has the right to name it. But, God gave this right to Adam. Therefore, Adam spoke for God and was meant to communicate God's love to the world. This made Adam the first prophet. Adam was also given dominion over all of God's creation. This means he was given power and authority over all that God made. He was meant to rule as a good king and govern according to the law of God.

When Adam and Eve sinned, the roles of priest, prophet, and king became distorted. Because of sin, Adam did not fulfill his roles as he was meant to. It became necessary for God to save Adam's descendants and restore them to these roles. All of humanity are the descendants of Adam. And so, God prepared us to receive salvation and revealed Himself throughout human history. Then, in the fullness of time, God entered into human history and assumed a human nature in the Person of Jesus Christ. God made His Son priest, prophet, and king to save us from sin and restore us and all of Creation to God's plan from the beginning.

1. What three roles did God give to Adam in the beginning?

   _____

   _____

2. In ancient times, what was the most important job of a priest? What was this meant to do?

   _____

   _____

   _____

3. What is a mediator? _____

4. In the ancient world, what did a prophet do? _____

5. What message did a prophet communicate and teach?

   _____

   _____

6. What does it mean for a king to have dominion?

   _____

7. How does a king govern?

   _____

8. What is the difference between a good king and a bad king?

   _____

   _____

9. How was Adam the first priest?

   _____

   _____

10. How was Adam the first prophet?

   _____

   _____

11. How was Adam the first king?

_____

_____

12. What happened to Adam's roles because of sin?

_____

_____

13. Who are the descendants of Adam? What did God do to save them from sin and restore them to His plan from the beginning?

_____

_____

_____

Reflection Question

At our Baptism, we are anointed as priest, prophet, and king. That means that we share in some way in Christ's threefold mission as priest, prophet, and king. Given the definitions of these roles, choose one role – priest, prophet, or king – and describe at least two ways in which you can live out that role in your own life today.

_____

_____

_____

_____

_____

_____

_____

Melchizedek

Directions: Read the brief story of Melchizedek from Genesis 14:18-20, then answer the questions that follow.

As Abram returned from his victory in battle, he met the priest-king Melchizedek. We read about this meeting in Genesis 14:18-20:

> Melchizedek, king of Salem, brought out bread and wine. He was a priest of God Most High. He blessed Abram with these words: "Blessed be Abram by God Most High, the creator of Heaven and earth; And blessed be God Most High, who delivered your foes into your hand." Then Abram gave him a tenth of everything.

1. Who was Melchizedek? _____

2. What did Melchizedek do when he met Abram (Abraham)?

   _____

3. Genesis 22:13 describes the typical animal sacrifice of the Old Testament: "Abraham looked up and saw a single ram caught by its horns in the thicket. So Abraham went and took the ram and offered it up as a burnt offering in place of his son." How was Melchizedek's offering different from other offerings?

   _____

   _____

4. How does Melchizekek, in his offering to Abram, foreshadow Jesus?

   _____

   _____

5. How was the offering made by Melchizedek similar to a modern-day Mass?

   _____

   _____

   _____

My Parish Priest

Directions: List at least five roles or duties of your parish priest.

1. _____

2. _____

3. _____

4. _____

5. _____

In the Person of Christ

Directions: Read the given Scripture passages and summarize each in your own words in the boxes. Then draw lines to match the Scripture passage about Jesus our High Priest with the Scripture passage about the priesthood of the Apostles and the ordained priests of today.

Jesus, our High Priest	Priests, in the Person of Christ
Mark 2:5	Luke 22:19-20
Matthew 15:30	John 20:21-23
1 Corinthians 15:3-4	Mark 6:7, 12-13

The Suffering Servant of Isaiah

Directions: Read Isaiah's prophecy of the Suffering Servant from Isaiah 53:1-12, then answer the questions.

1. To whom is Isaiah referring? How is the servant sinless?

   _____

   _____

2. In Isaiah's extraordinary account we learn about the Suffering Servant, the Messiah to come, whose voluntary suffering atones for the sins of the people and saves them from just punishment at the hands of God. Only in Jesus Christ is the prophecy perfectly fulfilled. Jesus is the Messiah of whom the prophet Isaiah foretold, and Jesus is the prophet like Moses whom God would raise up after him. Make a list of seven to ten references that Isaiah made to Jesus in this passage. Write the part of the passage that refers to Jesus on the line and then briefly explain why or how you think the passage refers to Jesus.

   ▶ _____

   Why? _____

   ▶ _____

   Why? _____

   ▶ _____

   Why? _____

   ▶ _____

   Why? _____

   ▶ _____

   Why? _____

➤ _____

Why? _____

➤ _____

Why? _____

➤ _____

Why? _____

➤ _____

Why? _____

➤ _____

Why? _____

Christ as the Suffering Redeemer,
by Andrea Mantegna.

Jesus the Prophet

Directions: Read the given Scripture passages and, in the boxes, summarize the words of Jesus in your own words. Then draw a line to match each Scripture passage about Jesus the prophet with a statement about what a prophet does.

What does a prophet do?	What did Jesus say?
1. The will of God.	Matthew 11:27
2. Reveals God to the people.	John 8:28
3. Speaks God's truth to the people.	Luke 22:42

Tu Rex Gloriae Christe
BY WILLIAM EARLEY (C. 1933)

St. Joseph's Church, Toomyvara, County Tipperary, Ireland.

Tu Rex Gloriae Christe

 Tu Rex Gloriae Christe, *by William Earley* (c. 1933)

Directions: Take some time to quietly view and reflect on the art. Let yourself be inspired in any way that happens naturally. Then think about the questions below, and discuss them with your classmates.

Conversation Questions

1. What do you first notice about Jesus in this picture?

2. What do you notice about the colors the artist chose for this picture? How does the light look? Where is it coming from?

3. The blue and gold ball in Jesus' left hand is a decorated globe that represents the earth. Why do you think the artist shows Jesus holding a globe in His hand?

4. Red is the color of blood, so it represents suffering and victory through suffering. Why do you think the artist shows Jesus wearing a red cape?

5. Jesus' bare or sandaled feet represent humility. To be humble means not to be proud or make oneself greater than others. It also represents being obedient and reflective. How does Jesus possess these qualities?

6. Jesus is standing on a cloud with stars sparkling inside of it. What do you think this symbolizes? Where does this suggest that Jesus' Kingdom comes from?

7. Notice the angels above and to the side of Jesus. What does it appear that they are doing? Why do you think so?

8. Jesus is wearing a crown and holding a scepter, which symbolize the power and rule of a king. Why do you think the artist showed Jesus with a crown and holding a scepter? What is Jesus the King of?

9. The title of this stained-glass window is *Tu Rex Gloriae Christe*, which is Latin for "You are the King of Glory, O Christ." Why do you think we call Christ the King of Glory? Why should we glorify Him?

The Corporal Works of Mercy

Directions: Read about the Corporal Works of Mercy from Matthew 25:31-46, then answer the questions.

1. List the six Corporal Works of Mercy Jesus teaches in this passage.

   _____

   _____

   _____

   _____

   _____

2. For whom does Jesus say one is doing each of these works of mercy when that person does them for the least among us?

   _____

   _____

3. What does Jesus say will be the consequence for those who do not do the works of mercy for the least among us?

   _____

   _____

4. What does Jesus say will be the reward for those who do the works of mercy for the least among us?

   _____

   _____

Living as the Image of God

Directions: Answer the following questions while viewing the video titled "Living as the Image of God" by Bishop Robert Barron.

1. What does it mean to be a king?

   _____

2. What is the common interpretation of Jesus' words to Peter, "The gates of hell shall not prevail against you"?

   _____

   _____

3. What is Bishop Barron's new interpretation of those same words to Peter?

   _____

   _____

4. Under what circumstances would our kingly mission not happen?

   _____

   _____

5. What is authentic Christianity?

   _____

   _____

6. What causes us to undermine our kingly mission?

   _____

   _____

7. Why does Bishop Barron describe Pontius Pilate as the first evangelist?

   _____

   _____

8. What does *Kaiser Kyrios* mean? What is St. Paul's revision of this phrase?

_____

_____

9. What does the visionary of the book of Revelation see?

_____

_____

10. What is the goal of our kingly mission?

_____

_____

Bishop Robert Barron

The Mystery of Faith

Directions: Read about the Memorial Acclamation at Mass and its different forms, then answer the questions about each one.

At every Mass we proclaim the Paschal Mystery in a prayer called the Memorial Acclamation. During the Liturgy of the Eucharist, after the priest has spoken the words of Consecration to transform the bread and wine into the Body and Blood of our Lord, the priest invites the congregation to pray together the "Mystery of Faith." Then, together as a Church, we acclaim this mystery by saying together one of the following forms of the prayer:

Option 1:   We proclaim your Death, O Lord, and profess your Resurrection until you come again.

Option 2:   When we eat this Bread and drink this Cup, we proclaim your Death, O Lord, until you come again.

Option 3:   Save us, Savior of the world, for by your Cross and Resurrection you have set us free.

Option 1

Read the first option for the Memorial Acclamation, then answer the questions.

1.   What do we proclaim and profess? _____

2.   What does this proclamation and profession say that we believe?

    _____

3.   What do we believe will happen at the end of time?

    _____

Option 2

Read the second option for the Memorial Acclamation, then answer the questions.

4.   How do we proclaim Christ's Death?

    _____

5. Where do we receive the Bread of Life and Cup of Christ's Blood?

_____

6. What do we believe will happen at the end of time?

_____

Option 3

Read the third option for the Memorial Acclamation, then answer the questions.

7. What do we ask of the Savior of the world?

_____

8. Who is the Savior of the World? _____

9. How are we set free? _____

10. What are we set free from? _____

Reflection Question

How do the three options for the Memorial Acclamation at Mass together fully express our belief in the Paschal Mystery?

_____

_____

_____

_____

_____

_____

_____

Christ and the Good Thief
BY TITIAN (C. 1566)

Pinacoteca Nazionale di Bologna, Italy.

Christ and the Good Thief

Directions: Read the story of Jesus' Crucifixion and conversation with the Good Thief from Luke 23:33, 39-43, then answer the questions.

1. With whom was Jesus Crucified? _____

2. What did Jesus ask of His Father for those who crucified Him? _____
    _____

3. What did they do with Jesus' garments? _____

4. What did the rulers say sneeringly to Jesus? _____

5. What did the inscription above Jesus' head say? _____
    _____

6. Did Jesus deserve to die? _____

7. Did the Good Thief deserve to die? _____

8. What did the Good Thief ask of Jesus? _____
    _____

9. What did the Good Thief have to believe in order to ask this of Jesus? _____
    _____

10. What did Jesus save the Good Thief from? _____

11. What are the wages of sin? _____

12. What did Jesus promise the Good Thief? _____
    _____

13. What did the Good Thief do in response? _____
    _____

The name Jesus means "God saves." This is exactly what the Good Thief believed. He believed that Jesus was God and that He could save him. Because the thief believed and repented, Jesus did save him. Jesus forgave him and gave him eternal life. Read the *Catechism of the Catholic Church* no. 620:

> Our salvation flows from God's initiative of love for us, because "he loved us and sent his Son to be the expiation for our sins" (1 Jn 4:10).

14. From where does our salvation flow? _____

15. Why did God send His Son? _____

16. How did Jesus show His love to the Good Thief? _____

17. Why does Jesus forgive us, save us, and give us eternal life? _____

_____

_____

The Resurrection

Directions: Read the Gospel account of Christ's Resurrection assigned to your group, then write a brief summary paragraph. Include all the details described in your Gospel. Then take turns sharing about your Gospel's account of the Resurrection with other students, completing the rest of the chart together.

Matthew 28	**Mark 16**
Luke 24	**John 20-21**

God's Covenants and Mercy

Directions: Every covenant has a promise, a mediator, and a sign. Each covenant also signifies a progression or growth in God's family. Fill in the following chart by placing the squares you receive from your teacher in the appropriate space.

Covenant Mediator	Covenant Promise	Covenant Sign	Covenant Progression
Adam			
Noah			
Abraham			

Covenant Mediator	Covenant Promise	Covenant Sign	Covenant Progression
Moses			
David			
Jesus			

The New Covenant in Scripture

Directions: Read each Scripture passage, then answer the questions.

Read Jeremiah 31:31-34, then answer:

1. What does the Lord say He will do with the House of Israel?

    _____

    _____

2. What covenant does God refer to when He says that the new covenant will not be like the ones before? How do you know?

    _____

    _____

    _____

3.   What did Israel do with the previous covenants? _____

4. What does God say He will place within and write upon the hearts of the people? What effect will this have?

    _____

    _____

    _____

5. Why does God say that in the new covenant everyone from the greatest to the least will know Him?

    _____

6. Based upon this prophecy of the new covenant over 600 years before the birth of Jesus, what would you say is the most important aspect of this covenant?

    _____

    _____

Read Luke 22:19-20, then answer:

7. What moment in the life of Jesus is this passage taken from? What happened at this event?

    _____

    _____

8. What does Jesus say about the cup of His Blood?

    _____

9. When did Jesus shed His Blood for us? Why?

    _____

    _____

Read Hebrews 9:11-15, then answer:

10. Recall how in the Old Testament, the Jewish people would offer animal sacrifices to make up in some small imperfect way for their sin. For one type of sacrifice, the high priest of the Temple would offer animal sacrifice to God on an altar in the sanctuary of the Temple. What does Jesus, the high priest, offer instead of animal sacrifice? What does He obtain with this offering that no animal sacrifice ever could?

    _____

    _____

    _____

11. What does St. Paul explain that animal sacrifices cleansed? What does the sacrifice of Christ cleanse?

    _____

    _____

    _____

12. What does Christ's sacrifice make Him? _____

13. In this New Covenant, how are we delivered from our transgressions (sins)?

    _____

14. What will those who are called receive? _____

Jesus Fulfills the Old Covenant

Directions: Read each Scripture passage about how Jesus fulfills each Old Testament covenant and then complete the chart by determining which Old Testament covenant mediator Jesus fulfills. Then describe how Jesus fulfilled each Old Testament covenant.

	Bible passage	Jesus is the new...	How does Jesus fulfill each Old Testament covenant?
1	**1 Corinthians 15:47-49** The first man was from the earth, earthly; the second man, from Heaven. As was the earthly one, so also are the earthly, and as is the Heavenly one, so also are the Heavenly. Just as we have borne the image of the earthly one, we shall also bear the image of the Heavenly one.		
2	**Luke 17:26-27, 30, 33** As it was in the days of Noah, so it will be in the days of the Son of Man; they were eating and drinking, marrying and giving in marriage up to the day that Noah entered the ark, and the flood came and destroyed them all. ...So it will be on the day the Son of Man is revealed. ...Whoever seeks to preserve his life will lose it, but whoever loses it will save it.		
3	**Luke 1:32-33** He will be great and will be called Son of the Most High, and the Lord God will give him the throne of David his father, and he will rule over the house of Jacob forever, and of his kingdom there will be no end.		

	Bible passage	Jesus is the new...	How does Jesus fulfill each Old Testament covenant?
4	**Galatians 3:7-9, 14** Realize then that it is those who have faith who are children of Abraham. Scripture, which saw in advance that God would justify the Gentiles by faith, foretold the good news to Abraham, saying, "Through you shall all the nations be blessed." Consequently, those who have faith are blessed along with Abraham who had faith...that the blessing of Abraham might be extended to the Gentiles through Christ Jesus, so that we might receive the promise of the Spirit through faith.		
5	**John 6:32-35** So Jesus said to them, "Amen, amen, I say to you, it was not Moses who gave the bread from Heaven; my Father gives you the true bread from Heaven. For the bread of God is that which comes down from Heaven and gives life to the world." So they said to him, "Sir, give us this bread always." Jesus said to them, "I am the bread of life; whoever comes to me will never hunger, and whoever believes in me will never thirst."		

The Effects of Baptism

Directions: Together as a group, read about the effects of the Sacrament of Baptism.

Forgiveness of Sins

The Sacrament of Baptism forgives all sin. This includes Original Sin, all personal sins, and any punishment for sin. Original Sin is the sin of Adam and Eve that is passed on to all of humanity. Personal sins are those sins that we commit. All sins have spiritual consequences, most especially mortal sin, which separates us from God. Baptism forgives all of these sins and removes all spiritual consequences. At the moment of Baptism, there is nothing that would prevent the baptized from entering Heaven.

Some earthly consequences of sin remain after Baptism. These include suffering, sickness, and death during our earthly lives. Also, all of humanity experiences a tendency to sin called concupiscence. This is a kind of human weakness that can be resisted with the help of God's grace.

New Creation

The Sacrament of Baptism makes the baptized new creations in the eyes of God. We are made adopted sons and daughters of God and sharers in His divine life. As God's children, through Baptism, we also receive the benefit of all of God's promises, and our bodies become temples of the Holy Spirit.

This is all possible because Baptism gives us sanctifying grace. Sanctifying grace is the undeserved gift of God's life within us. It makes us able to believe in God, to hope in His promises of salvation, and to love Him and all that He has made. Sanctifying grace also gives us the power to live a holy life with the help of the Holy Spirit. Baptism is the foundation of the Christian life.

Members of the Church

The Sacrament of Baptism makes those who are baptized members of the Church, the Body of Christ. We become united to everyone else who has been baptized and together become one People of God. Scripture explains that Baptism makes us "a chosen race, a royal priesthood, a holy nation, God's own people." This means that the baptized are made into a common priesthood of all believers, who are called to serve one another in love and sacrifice.

As members of Christ's Church, we are given all of the rights and privileges that come with membership. This means we can now go on to receive all of the other Sacraments, to worship fully at Mass, and to receive all of the other spiritual help of the Church. We are also given the mission of the Church, which is to share the Good News of Jesus Christ with all who will hear it. We who are baptized and profess the Faith of the Church must also be obedient to the teachings and leaders of the Church who were appointed by Jesus Himself.

Bond of Unity

The Sacrament of Baptism goes beyond any barriers made by race, nationality, culture, or gender and makes us one Body of Christ. Other Christian faiths that are not in communion with the Catholic Church also celebrate Baptism. We recognize the truth of Baptism that occurs outside the Catholic Church as long as it is done "in the name of the Father, and of the Son, and of the Holy Spirit." Therefore, Baptism makes us all brothers and sisters in Christ and rightly called Christians. Baptism forms a sacramental bond of unity among everyone who is reborn through it.

Indelible Mark

The Sacrament of Baptism gives each person an indelible, or permanent, spiritual mark on his or her soul as belonging to Christ. This spiritual seal is not removable, even if the baptized person sins and gives up the Faith. Therefore, the Sacrament of Baptism can be received only once.

The Holy Spirit places this mark upon our souls to set us apart for the day of redemption. Over the course of our lives, this indelible mark enables us to participate fully in the Mass. It also allows us to use the gifts of the Holy Spirit given to us at our Baptism to live a life of holiness. If we remain faithful to the demands of our baptism, we will leave this life "marked with the sign of faith" and expect to enter the Kingdom of God and be saved.

Baptism is new life in Christ and His Church. With only a few strict exceptions (such as people who die for the faith, those who die while preparing for Baptism, people who have never heard of the Gospel but seek God and try to do His will, and unbaptized babies whom we entrust to the mercy of God), both Baptism and the Church are necessary for salvation. If there is no other option, any person can baptize another person, provided he intends to do what the Church does, and as long as he pours water on the candidate's head while saying, "I baptize you in the name of the Father, and of the Son, and of the Holy Spirit."

Members of the New Covenant

Directions: Using all that you have learned in the past few lessons about the New Covenant, create a poster or flier that advertises for membership in the New Covenant. Include in the advertisement essential information about the New Covenant and descriptions of at least two of the effects of Baptism, the membership requirement for the New Covenant. Your advertisement should also be creatively illustrated. Keep in mind that an advertisement is meant to convince people of the need for the product in the ad.

UNIT 8

God with Us

In this unit, you will learn about...

> The Church as a visible sign of God's presence.

> Mary as the greatest example of a follower of Christ.

> The four marks of the Church: the Church is one, holy, catholic, and apostolic.

> The precepts of the Church.

Introduction

The Church is the People of God whom He has called to communion with Him and with each other. The Church is experienced as the local community (parishes and dioceses), the liturgical assembly (the Mass and other Sacraments of the Church), and the universal community (the worldwide Church). Throughout the world, you can see diverse liturgical traditions or rites that are recognized by the Church. For example, Byzantine rite or Melkite rite churches are in communion with the Catholic Church. Though these rites may appear different, the quality that keeps them unified is their faithfulness to apostolic tradition–the communion in our Faith and the Sacraments received from the Apostles and transmitted by the Holy Spirit through apostolic succession. These rites make known to us the catholicity, or universal nature of the Church. They signify and communicate to us the same mystery of Christ. As a both human and divine institution, the Church was established by Jesus Christ Himself, and is made up of imperfect human beings. Jesus gave the Church four defining characteristics, called the four marks of the Church. They are: the Church is one, the Church is holy, the Church is catholic, and the Church is apostolic. The precepts of the Church present to the faithful.

Are there any questions you still have about the topics you learned last month? What steps can you take to find out the answers?

_____

_____

What questions do you have right now about the topics you will be learning about in this unit?

_____

_____

_____

Abstinence: Intentionally refraining from, or not doing, something. Catholics are required to abstain from eating meat Fridays during Lent and are encouraged to do so on other days throughout the year. (2043, 2193)

Apostle: A person who is sent out as a representative of someone else. Jesus chose twelve men to be His Apostles. They preached Jesus' message of salvation and worked miracles in His name. Jesus gave the Apostles special authority and made them the first leaders (bishops) of the Church.

Apostolic Succession: The handing on of apostolic preaching and authority from the Apostles to their successors the bishops through the laying on of hands, as a permanent office in the Church. The fourth mark of the Church is that the Church is apostolic, which means that the Church is built on the lasting foundation of the Apostles.

Authority: Power or influence over another's thought, opinion, or behavior. Jesus gave His authority to Peter and the Apostles and to their successors, the bishops.

Bishop: The leader of a particular diocese and a main teacher of the Catholic faith. A bishop also makes the Sacraments available to the people of his diocese. The bishops of the Church are the successors to the Apostles. They guard and protect the teachings of the Church to make sure they are handed on faithfully.

Catholic: Universal. The third mark of the Church is that the Church is catholic, or universal. This means that the Church is for all people in every time and place. Her truths apply to all people throughout time.

Church: The community of disciples founded by Jesus that will exist until the end of time. The Church is at the same time human and divine. It is the gathering of God's people, whom He calls, on earth and it is the mystical Body of Christ. The Church is also the Temple of the Holy Spirit, who gives life to the Body of Christ and unites its members.

Disciple: Student. The disciples were followers, or students, of Jesus. Jesus had thousands of disciples. All Christians are His disciples today.

***Ecclesia*:** Latin word used for the Church. It is derived from the Greek word, *ekkalein*, which means "to call out of." The Greek form of the word is used frequently in the Old Testament for the assembly of the Chosen People before God. The early Church adopted the word to describe themselves and to be connected to the assembly of God's people from the Old Testament.

Ecumenism: The work of restoring unity among all Christians.

Evangelization: Sharing the Good News of the Gospel message of salvation with all the world. At the command of Jesus, the Church's mission is to evangelize the whole world.

Fasting: Intentionally refraining from eating and drinking. Catholics over the age of 14 are required to fast on Ash Wednesday and Good Friday and are encouraged to do so at other times throughout the year as an intentional sacrifice.

Heretic: One who teaches false things about God, Jesus, salvation, and the Church.

Holy Days of Obligation: On special days throughout the liturgical year, Catholics are required to attend Mass to celebrate important events in the life of the Church.

Holy/Holiness: Holy means sacred or set apart by God. We do not make ourselves holy; rather, holiness comes from God's initiative. We are holy because God is holy and he calls us to Himself. The second mark of the Church is that the Church is holy.

Infallibility: Being without error. The Magisterium of the Catholic Church (the pope and all of the world's bishops in union with the pope) are incapable of error when teaching about matters of faith and morals in a definitive way.

Kyriake: Greek for "church." See *ecclesia*.

Pope: The bishop of Rome and successor of St. Peter. The pope has the special responsibility of being the head of the entire Church on earth. He unites and guides all of the world's bishops and leads all of God's people on earth. He is Christ's chief representative on earth.

Precepts of the Church: The minimum of what is required of us for Christian living. The precepts are: to attend Mass and to rest from servile work on Sundays and Holy Days of Obligation, to confess our sins to a priest at least once a year, to receive our Lord Jesus Christ in the Holy Eucharist at least once a year during the Easter Season, to observe the days of abstinence and fasting, and to contribute to the support of the Church.

Priest: Co-workers with their bishops who serve the faithful by building up and guiding the Church. Priests preach the Gospel of Christ and make available the Sacraments to the People of God, especially the Holy Eucharist. In a special way, priests act in the person of Christ, making Jesus present to us, when they present the Sacraments.

Schism: Division within the Church.

Unity: The quality of being together as one. Jesus founded one Church and desires for His Church to be one and come together as one People of God united by one belief, one worship, and one liturgy.

Coronation of Mary

Dome of the Basilica of Santa Maria, Trastevere, Italy.

Coronation of Mary

Coronation of Mary, *dome at the Basilica of Santa Maria, Trastevere*

Directions: Take some time to quietly view and reflect on the art. Let yourself be inspired in any way that happens naturally. Then think about the questions below, and discuss them with your classmates.

Conversation Questions

1. Who are the man and the woman in the center of the mosaic? Can you identify other people?

2. Read Matthew 28:18-20, a passage known as the Great Commission. The Apostles have gathered to witness Jesus' Ascension into Heaven. Before He ascends, Jesus gives them these commands and reassures them. What three things does Jesus command the Apostles to do? How does He reassure them?

3. Read *Catechism of the Catholic Church* no. 752:

   In Christian usage, the word "church" designates the liturgical assembly, but also the local community or the whole universal community of believers. These three meanings are inseparable. "The Church" is the People that God gathers in the whole world. She exists in local communities and is made real as a liturgical, above all a Eucharistic, assembly. She draws her life from the word and the Body of Christ and so herself becomes Christ's Body.

   What are the three meanings of *church* given in this passage? How would you explain these three meanings in your own words?

4. Which meaning of the word *church* is used in the sentence, "This mosaic was made by an artist in our church community"?

5. Which meaning of the word *church* is used in the sentence, "We see the Church in the people gathered for Mass"?

6. Which meaning of the word *church* is used in the sentence, "We are members of the Catholic Church"?

7. Where do we find the word of Christ in a church? Where do we find the body of Christ? How are the word and body of Christ illustrated in this mosaic?

8. The Church of Santa Maria in Trastevere is shaped like a cross. How does the shape of this church illustrate the truth that the Church is the Body of Christ?

Matthew 28:18-20

Then Jesus approached and said to them, "All power in Heaven and on earth has been given to me. Go, therefore, and make disciples of all nations, baptizing them in the name of the Father, and of the Son, and of the Holy Spirit, teaching them to observe all that I have commanded you. And behold, I am with you always, until the end of the age."

Matthew 16:18

And so I say to you, you are Peter, and upon this rock I will build my church, and the gates of the netherworld shall not prevail against it.

John 17:20-21

I pray not only for them, but also for those who will believe in me through their word, so that they may all be one, as you, Father, are in me and I in you, that they also may be in us, that the world may believe that you sent me.

Leviticus 20:26

To me, therefore, you shall be holy; for I, the LORD, am holy, and I have set you apart from other peoples to be my own.

Acts 1:8

But you will receive power when the Holy Spirit comes upon you, and you will be my witnesses in Jerusalem, throughout Judea and Samaria, and to the ends of the earth.

Luke 10:16

Whoever listens to you listens to me.
Whoever rejects you rejects me. And whoever
rejects me rejects the one who sent me.

Exodus 19:5

Now, if you obey me completely and keep my covenant, you will be my treasured possession among all peoples, though all the earth is mine.

The Church: A Visible and Spiritual Reality

Directions: Read the following paragraphs from the *Catechism of the Catholic Church* nos. 770-776 out loud as a class, then answer the questions that follow.

The Mystery of the Church

770 The Church is in history, but at the same time she transcends it. It is only "with the eyes of faith" that one can see her in her visible reality and at the same time in her spiritual reality as bearer of divine life.

The Church – both visible and spiritual

771 "The one mediator, Christ, established and ever sustains here on earth his holy Church, the community of faith, hope, and charity, as a visible organization through which he communicates truth and grace to all men." The Church is at the same time:

> a "society structured with hierarchical organs and the mystical body of Christ;

> the visible society and the spiritual community;

> the earthly Church and the Church endowed with heavenly riches."

These dimensions together constitute "one complex reality which comes together from a human and a divine element":

The Church is essentially both human and divine, visible but endowed with invisible realities, zealous in action and dedicated to contemplation, present in the world, but as a pilgrim, so constituted that in her the human is directed toward and subordinated to the divine, the visible to the invisible, action to contemplation, and this present world to that city yet to come, the object of our quest.

O humility! O sublimity! Both tabernacle of cedar and sanctuary of God; earthly dwelling and celestial palace; house of clay and royal hall; body of death and temple of light; and at last both object of scorn to the proud and bride of Christ! She is black but beautiful, O daughters of Jerusalem, for even if the labor and pain of her long exile may have discolored her, yet heaven's beauty has adorned her.

The Church – mystery of man's union with God

772 It is in the Church that Christ fulfills and reveals his own mystery as the purpose of God's plan: "to unite all things in him." St. Paul calls the nuptial union of Christ and the Church "a great mystery." Because she is united to Christ as to her bridegroom, she becomes a mystery in her turn. Contemplating this mystery in her, Paul exclaims: "Christ in you, the hope of glory."

773   In the Church this communion of men with God, in the "love [that] never ends," is the purpose which governs everything in her that is a sacramental means, tied to this passing world. "[The Church's] structure is totally ordered to the holiness of Christ's members. And holiness is measured according to the 'great mystery' in which the Bride responds with the gift of love to the gift of the Bridegroom." Mary goes before us all in the holiness that is the Church's mystery as "the bride without spot or wrinkle." This is why the "Marian" dimension of the Church precedes the "Petrine."

The universal Sacrament of Salvation

774   The Greek word *mysterion* was translated into Latin by two terms: *mysterium* and *sacramentum*. In later usage the term *sacramentum* emphasizes the visible sign of the hidden reality of salvation which was indicated by the term *mysterium*. In this sense, Christ himself is the mystery of salvation: "For there is no other mystery of God, except Christ." The saving work of his holy and sanctifying humanity is the sacrament of salvation, which is revealed and active in the Church's sacraments (which the Eastern Churches also call "the holy mysteries"). The seven sacraments are the signs and instruments by which the Holy Spirit spreads the grace of Christ the head throughout the Church which is his Body. The Church, then, both contains and communicates the invisible grace she signifies. It is in this analogical sense, that the Church is called a "sacrament."

775   "The Church, in Christ, is like a sacrament–a sign and instrument, that is, of communion with God and of unity among all men." The Church's first purpose is to be the sacrament of the *inner union of men* with God. Because men's communion with one another is rooted in that union with God, the Church is also the sacrament of the *unity of the human race*. In her, this unity is already begun, since she gathers men "from every nation, from all tribes and peoples and tongues"; at the same time, the Church is the "sign and instrument" of the full realization of the unity yet to come.

776   As sacrament, the Church is Christ's instrument. "She is taken up by him also as the instrument for the salvation of all," "the universal sacrament of salvation," by which Christ is "at once manifesting and actualizing the mystery of God's love for men." The Church "is the visible plan of God's love for humanity," because God desires "that the whole human race may become one People of God, form one Body of Christ, and be built up into one temple of the Holy Spirit."

1. What does it mean when we say the Church is both human and divine?

   _____

   _____

2. How does the Church reveal the mystery and purpose of God's plan?

   _____

   _____

3. What is meant by the statement: the "Marian" dimension of the Church precedes the "Petrine."

   _____

   _____

4. What is meant by saying that the Church is a *Sacrament*?

   _____

   _____

5. How does seeing the Church in light of the way the *Catechism* describes her change your perception of her?

   _____

   _____

   _____

Disputation of the Sacrament
BY RAPHAEL (1509-1510)

Fresco, Apostolic Palace, Vatican City.

The Story of the Church

Directions: Read the following readings from the *Catechism* and Scripture. Then have a discussion in your group and complete the assignment that follows.

Catechism of the Catholic Church 758-762

758 We begin our investigation of the Church's mystery by meditating on her origin in the Holy Trinity's plan and her progressive realization in history.

A plan born in the Father's heart

759 "The eternal Father, in accordance with the utterly gratuitous and mysterious design of his wisdom and goodness, created the whole universe and chose to raise up men to share in his own divine life," to which he calls all men in his Son. "The Father...determined to call together in a holy Church those who should believe in Christ." This "family of God" is gradually formed and takes shape during the stages of human history, in keeping with the Father's plan. In fact, "already present in figure at the beginning of the world, this Church was prepared in marvelous fashion in the history of the people of Israel and the old Alliance. Established in this last age of the world and made manifest in the outpouring of the Spirit, it will be brought to glorious completion at the end of time."

The Church – foreshadowed from the world's beginning

760 Christians of the first centuries said, "The world was created for the sake of the Church." God created the world for the sake of communion with his divine life, a communion brought about by the "convocation" of men in Christ, and this "convocation" is the Church. The Church is the goal of all things, and God permitted such painful upheavals as the angels' fall and man's sin only as occasions and means for displaying all the power of his arm and the whole measure of the love he wanted to give the world: Just as God's will is creation and is called "the world," so his intention is the salvation of men, and it is called "the Church."

The Church – prepared for in the Old Covenant

761 The gathering together of the People of God began at the moment when sin destroyed the communion of men with God, and that of men among themselves. The gathering together of the Church is, as it were, God's reaction to the chaos provoked by sin. This reunification is achieved secretly in the heart of all peoples: "In every nation anyone who fears him and does what is right is acceptable" to God.

762 The remote *preparation* for this gathering together of the People of God begins when he calls Abraham and promises that he will become the father of a great people. Its immediate preparation begins with Israel's election as the People of God. By this election, Israel is to be the sign of the future gathering of all nations. But the prophets accuse Israel of breaking the covenant and behaving like a prostitute. They announce a new and eternal covenant. "Christ instituted this New Covenant."

Scripture Passages

- Matthew 10:1-10
- Matthew 16:13-19
- John 20:19-23
- Matthew 28:16-20

Discussion Questions

1. Summarize how the Church came into being.

2. How does reading these passages help us to see the Church as having both a human element and a divine element?

Assignment

Create a cartoon/comic that summarizes the origins and founding of the Church and shows both the visible (human) and spiritual (divine) aspects of it.

The Church and I

Directions: Write two well-constructed five- to seven-sentence paragraphs that reflect on the following questions:

1. How strong is my faith in the Church? Why?

2. Has my understanding of the Church changed at all with the knowledge I gained today?

3. Is it possible to have a true and authentic relationship with Christ without the Church? Why or why not?

4. What part am I called to play in the Church?

_____

_____

_____

_____

_____

_____

_____

_____

_____

_____

_____

_____

"The Church's One Foundation"

The Church's one foundation
Is Jesus Christ her Lord,
She is His new creation
By water and the Word.
From Heav'n He came and sought her
To be His holy bride;
With His own blood He bought her
And for her life He died.

She is from every nation,
Yet one o'er all the earth;
Her charter of salvation,
One Lord, one faith, one birth;
One holy name she blesses,
Partakes one holy food,
And to one hope she presses,
With every grace endued.

The Church shall never perish!
Her dear Lord to defend,
To guide, sustain, and cherish,
Is with her to the end:
Though there be those who hate her,
And false sons in her pale,
Against both foe or traitor
She ever shall prevail.

Though with a scornful wonder
Men see her sore oppressed,
By schisms rent asunder,
By heresies distressed:

Yet saints their watch are keeping,
Their cry goes up, How long?
And soon the night of weeping
Shall be the morn of song!

'Mid toil and tribulation,
And tumult of her war,
She waits the consummation
Of peace forevermore;
Till, with the vision glorious,
Her longing eyes are blest,
And the great Church victorious
Shall be the Church at rest.

Yet she on earth hath union
With God the Three in One,
And mystic sweet communion
With those whose rest is won,
With all her sons and daughters
Who, by the Master's hand
Led through the deathly waters,
Repose in Eden land.

O happy ones and holy!
Lord, give us grace that we
Like them, the meek and lowly,
On high may dwell with Thee:
There, past the border mountains,
Where in sweet vales the Bride
With Thee by living fountains
Forever shall abide!

Words: Samuel J. Stone, *Lyra Fidelium: Twelve Hymns of the Twelve Articles of the Apostle's Creed* (London: Messrs. Parker, 1866). **Music:** Samuel S. Wesley, AURELIA in *A Selection of Psalms and Hymns*, by Charles Kemble (London: John F. Shaw, 1864).

The Church's One Foundation

1 The Church's one foun - da - tion is Je - sus Christ her
2 E - lect from ev - ery na - tion, yet one o'er all the
3 Though with a scorn-ful won - der we see her sore op -
4 'Mid toil and tri - bu - la - tion, and tu-mult of her
5 Yet she on earth hath u - nion with God,the Three in

Lord; she is his new cre - a - tion, by wa - ter and the
earth, her char - ter of sal - va - tion: one Lord, one faith, one
pressed, by schisms rent a - sun - der, by he - re - sies dis-
war, she waits the con - sum - ma - tion of peace for - e - ver-
One, and my - stic sweet com - mu - nion With those whose rest is

word: from heaven he came and sought her to be his ho - ly
birth; one ho - ly name she bles - ses, par-takes one ho - ly
tressed: yet saints their watch are keep - ing, their cry goes up,"How
more, till with the vi - sion glo -rious her long-ing eyes are
won: O hap - py ones and ho - ly! Lord, give us grace that

bride; with his own blood he
food, and to one hope she
long?" and soon the night of
blest, and the great Church vic -
we, like them, the meek and

bought her, and for her life he died.
pres - ses with ev - ery grace en - dued.
weep - ing shall be the morn of song.
to - rious shall be the Church at rest.
low - ly, on high may dwell with thee.

Hymnary.org

The First Mark of the Church: The Church is One

Directions: Read about the first mark of the Church, the Church is one, and then answer the focus questions.

The first mark of the Church tells us the Church is one. This means that there is unity to the Church. Jesus founded one Church; therefore the Church must be one. The fact that other Christian churches exist is a sign of our fallen human nature due to sin, because those churches were founded by human beings, not by Jesus. Jesus said in John 17:20-21: "I pray...for those who will believe in me through their word, so that they may all be one, as you, Father, are in me and I in you, that they also may be in us, that the world may believe that you sent me. Jesus wants all of God's people to be one people. He desires unity among all the faithful. God's will for the Church is for it to be one Church, not many.

We believe that the Church is one in belief. This means we have one creed and one set of doctrines that we all profess to believe, no matter where in the world we are. The teachings of the Church are one no matter where you live, what parish you attend, or who your bishop is. Therefore, we are united as one Church because of the unity of what we believe.

The Church is one in worship and liturgy. This means we all say the same prayers and share the same Sacraments. The Mass remains the same no matter what language or what part of the world it is celebrated in. We share the same prayers, and participate and receive the same Sacraments from parish to parish and diocese to diocese. The worship and liturgy of the Church make us one.

The Church is one in government. We are all governed by one pope and one Magisterium, or teaching authority of the Church. We have one central hierarchy that governs the Church and one central authority that guides our beliefs and shepherds all of God's people.

Unfortunately, because of sin and its effects on human nature, there are many wounds to the unity of the Church. From the very beginning even through to today, there have been people who have taught incorrect things about God, Jesus, salvation, and the Church. These kinds of false teachings are called heresy. Heresy often leads to division in the Church, or schism. The Apostles and their successors have always been quick to oppose and correct heresy, but the effects of heresy linger and can hurt people's faith and deeply wound the unity of the Church. One of the largest schisms in the history of the Church was the Protestant Reformation led by Martin Luther, which began in the 1500's. Today, there are thousands of non-Catholic Christian churches around the world who for various reasons are not in union with the Catholic Church. We cannot, however, charge with the sin of separation, those who through no fault of their own have been born into communities not in union with the Church. Anyone who has been Baptized in faith has the right to be called a Christian. As a Church, we must continue the work of ecumenism, or the work of restoring unity among all Christians.

1. What is the first mark of the Church? What does this mean about the Church?

_____

_____

2. Why must the Church be one? _____

3. What does Jesus want for His Church? _____

4. What does it mean that the Church is one in belief?

_____

5. What does it mean that the Church is one in worship and liturgy?

_____

6. What does it mean that the Church is one in government?

_____

7. Why are there wounds to the unity of the Church? _____

8. What is a heresy? _____

9. What is a schism? _____

10. What is one of the largest schisms in the history of the Church?

_____

11. Why is it not a sin of separation for those born in other Christian churches?

_____

12. What is ecumenism? _____

_____

How Can I Help Make the Church One?

Directions: Reflect on what you have learned about the first mark of the Church, the Church is one, then answer the questions.

1. What does it mean to you that the Church is one?

    _____

    _____

    _____

2. What are two things you notice in the world around you that hurt the unity of the Church?

    _____

    _____

    _____

3. What are three things you can do to help build unity in the Church and make the Church one?

    _____

    _____

    _____

    _____

Understanding the Second Mark of the Church

Directions: Read the following paragraphs taken from the *Catechism of the Catholic Church* and then answer the focus questions.

II. The Church Is Holy

823 "The Church...is held, as a matter of faith, to be unfailingly holy. This is because Christ, the Son of God, who with the Father and the Spirit is hailed as 'alone holy,' loved the Church as his Bride, giving himself up for her so as to sanctify her; he joined her to himself as his body and endowed her with the gift of the Holy Spirit for the glory of God." The Church, then, is "the holy People of God," and her members are called "saints."

1. What do we hold as a matter of faith about the Church?

   _____

   _____

2. What did Jesus do for the Church? What did He give the Church?

   _____

   _____

   _____

3. What is the Church and what do we call her members?

   _____

   _____

824 United with Christ, the Church is sanctified by him; through him and with him she becomes sanctifying. "All the activities of the Church are directed, as toward their end, to the sanctification of men in Christ and the glorification of God." It is in the Church that "the fullness of the means of salvation" has been deposited. It is in her that "by the grace of God we acquire holiness."

4. To sanctify means to make holy. Sanctity is holiness. How is the Church sanctified?

   _____

5. How does the Church sanctify others?

_____

_____

6. What do we find the fullness of in the Church?

_____

_____

825 "The Church on earth is endowed already with a sanctity that is real though imperfect."
In her members perfect holiness is something yet to be acquired: "Strengthened by so many
and such great means of salvation, all the faithful, whatever their condition or state – though
each in his own way – are called by the Lord to that perfection of sanctity by which the Father
himself is perfect."

7. What is the sanctity of the Church on earth like?

_____

8. What does the Lord call all the faithful to?

_____

_____

827 "Christ, 'holy, innocent, and undefiled,' knew nothing of sin, but came only to expiate the
sins of the people. The Church, however, clasping sinners to her bosom, at once holy and always
in need of purification, follows constantly the path of penance and renewal." All members of
the Church, including her ministers, must acknowledge that they are sinners. In everyone,
the weeds of sin will still be mixed with the good wheat of the Gospel until the end of time.
Hence the Church gathers sinners already caught up in Christ's salvation but still on the way
to holiness: The Church is therefore holy, though having sinners in her midst, because she
herself has no other life but the life of grace. If they live her life, her members are sanctified;
if they move away from her life, they fall into sins and disorders that prevent the radiation of
her sanctity. This is why she suffers and does penance for those offenses, of which she has the
power to free her children through the blood of Christ and the gift of the Holy Spirit.

9. What must all members of the Church acknowledge?

_____

10. Whom does the Church gather?

_____

_____

11. How are the faithful sanctified? How do they fall into sin?

_____

_____

828 By canonizing some of the faithful, i.e., by solemnly proclaiming that they practiced heroic virtue and lived in fidelity to God's grace, the Church recognizes the power of the Spirit of holiness within her and sustains the hope of believers by proposing the saints to them as models and intercessors. "The saints have always been the source and origin of renewal in the most difficult moments in the Church's history." Indeed, "holiness is the hidden source and infallible measure of her apostolic activity and missionary zeal."

12. What does it mean to canonize?

_____

_____

13. We call a soul who has been canonized a saint. Why does the Church propose the saints to us?

_____

_____

14. What have the saints always been in the Church?

_____

_____

Reflecting on Holiness

Directions: Write a short, one-paragraph reflection in response to any two of the following questions you choose:

1. Who in your life do you consider to be an example of holiness? Why or how?

2. Think of an encounter you've had with something or someone holy in the Church. How did that encounter impact your own faith?

3. What are things you can work on in your own life to assist you in becoming holy?

4. What are some ways that you can view the Church as holy despite the sinfulness of her members?

5. Which saint most inspires you to holiness? Why or how?

Question 1:

_____

_____

_____

_____

_____

_____

_____

_____

_____

_____

_____

Question 2:

_____

_____

_____

_____

_____

_____

_____

_____

_____

_____

Portraits of Mary

Our Lady of Guadalupe

Our Lady of Czestochowa

The Virgin of the Lilies

Our Lady of Deliverance,
Empress of China

The Third Mark of the Church Fill-in-the-Blank

Directions: Fill in the blanks as you follow along with your teacher.

1. The third mark of the Church is _____.

2. The word Catholic means _____.

3. The many images of _____ from different cultures show that the truth and beauty of our faith is in fact _____ and meant for _____.

4. Our Lady's appearances to different cultures speak to a need for _____ and spreading the _____ to the ends of the earth.

5. The first reason the Church is catholic is because _____ is present in her.

6. "Where there is _____ there is the _____."

7. In the Church is the fullness of _____ for _____ everywhere.

8. The second reason the Church is catholic is because Jesus sent the Church on a mission to _____ all people everywhere in the _____ of God.

9. Christ's message of _____ is to be shared throughout the _____ for all time.

10. At His _____, Jesus told His disciples, "Go, therefore and make _____ of all _____."

11. We have a responsibility as Catholics to share our _____ with others.

12. In order to do this, we simply need to _____ to the love of Christ in our lives.

Delivery of the Keys
BY PERUGINO (C 1481-1482)

Sistine Chapel, Vatican City, Rome.

What Kind of Authority Did Jesus Give the Apostles?

Directions: Read each of the following Scripture passages, then determine and record what power Jesus gave the Apostles. Finally, answer the question that follow.

Matthew 28:18-20

Then Jesus approached and said to them, "All power in heaven and on earth has been given to me. Go, therefore, and make disciples of all nations, baptizing them in the name of the Father, and of the Son, and of the holy Spirit, teaching them to observe all that I have commanded you. And behold, I am with you always, until the end of the age."

1.   Power given: _____

John 20:23

Whose sins you forgive are forgiven them, and whose sins you retain are retained.

2.   Power given: _____

1 Corinthians 11:23-24

For I received from the Lord what I also handed on to you, that the Lord Jesus, on the night he was handed over, took bread, and, after he had given thanks, broke it and said, "This is my body that is for you. Do this in remembrance of me."

3.   Power given: _____

Luke 10:16

Whoever listens to you listens to me. Whoever rejects you rejects me. And whoever rejects me rejects the one who sent me.

4.   Power given: _____

Matthew 18:17

If he refuses to listen to them, tell the church. If he refuses to listen even to the church, then treat him as you would a Gentile or a tax collector.

5. Power given: _____

Matthew 18:18

Amen, I say to you, whatever you bind on earth shall be bound in heaven, and whatever you loose on earth shall be loosed in heaven.

6. Power given: _____

Critical Thinking Questions

1. Why do you think Jesus gave the Apostles these powers?

   _____

   _____

   _____

2. What conclusion must we draw from the fact that Jesus gave the Apostles these powers and that the Church still exists today?

   _____

   _____

   _____

Reflection Question

On your own paper, describe a time when you were given a responsibility. What was it like to be trusted in that way? Who gave you the responsibility? Why? How did you handle the responsibility you were given? Was it easy or difficult to use your responsibility? Why? What help did you need?

The Gift of Apostolic Succession

Directions: Think about a pope, bishop, or priest who has inspired you and had an impact on your life. Write that person a letter telling him why he inspires you. Even though priests are not successors of the Apostles, they share in their ministry and assist those who are. Even if the person may never read this letter, think of it as a way also to thank God for the gift of this mark of the Church.

Dear _____,

_____

_____

_____

_____

_____

_____

_____

_____

_____

_____

_____

_____

_____

Sincerely,

_____

The Bare Minimum

Directions: Read each of the following scenarios, then answer the questions that follow.

Scenario 1: The Vikings

The Sacred Heart School Vikings are a football team made up of a great group of naturally talented and athletic guys. They practice only three days a week, as opposed to other teams in the area that practice five days a week. The Vikings' practices are only 45 minutes long, and they run laps and lift weights only once a week. The other teams in the area practice for 2 hours and run laps and lift weights every day. The Vikings all enjoy playing but usually win only a few games each season. They have never made it to the playoffs or won a state championship.

1. Do the Vikings still meet all the requirements of a football team? _____

2. Would you want to be a part of that team? Why or why not?

_____

_____

_____

Scenario 2: Allison

Allison is a young girl who attends St. Joseph's Academy. She is an actress and has a lot of natural talent. All of the other actors and actresses at her school are taking acting classes, are enrolled in choir, and take private voice lessons. Allison doesn't do any of these things. She simply relies on her natural talent when she auditions for school plays and musicals. She has been cast in every show she has auditioned for, but only in small bit parts or in the chorus. She has never been cast in a lead role.

3. Can you still consider Allison an actress?_____

4. Is she the best actress she could be? Why or why not?

_____

_____

_____

Scenario 3: Mark

Mark is a young man who attends All Saints School in Florida. Last summer, Mark's parents told him he had to get a job, so he started his own lawn-mowing business. He got the idea from a friend of his who started his own mowing business. Mark had only five customers that summer and didn't do anything to promote himself or his business. He made enough money to be able to go out with his friends on the weekend, but he never saved any money. Mark's friend promoted himself, had twenty customers, and made enough money not only to go out with his friends but also to save enough to buy himself a car and to put money away for college.

5. Did Mark get a job as his parents asked him?_____

6. Did he make the most out of the opportunity? Why or why not?

_____

_____

The Precepts of the Church Note-Taking Guide

Directions:

The Precepts of the Church

- Set in the context of the _____.

- Nourished by _____.

- _____ requirements for growth in love of _____

  and _____.

What are the Precepts of the Church? Define each precept.

1. _____

   _____

2. _____

   _____

3. _____

   _____

4. _____

   _____

5. _____

   _____

Living the Precepts of the Church in My Life

Directions: Write a one- or two-paragraph reflection that addresses the following questions.

> What is one precept of the Church you struggle with most? Why?

> What are three ways you can strive to live it more perfectly?

> Write a prayer asking Jesus to give you the strength and understanding to live this precept.

_____

_____

_____

_____

_____

_____

_____

_____

_____

_____

_____

_____

_____

_____

Identifying the Precepts of the Church

Directions: Read each of the following scenarios and identify which precept of the Church is being upheld or violated.

Precepts of the Church

A. To attend Mass and rest from servile work on Sundays and Holy Days of Obligation.

B. To confess our sins to a priest, at least once a year.

C. To receive our Lord Jesus Christ in the Holy Eucharist at least once a year during Easter Season.

D. To observe the days of abstinence and fasting.

E. To contribute to the support of the Church.

_____ 1. Mark is out with his friends on Good Friday. They go to a fast-food restaurant. He really doesn't like the fish sandwich so he decides to order a burger.

_____ 2. Cory goes to Mass every Sunday with his family and often tries to go to daily Mass once or twice a week on his own.

_____ 3. Theresa does not like going to Confession. She hasn't been in over five years.

_____ 4. Andrew works hard as a waiter on the weekends. Every Sunday at Mass, he gives 8 percent of the tips he has earned that weekend to the Church.

_____ 5. Colleen is in love with the gift of the Eucharist. She feels so blessed to be able to receive Jesus in the Eucharist every week.

_____ 6. Brady and his family attend Mass only on Christmas and Easter.

_____ 7. Michael goes to Confession every other Saturday.

_____ 8. Steven makes $100,000 a year. He works hard for his money and doesn't think he should give anything to the Church or anyone else.

UNIT 9

Your Kingdom Come

In this unit, you will learn about...

> The Kingdom of God and the reign of God over all things.

> The purpose of time.

> The liturgical calendar.

> The Last Things: death, judgment, Heaven, Purgatory, and Hell.

> The renewal of all things at the end of time in the New Heavens and the New Earth.

Introduction

During His earthly life, Jesus proclaimed the coming of the Kingdom of God. God's kingdom is not a physical or geographical place, but rather the reign of God over all things throughout creation. Our time on earth is meant for us to prepare to enter the Kingdom of God. We will experience the Last Things: death and judgment, Heaven, Purgatory, or Hell. When Jesus in glory comes at the end of time, He will judge the living and the dead. He will reveal the secrets of everyone's hearts, and will give to each person according to how He has lived, and whether he chose to accept or reject God's grace. Then, at the end of time when Jesus returns, God's reign over all of creation will be fulfilled and the universe will be renewed in a New Heavens and a New Earth.

Are there any questions you still have about the topics you learned last month? What steps can you take to find out the answers?

_____

_____

_____

_____

What questions do you have right now about the topics you will be learning about in this unit?

_____

_____

_____

_____

Advent: The season that begins the liturgical year. It is a time when we reflect on the Incarnation, and prepare ourselves to celebrate the birth of Jesus, our King, on Christmas Day. We also prepare for His Second Coming at the end of time. This season is represented by the color violet, or purple, which represents penance and humility.

Christmas: A liturgical season to spend time celebrating the joy of the Incarnation and the birth of our Savior Jesus Christ. This season is represented by the color white, which represents light, purity, and joy, or gold, which represents joy.

Communion of Saints: All the members of Christ and His Church: those here on earth, those in Purgatory, and those in Heaven.

Easter: The liturgical season following Lent in which we celebrate the Resurrection of Jesus on Easter Sunday. All of Jesus' suffering was redeemed by the glory of His Resurrection. We are reminded that, because of Jesus' death and resurrection, we may gain the reward of eternal salvation. Jesus' Resurrection is the principle of our own resurrection. Just as Christ rose from the dead and lives forever, so all of us will rise in our own bodies at the last day. Easter is more than just a day; it is an entire season. Like the Christmas season, the Easter season is a time of joy and celebration, and so it is represented by the color white or gold.

Eulogy: A written or spoken tribute to someone who has died.

General (or Last) Judgment: At the end of time, the light of Christ, who is Truth itself, will illuminate everything. Nothing will remain hidden. We will see not only all of our own individual choices for or against God, but how each one affected everyone else and the whole order of creation. On this, then, we will be judged and welcomed to eternal life with Christ in the New Heavens and the New Earth, or banished into the eternal torment of Hell.

Heaven: The state of being after death in which "those who die in God's grace and friendship and are perfectly purified live forever with Christ" (CCC 1023). The souls in Heaven enjoy perfect communion and relationship with God, His angels, and all of the saints. In Heaven we will see God face-to-face, as He is. This is called the Beatific Vision.

Hell: The state of being after death in which those who die unrepentant of mortal sin and refuse the love and mercy of God to the end experience eternal separation from God and the Communion of Saints. The primary punishment in Hell is the eternal separation from God while continually thirsting for Him.

Holy Week (Triduum): The shortest liturgical season. It is the three days between Lent and Easter in which we reflect in a particular way upon Christ's suffering and death. It is represented by the color red, which represents fire, love, Jesus' Passion, and the blood of the martyrs.

Lent: The liturgical season in which we focus on the Paschal Mystery by reflecting upon Jesus' life, Passion, Death, and Resurrection, and how He redeemed us of our sins. During Lent we do penance and prepare our hearts to receive the salvation won for us by Christ. The color of this season is violet, or purple for penance and humility.

Liturgical Calendar: A calendar that charts the various seasons, remembrances, feasts, and celebrations in the life of the Church over the course of a year. The liturgical year begins with Advent and includes the seasons of Christmas, Lent, Holy Week or Triduum, Easter, and the two larger periods of Ordinary Time.

New Heavens and New Earth: The mysterious renewal of all things that will occur at the end of time when Jesus returns to usher in the reign of God. It will be the definitive realization of God's plan to bring the universe under the rule of His Son. God will dwell among men and there will no suffering, pain, or death. Human beings will be filled forever with happiness, peace, and mutual communion with each and with God. The world will be restored to its original state.

Ordinary Time: The liturgical season when we learn about the life of Christ. There are two periods of Ordinary Time during the year: between the end of the Christmas season and the beginning of Lent, and between the end of the Easter season and the beginning of Advent. Ordinary Time is represented by the color green, which represents life and hope. Ordinary Time is not called ordinary because it is uninteresting or common. Rather, the name comes from the Latin word ordo, which is where we get the English word order. In other words, Ordinary Time reflects the order of the Church year. The weeks of Ordinary Time are numbered and point us toward the goal that all history is ordered towards: the reign of Christ the King. On the final Sunday in Ordinary time, we celebrate the Solemnity of Our Lord Jesus Christ, King of the Universe.

Particular Judgment: A judgment by God at the moment of death, in which we will receive from Him what we deserve, based on our faith and our good works throughout our lives. In other words, we will be judged by our love – how we loved God and how we loved others. All who die in God's grace and friendship are assured of their eternal salvation in Heaven, while those who die in mortal sin accept eternal separation from God in Hell.

Purgatory: The state of being after death in which those who "die in God's grace and friendship, but [are] still imperfectly purified, are indeed assured of their eternal salvation; but after death they undergo purification, so as to achieve the holiness necessary to enter the joy of Heaven" (CCC 1030). The souls in Purgatory endure great suffering in order to be purified of any unconfessed venial sins and for the reparation of the remaining effects of confessed mortal and venial sins.

Sanctoral Cycle: The sequence of saints' feast days throughout the liturgical year.

Parable of the Wedding Feast

BY ANDREI MIRONOV (C. 2014)

404

Parable of the Wedding Feast

Parable of the Wedding Feast, by Andrei Mironov (c. 2014)

Directions: Take some time to quietly view and reflect on the art. Let yourself be inspired in any way that happens naturally. Then think about the questions below, and discuss them with your classmates.

Conversation Questions

1. Read Matthew 22:1-14. What part of the parable does this picture show?

   Jesus again in reply spoke to them in parables, saying, "The kingdom of Heaven may be likened to a king who gave a wedding feast for his son. He dispatched his servants to summon the invited guests to the feast, but they refused to come. A second time he sent other servants, saying, 'Tell those invited: "Behold, I have prepared my banquet, my calves and fattened cattle are killed, and everything is ready; come to the feast."' Some ignored the invitation and went away, one to his farm, another to his business. The rest laid hold of his servants, mistreated them, and killed them. The king was enraged and sent his troops, destroyed those murderers, and burned their city. Then he said to his servants, 'The feast is ready, but those who were invited were not worthy to come. Go out, therefore, into the main roads and invite to the feast whomever you find.' The servants went out into the streets and gathered all they found, bad and good alike, and the hall was filled with guests. But when the king came in to meet the guests he saw a man there not dressed in a wedding garment. He said to him, 'My friend, how is it that you came in here without a wedding garment?' But he was reduced to silence. Then the king said to his attendants, 'Bind his hands and feet, and cast him into the darkness outside, where there will be wailing and grinding of teeth.' Many are invited, but few are chosen."

2. Why do you think the artist chose to paint this particular moment from the parable?

3. Why is this particular moment from the parable important?

4. Who is listening to the man in blue, and who is not?

5. Why do you think the artist chose to paint the Parable of the Wedding Feast to look also like Jesus preaching?

6. In the parable, what were the servants calling people to come to? What does Jesus call us to?

7. In what ways is the parable of the wedding feast similar to Jesus' life?

8. What are some important moments in our lives when we can choose to follow or ignore God's invitation to enter His Kingdom?

The Kingdom of Heaven Is Like...

Directions: Read the parable assigned by your teacher and write in the chapter and verse numbers. Then answer the questions.

Name of the parable: _____

Chapter and verse in the Bible where this parable is found: _____

1. Summarize this parable in your own words:

    _____

    _____

    _____

2. What point do you think Jesus is making about the Kingdom of Heaven?

    _____

    _____

    _____

3. Why do you think this truth about the Kingdom of Heaven is important for us to know?

    _____

    _____

    _____

4. How would you describe the Kingdom of Heaven based on this parable?

    _____

    _____

    _____

Matthew 22:9

Then he said to his servants, 'The feast is ready, but those who were invited were not worthy to come. Go out, therefore, into the main roads and invite to the feast whomever you find."

Ecclesiastes 3:11

He has made everything appropriate to its time,
and has put the timeless into their hearts.

1 Corinthians 9:24

Do you not know that the runners in the stadium all run in the race, but only one wins the prize? Run so as to win.

John 3:16

For God so loved the world that he gave his only Son, so that everyone who believes in him might not perish but might have eternal life.

Revelation 21:3-4

God's dwelling is with the human race. He will dwell with them and they will be his people and God himself will always be with them [as their God]. He will wipe every tear from their eyes, and there shall be no more death or mourning, wailing or pain, [for] the old order has passed away.

1 Corinthians 15:54-55

Death is swallowed up in victory. Where, O death, is your victory? Where, O death, is your sting?

Me and Time

Directions: In our lives, time is something we live with. It is an important and influential part of our human experience. Time can bring about various feelings and reactions from us. For example, it can make us excited, nervous, tired, comfortable — you name it! The questions below are meant to help you evaluate your experience of time.

1. Describe three experiences or moments in time that you would want to go by slowly, and explain why for each one.

   _____

   _____

   _____

   _____

   _____

2. Describe three experiences or moments in time that you would want to go by quickly, and explain why for each one.

   _____

   _____

   _____

   _____

   _____

3. Using the chart on the next page, complete a typical weekly schedule that you follow.

	7:00am–9:00am	9:00am–11:00am	11:00am–1:00pm	1:00pm–3:00pm	3:00pm–5:00pm	5:00pm–7:00pm	7:00pm–Bedtime
Sunday							
Monday							
Tuesday							
Wednesday							
Thursday							
Friday							
Saturday							

4. Take a look at your completed weekly schedule. What are the top three things that you spend your time doing?

_____

_____

_____

5. Sometimes people are unhappy with their schedules and routines. You may have heard others complain that they do not have time to do the things they want to do. Thinking about your own schedule, what are the things you will always want to make time for in your life, no matter how "full" your schedule becomes?

_____

_____

_____

_____

416

Living the Works of Mercy in Our Time

Matthew 25:31-46

When the Son of Man comes in his glory, and all the angels with him, he will sit upon his glorious throne, and all the nations will be assembled before him. And he will separate them one from another, as a shepherd separates the sheep from the goats. He will place the sheep on his right and the goats on his left. Then the king will say to those on his right, "Come, you who are blessed by my Father. Inherit the kingdom prepared for you from the foundation of the world. For I was hungry and you gave me food, I was thirsty and you gave me drink, a stranger and you welcomed me, naked and you clothed me, ill and you cared for me, in prison and you visited me." Then the righteous will answer him and say, "Lord, when did we see you hungry and feed you, or thirsty and give you drink? When did we see you a stranger and welcome you, or naked and clothe you?

When did we see you ill or in prison, and visit you?" And the king will say to them in reply, "Amen, I say to you, whatever you did for one of these least brothers of mine, you did for me." Then he will say to those on his left, "Depart from me, you accursed, into the eternal fire prepared for the devil and his angels. For I was hungry and you gave me no food, I was thirsty and you gave me no drink, a stranger and you gave me no welcome, naked and you gave me no clothing, ill and in prison, and you did not care for me." Then they will answer and say, "Lord, when did we see you hungry or thirsty or a stranger or naked or ill or in prison, and not minister to your needs?" He will answer them, "Amen, I say to you, what you did not do for one of these least ones, you did not do for me." And these will go off to eternal punishment, but the righteous to eternal life.

Directions: The **Corporal and Spiritual Works of Mercy** are things we must do to show love to our neighbor. In fact, Jesus tells us that at the end of time, we will all be judged according to whether and how we performed these actions!

Working adults spend a lot of their time at their jobs. Sometimes it can be difficult to balance love for God, neighbor, and self in daily life. What we don't want to do is give our heart and efforts to God only once a week. We want to do it every moment of every day. It is possible!

On the next page are several types of common careers. Choose one that you are familiar with, and, for each of the Corporal and Spiritual Works of Mercy, try to give examples of how a person with that career could incorporate these actions and efforts into his or her daily work life.

Choose a career:

Stay-at-home-parent	Social Worker	Engineer	Priest/Clergy/
Actor/Actress	Musician	Accountant	Religious Brother
Psychologist/	Teacher	Author	or Sister
Psychiatrist	Nurse/EMT	Journalist	Physical Trainer
Lawyer	Chemist	Business Manager	Firefighter
Doctor	Politician	Photographer	Pilot/Bus, Taxi,
Police Officer	Coach	Meteorologist	or Truck Driver

1. How could a person with this career live out the Corporal Works of Mercy?

   Feeding the hungry: _____

   Clothing the naked: _____

   Visiting the sick: _____

   Visiting the imprisoned: _____

   Sheltering the homeless: _____

   Burying the dead (Ecclesiastes 6:3): _____

2. How could a person with this career live out the Spiritual Works of Mercy?

   Instructing the ignorant (Mark 16:1): _____

   _____

   Advising against sin (Luke 15:7): _____

   _____

   Consoling the doubtful (John 14:27): _____

   _____

   Comforting the afflicted (Matthew 11:28): _____

   _____

   Forgiving offenses willingly (Matthew 6:12): _____

   _____

   Praying for the living and the dead (John 17:24): _____

   _____

St. Augustine's Perspective on Time

Introduction

St. Augustine of Hippo lived from AD 344 to 430. He spent his youth living sinfully and contrary to the gospel. He was highly intelligent, but, despite the prayers of his mother, he remained firmly against the truth of Christianity. At the age of 33, St. Augustine experienced a deep conversion to Christianity through God's speaking to him in the Scriptures. At 36 he was ordained a priest, and by 41 he was appointed the bishop of Hippo, a region in northern Africa. St. Augustine had a great influence on many matters of theology, and he wrote many books. Two books in particular have been very important to Western thought and are still widely read today. *The Confessions* is St. Augustine's telling of his life story and conversion. *The City of God* reflects upon the differences between the world of man and the Kingdom of God. St. Augustine is a Doctor of the Church because of the influence of his writings and his example of holiness. In his *Confessions*, St. Augustine wrote about time. Reflect on the quote below:

> "Perhaps it is best to say, 'There are three times, a present of things past, a present of things present, and a present of things future.'"

–CONFESSIONS XI, 20

To St. Augustine, the only time that has any real existence is the present moment. So he divided our experience or perspective of time into three categories: Remembrance (the past), Consideration (the present), and Expectation (the future).

Now, let's try to use this expression of St. Augustine in the context of a short video. Your instructor is going to show you a video but will pause it at certain points for consideration. When the video is paused, identify these three parts.

First Pause (at 2:57)

1. What is the **Remembrance**? *What has happened so far in this video?*

_____

_____

_____

2. What is the **Consideration**? *What is currently happening in the video?*

_____

_____

_____

3. What is the **Expectation**? *What do you expect to happen in the rest of the video?*

_____

_____

_____

Second Pause (at 4:57)

4. What is the **Remembrance**? *What has happened so far in this video?*

_____

_____

_____

5. What is the **Consideration**? *What is currently happening in the video?*

_____

_____

_____

6. What is the **Expectation**? *What do you expect to happen in the rest of the video?*

_____

_____

_____

Critical Thinking and Reflection

You have watched the video *Once Upon a Tandem* and have paused to think about it, and the final outcome may or may not have happened the way you expected it to. The original owner and rider of the bicycle certainly was surprised, confused, upset, disappointed, nervous, and so forth.

7. Do you think the original owner and rider of the bicycle expected things to end up the way they did? Why or why not?

    _____

    _____

    _____

Likewise, throughout our lives, what we expect to happen doesn't always happen! Many times our expectations are shattered. The video is a made-up story, but it expresses a profound truth. As Christians we believe that God is **omnipresent**, which means that He is present in all of human history (past, present, and future). He is not a mere observer, but is active in human history. We call the presence of God and His salvation of mankind in history **salvation history**. We can use the *faithful* remembrance of God's saving actions in the past and look forward with *hope* to the fulfillment of His promises in the future as *loving inspiration* for the present moments in our lives!

Below, work with a group of other students to complete a recounting of salvation history using St. Augustine's three-part division of time.

8. How do we as Christians **faithfully remember** God's saving actions in salvation history?

    _____

    _____

9. How do we as Christians **look forward** with **hope** to the fulfillment of God's promises?

    _____

    _____

10. How does the **love** God has shown us **inspire** our present moments as Christians?

    _____

    _____

The Liturgical Calendar

As we've discussed, sometimes time can move slowly when we do not want it to. The Church understands this! Our perspective of time can sometimes be challenging. It's easy to forget reasons to be happy when we are experiencing hard or sad times. Or when things seem to be great, it may be hard to remember that we still have things to improve on.

Likewise, to have a fuller experience of time, we need to have Remembrance (of things past), Consideration (of things present), and Expectation (of things future). If we examine the Church's **liturgical cycle**, we can see that the Church wants us to make the most of time! One liturgical year in the Church is marked by many seasons, remembrances, feasts, celebrations, and so forth. A careful examination of the seasons in the cycle reveals that we spend time as a Church preparing, celebrating, focusing, and remembering.

The liturgical year begins with **Advent**, a time when we reflect on the Incarnation (the Second Person of the Holy Trinity, the Son of God, assumed a human nature in the Person of Jesus Christ), and prepare ourselves to celebrate the birth of Jesus, our King, on Christmas Day. We don't just prepare for the coming of Jesus as a baby, but also for His Second Coming at the end of time. This season is represented by the color violet, or purple, which represents penance and humility. (On your chart, color the Advent-season space purple.)

Then, during the **Christmas** season, we spend time celebrating the birth of our Lord Jesus Christ. There's a lot to be joyful about during Christmas! Not only do we receive gifts, but we celebrate the birth of our Savior Jesus Christ, the best gift ever! This season is represented by the color white, which represents light, purity, and joy, or gold, which represents joy. (On your chart, leave the Christmas-season space white or color it yellow or gold.)

During Lent we focus on the Paschal Mystery. We reflect upon Jesus' life, Passion, Death, and Resurrection, and how He redeemed us from our sins! That's good news for sure, but we have to remember how this victory was achieved, and the suffering that Christ endured for us. During Lent we do penance and prepare our hearts to receive the salvation won for us by Christ, so the color of this season is violet, or purple. (On your chart, color the space for the season of Lent purple.)

Following Lent, we have the great celebration of the Resurrection of Jesus called **Easter**. All of Jesus' suffering was redeemed by the glory of His Resurrection. This is inspiring to us! We are reminded that we may eventually gain the reward of eternal salvation despite the difficulties of our own crosses. Notice that Easter is more than just a day; it's a season! Like the Christmas season, the Easter season is a time of joy and celebration, and so it is represented by the color white or gold. (On your chart, leave the Easter-season space white or color it yellow or gold.)

Much of the liturgical calendar is made up of **Ordinary Time**. There are two periods of Ordinary Time during the year: between the end of the Christmas season and the beginning of Lent, and between the end of the Easter season and the beginning of Advent. During this liturgical season we learn about the life of Christ. Ordinary Time is represented by the color green, which represents life and hope. Ordinary Time is not called ordinary because it is uninteresting or common. Rather, the name comes from the Latin word *ordo*, which is where we get the English word order. In other words, Ordinary Time reflects the order of the Church year.

The weeks of Ordinary Time are numbered and point us toward the goal that all history is ordered toward: the reign of Christ the King. On the final Sunday in Ordinary time, we celebrate the Solemnity of Our Lord Jesus Christ, King of the Universe. (On your chart, color all of the Ordinary Time spaces green.)

Throughout the liturgical season, we remember special events in the life of the Church or celebrate the saints. For example, fifty days after Easter, we celebrate the coming

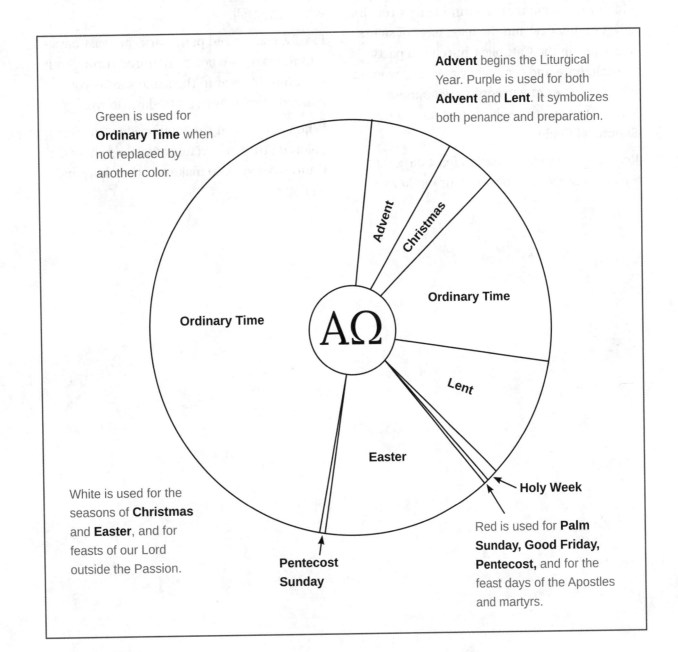

Green is used for **Ordinary Time** when not replaced by another color.

Advent begins the Liturgical Year. Purple is used for both **Advent** and **Lent**. It symbolizes both penance and preparation.

Advent

Christmas

Ordinary Time

AΩ

Ordinary Time

Lent

Easter

Holy Week

Pentecost Sunday

White is used for the seasons of **Christmas** and **Easter**, and for feasts of our Lord outside the Passion.

Red is used for **Palm Sunday, Good Friday, Pentecost,** and for the feast days of the Apostles and martyrs.

of the Holy Spirit at Pentecost. Another example would be Holy Week, or the Triduum. During this three-day period, we reflect in a particular way upon Christ's suffering and death. Pentecost and Triduum are represented by the color red, which represents fire, love, Jesus' Passion, and the blood of the martyrs. (On your charts, color the Pentecost and Triduum spaces red.)

Throughout the liturgical year, we also celebrate various Marian feast days (on which we remember the Virgin Mary's role in salvation history) and the feast days of saints. Every day in the Catholic Church is a party! We celebrate and remember men and women who lived lives of extraordinary holiness. We call the cycle of saints' feast days the **Sanctoral Cycle**.

Research the various Marian feast days that we celebrate. (Use a blue pen or marker to draw a blue line on the cycle in the general vicinity of where these feast days fall, and label them and the date on which they fall.)

Next, using a black pen, mark the feast days of 5 to 10 saints (not martyrs) you are familiar with – perhaps the feast day of the saint whose name you share, or common names in your family, or maybe a saint you relate to in some way. You choose! Draw a line in the general vicinity of where each of these feast days falls, and label them and the date on which they fall.

Finally, using a red pen, mark the feast days of 5 to 10 martyrs who are honored throughout the Church's year in the same way as you marked Marian and saints' days above.

When you look at the final product of your colored liturgical cycle, you can see how the Church helps us to make our time holy and well spent!

What Do You Know About Heaven, Hell, and Purgatory?

Directions   With your group, list as many things as you know about Heaven, Hell, and Purgatory in response to the questions.

	Heaven	Hell	Purgatory
What is it?			
How does one "go" there?			
What happens there?			
Who is there?			
What are other important things to know about it?			

The Last Things Scripture Scavenger Hunt

Directions: Read about Heaven, Hell, and Purgatory in the given Scripture passages. Then determine and record what each passages teaches us about Heaven, Hell, or Purgatory. Think about what each passage teaches about what it is, who "goes" there, what happens there, who is there, and anything else important that the passage might teach us.

Scripture	What does this passage teach us about Heaven?
1. John 14:2-3	
2. John 3:16	
3. Luke 23:42-43	
4. Matthew 25:45-46	
5. 1 John 3:2	
6. 1 Corinthians 13:12	

Scripture	What does this passage teach us about Hell?
7. Matthew 10:28	
8. Matthew 13:49-50	
9. Matthew 25:46	
10. 2 Thessalonians 1:6, 9	
11. Job 10:21-22	
12. Matthew 16:18	

Scripture	What does this passage teach us about Purgatory ?
13. Matthew 12:32	
14. Luke 12:58-59	
15. 2 Maccabees 12:39-46	
16. 1 Peter 1:6-7	
17. Isaiah 4:4	
18. 1 Corinthians 3:15	

Judgment

Directions: Read the excerpts from the *Catechism of the Catholic Church* about the particular judgment and the Last Judgment, then answer the questions that follow each excerpt.

The Particular Judgment

1021 Death puts an end to human life as the time open to either accepting or rejecting the divine grace manifested in Christ. The New Testament speaks of judgment primarily in its aspect of the final encounter with Christ in his second coming, but also repeatedly affirms that each will be rewarded immediately after death in accordance with his works and faith. The parable of the poor man Lazarus and the words of Christ on the cross to the good thief, as well as other New Testament texts speak of a final destiny of the soul–a destiny which can be different for some and for others.

1. When is the time for either accepting or rejecting the divine grace given to us by Christ?

_____

2. Which judgment does the New Testament primarily speak of?

_____

3. Which Gospel stories affirm the existence of the particular judgment immediately after death?

_____

_____

_____

1022 Each man receives his eternal retribution in his immortal soul at the very moment of his death, in a particular judgment that refers his life to Christ: either entrance into the blessedness of heaven–through a purification or immediately–or immediate and everlasting damnation.

At the evening of life, we shall be judged on our love.

4. What happens in the particular judgment at the very moment of our death?

_____

5. Upon what will we be judged? _____

_____

The Last Judgment

1038 The resurrection of all the dead, "of both the just and the unjust," will precede the Last Judgment. This will be "the hour when all who are in the tombs will hear [the Son of man's] voice and come forth, those who have done good, to the resurrection of life, and those who have done evil, to the resurrection of judgment." Then Christ will come "in his glory, and all the angels with him. ...Before him will be gathered all the nations, and he will separate them one from another as a shepherd separates the sheep from the goats, and he will place the sheep at his right hand, but the goats at the left. ...And they will go away into eternal punishment, but the righteous into eternal life."

6. What will come before the Last Judgment? _____

7. Who will be gathered before Christ at His second coming? What will He do with them?

_____

_____

1039 In the presence of Christ, who is Truth itself, the truth of each man's relationship with God will be laid bare. The Last Judgment will reveal even to its furthest consequences the good each person has done or failed to do during his earthly life.

8. Who is Truth itself? _____

9. What will be revealed in the presence of Christ? _____

_____

10. What will be revealed even to its furthest consequences? _____

_____

1040 The Last Judgment will come when Christ returns in glory. Only the Father knows the day and the hour; only he determines the moment of its coming. Then through his Son Jesus Christ he will pronounce the final word on all history. We shall know the ultimate meaning of the whole work of creation and of the entire economy of salvation and understand the marvelous ways by which his Providence led everything towards its final end. The Last Judgment will reveal that God's justice triumphs over all the injustices committed by his creatures and that God's love is stronger than death.

11. When will the Last Judgment occur? Who knows when this will be?

_____

_____

12. What will we know when the Father pronounces the final word on all history?

_____

_____

13. What will triumph in the end? What is stronger than death?

_____

_____

An Examination of Conscience for Children

Responsibilities to God

› Have I prayed every day?

› Have I prayed my morning prayers and night prayers?

› Have I prayed with my parents and family?

› Have I been moody and rebellious about praying and going to church on Sunday?

› Have I asked the Holy Spirit to help me whenever I have been tempted to sin?

› Have I asked the Holy Spirit to help me do what is right?

Responsibilities to others

› Have I been obedient and respectful to my parents?

› Have I lied or been deceitful to them or to others?

› Have I been arrogant, stubborn, or rebellious?

› Have I talked back to parents, teachers, or other adults?

› Have I pouted and been moody?

› Have I been selfish toward my parents, my brothers and sisters, my teachers, or my friends and schoolmates?

› Have I gotten angry at them? Have I hit anyone?

› Have I held grudges or not forgiven others?

› Have I treated other children with respect, or have I made fun of them and called them names?

› Have I used bad language?

› Have I stolen anything? Have I returned it?

› Have I performed my responsibilities, such as homework and household chores?

› Have I been helpful and affectionate toward my family?

› Have I been kind and generous with my friends?

Write Your Own Eulogy

Section 1: Interviews

Ask three to five of your classmates the following questions and record your answers below.

> What is my best personality trait?

> Have I taught you anything?

> What is something that would always remind you of me if I were not around (a song, a food, a memory, etc.)?

_____

_____

_____

_____

_____

Section 2: Write Your Eulogy, Part 1

Write your own eulogy using *only* information from the answers given in Section 1.

_____

_____

_____

_____

_____

_____

Section 3: Write Your Eulogy, Part 2

Reflect on the process you just followed. Based on what you learned, are you living your life as an example of how to live as a disciple of Christ and get to Heaven? If not, what do you need to change? Now, write the eulogy you would be proud to have read at your funeral. Write a eulogy based on how you should live in order to go to Heaven after you die.

The New Heavens and the New Earth

Sin causes all sorts of consequences for mankind. We experience these consequences during our earthly lives. But Scripture makes clear that we will no longer experience these consequences in the New Heavens and the New Earth at the end of time. Revelation 21:4 says God "will wipe every tear from their eyes, and there shall be no more death or mourning, wailing or pain, [for] the old order has passed away." We can begin to think about what the New Heavens and the New Earth will be like by thinking about what they *won't* be like.

Directions: Listed below are some of the consequences or effects of sin. Think about each of these consequences and then, in the space below each, describe what the world would be like without each of these consequences of sin.

Effects of sin	What the world would be like without this effect
Loss of Union with God	
Loss of Eternal Life	
Loss of Perfect Faith	
Failure to Act out of Love for God and One Another	
Tendency to Sin	
Suffering	
Death	

What the Church Teaches about the New Heavens and the New Earth

Directions: Read in the *Catechism of the Catholic Church* nos. 1042-1048 what the Church teaches about the New Heavens and the New Earth, then answer the questions that follow each excerpt.

1042 At the end of time, the Kingdom of God will come in its fullness. After the universal judgment, the righteous will reign for ever with Christ, glorified in body and soul. The universe itself will be renewed:

The Church...will receive her perfection only in the glory of heaven, when will come the time of the renewal of all things. At that time, together with the human race, the universe itself, which is so closely related to man and which attains its destiny through him, will be perfectly re-established in Christ.

1. When will the Kingdom of God come in its fullness? _____

2. What will the righteous do after the universal judgment? What will happen to the universe?

   _____

   _____

3. What will be perfected in the glory of Heaven? _____

1043 Sacred Scripture calls this mysterious renewal, which will transform humanity and the world, "new heavens and a new earth." It will be the definitive realization of God's plan to bring under a single head "all things in [Christ], things in heaven and things on earth."

4. What does Scripture call the mysterious renewal? _____

5. What is God's plan that will be definitively realized?

   _____

   _____

1044 In this new universe, the heavenly Jerusalem, God will have his dwelling among men. "He will wipe away every tear from their eyes, and death shall be no more, neither shall there be mourning nor crying nor pain any more, for the former things have passed away."

6. Where will God's dwelling be in this new universe? _____

7. What will there no longer be? _____

   _____

1045 For man, this consummation will be the final realization of the unity of the human race, which God willed from creation and of which the pilgrim Church has been "in the nature of sacrament." Those who are united with Christ will form the community of the redeemed, "the holy city" of God, "the Bride, the wife of the Lamb." She will not be wounded any longer by sin, stains, self-love, that destroy or wound the earthly community. The beatific vision, in which God opens himself in an inexhaustible way to the elect, will be the ever-flowing well-spring of happiness, peace, and mutual communion.

8. What will be finally realized for man? _____

   _____

9. Who will form the community of the redeemed? What will they be called?

   _____

   _____

10. What will no longer destroy or wound the earthly community? _____

11. The Beatific Vision is the privilege of the souls in Heaven to look upon God as He is, face-to-face. What will flow from the Beatific Vision?

    _____

    _____

    _____

1047 The visible universe, then, is itself destined to be transformed, "so that the world itself, restored to its original state, facing no further obstacles, should be at the service of the just," sharing their glorification in the risen Jesus Christ.

12. What is the destiny of the visible universe?

    _____

    _____

1048 "We know neither the moment of the consummation of the earth and of man, nor the way in which the universe will be transformed. The form of this world, distorted by sin, is passing away, and we are taught that God is preparing a new dwelling and a new earth in which righteousness dwells, in which happiness will fill and surpass all the desires of peace arising in the hearts of men."

13. When will the consummation (the ultimate end or finishing) of the earth and man occur? How will that happen?

_____

14. What do we know about the ultimate end?

_____

_____

_____

Life Plan

Directions: Consider the eulogy you wrote for yourself as you answer the questions below.

1. How is the eulogy that you wrote based on your classmates' answers to the interview questions different from the second one that you wrote for yourself?

    _____

    _____

2. What must change in your life for that second eulogy to be true?

    _____

    _____

3. What change can you make today to direct your life more toward God?

    _____

    _____

4. What change can you make over the next week to direct your life more toward God?

    _____

    _____

5. What change can you make over the next month to direct your life more toward God?

    _____

    _____

6. What change can you make over the next year to direct your life more toward God?

    _____

    _____

7. On your own paper, write a prayer in your own words asking for God's grace and help in directing your life toward Him and His Kingdom.